Business Decisions!

Other Books by Michael E. McGrath

Decide Better! For a Better Life

Decide Better! For College (with Christopher K. McGrath)

*Next Generation Product Development: How to Increase Productivity, Cut Costs, and Reduce Cycle Times**

*Product Strategy for High-Technology Companies**

*Setting the PACE® in Product Development: A Guide to Product and Cycle-time Excellence***

*Published by McGraw-Hill

**Published by Butterworth-Heinemann

Decide **Better!**  BUSINESS SERIES

Business Decisions!

How to Be More Decisive While Reducing Risk in Today's Economy

Michael E. McGrath

MOTIVATION
PUBLISHING

ADDISON, TEXAS

MOTIVATION
PUBLISHING

Business Decisions!
How to Be More Decisive While Reducing Risk in Today's Economy

Motivation Publishing
16633 Dallas Pkwy, Suite 280
Addison, TX 75001

For more information, visit DecideBetter.com.
PACE® is a registered trademark of Pittiglio Rabin Todd & McGrath (PRTM)
iPhone™ is a trademark of Apple Inc.
iPod® is a registered trademark of Apple Inc.

Printed in the United States of America
Jacket and text design by Mayapriya Long, Bookwrights
Author photography by Peter Cao, Greg Booth and Associates

Library of Congress Control Number: 2009931498
ISBN-13: 978-1-935112-15-0
First Edition

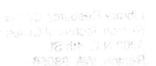

This book is dedicated to my wife Diane.

Acknowledgments

Many people were involved with the production of this third book in the *Decide Better!* series — too many to mention — but a number of people were absolutely crucial to its completion. My son Chris helped write this book, as he did with the other *Decide Better!* books. Jennifer Cary helped to create the new *Decide Better!* Business Decisions Series, and as publisher of Motivation Publishing, she was responsible for the production, marketing, and promotion of the book. Trudi Pevehouse was indispensible in doing all of the many tasks required in a project like this.

Barbara Darling, Becca McGrath, Bob Land, and Sarah McGrath helped with revisions and editing, providing a more readable book. Mayapriya Long designed the book and the cover, and also provided advice throughout the project. David Johnson and Laura Ward at Strategic Vision were invaluable in marketing and promoting the book and the *Decide Better!* vision.

Over the last 30 years, I have learned a great deal about making decisions thanks to many people. The directors and consultants at PRTM worked with me to solve challenging client problems for 28 years. I also learned a lot about decisions from the many clients throughout the world I worked with over that period of time. My experiences as CEO of i2 Technologies, executive chairman of Thomas Group, and chairman of Entrust all helped to further my experience at making decisions.

Finally, I would like to thank my family: my wife Diane and my daughter Molly for putting up with me when I write; Mike and Sarah; Chris and Becca; Jill and Carmen; and Matthew, Callie, and Drew.

Contents

Introduction

Businesses succeed or fail based on the decisions they make. It is as simple as that. Successful businesses make better strategic decisions, as well as better hiring, product selection, project management, pricing, planning, and marketing decisions. Businesses fail because of a bad decision that turned out to be fatal, or because of an accumulation of bad decisions. Mediocre businesses may have mixed success with decisions or, more often than not, just miss opportunities because of neglected decisions.

The importance of business decisions has never been more apparent than it was at the end of 2008. As the economy collapsed across the globe, it became clear that dreadful business decisions were the cause. Some prominent financial institutions were destroyed, and many others weakened, by incredibly risky decisions. Even long-standing institutions, such as General Motors, were eventually forced into bankruptcy as the result of many years of poor decisions. The consequences of these bad decisions were so severe that they reached beyond the companies themselves to the entire economy. While we need to avoid these same decision mistakes in the future, it is even more important that we delve more deeply to understand the underlying causes, which can be more broadly applied to decision making.

As a result of the magnitude of this collapse, businesses and other organizations all over the world are reexamining the way they make decisions. Unlike years past where a growing economy hid bad decisions, businesses today have little margin for error; they consistently must make sound choices or risk complete failure. *Business Decisions!* provides a timely solution for improving these decisions. It is a singularly comprehensive guide to skills, practices, and insights for making great business decisions.

While many popular business books have chronicled the reasons that businesses succeed or fail, presenting useful theories for success, opinions shift over time about which success stories to emulate and which theories to follow. Fundamental to all of these success stories, however, is one indisputable fact: successful businesses make better decisions.

When you get down to basics, a business is just made up of numerous decisions, beginning with the one to start the business and continuing with those that shape virtually everything the business does. A typical mid-sized business makes hundreds of decisions every day, while a large business makes thousands. Decisions are made by every executive and manager in the business, and by nearly every worker.

Successful executives and managers are known for their ability to make good decisions. How is it that they make good decisions while others struggle and make choices they later regret? Why do some organizations seem to consistently make good decisions while others seem to make one bad one after another? Answering these questions is the quest of this book.

I have devoted my career to making winning decisions — advising some of the largest companies in the world and innovating new decision techniques used by hundreds of successful businesses. I have made countless decisions as a CEO building a world-class consulting firm and leading a public company turnaround. In addition to my personal experiences and the vast experience of my consulting firm, for more than 20 years I have studied the way businesses make decisions and how these decisions affect their success. I have always been fascinated by decision making and its combination of inherent abilities, skills, techniques, processes, and thoughtful reflection. I concluded that executives and managers can learn how to make better decisions, and in *Business Decisions!* I have tried to present the most important lessons and techniques to improve decisions, especially in today's economy.

Selecting from the vast body of knowledge on decision making was a challenge. There is just too much information to include in the scope of one book, so I selected a range of lessons and techniques that I believe are the most practical and useful. *Business Decisions!* combines new, but proven, approaches to decisions along with some unique views on traditional techniques. Even though I have a quantitative mathematics background and value quantitative decision techniques, *Business Decisions!* does not include mathematical decision theory; the emphasis is on the practical. I believe that the best way to learn is from the experience of others, so I use many examples throughout the book. Those examples with real company names are derived from publicly available information, while others are disguised, modified, and composite examples.

There are different aspects to improving business decisions. The first is to understand your own skills, weaknesses, and tendencies. This self-understanding is addressed in several ways throughout the book. The second is to master decision techniques. There are many different skills to learn, so I focus on those I think are the most important, including some that I have relied on for years but which may be new to you. Third, you need to learn about decision pitfalls. These are the traps that you can easily fall into if you are not careful. Finally, it helps to understand how others make decisions and how decisions are made by teams and organizations.

Examining the dreadful decisions that caused the collapse of the world economy in late 2008 provides the best starting point. In the first section, I explore what I believe are some of the most perilous decision pitfalls, starting with those that led to this economic collapse, and continuing to other prevalent business decision pitfalls.

In several decades of working with executives and managers, I learned that those who are successful are more skilled at making decisions. They study decision techniques, adapt methods from others, and learn from their own mistakes. There is a wide range of techniques for business decisions; no one practice fits all situations. In section II, I have included a selection of business decision techniques that I believe are particularly useful in today's economy.

Some of the most critical decisions are not routine and have significant implications, but since these are not routine, executives and managers involved with them may be facing them for the first time. Therefore, the topics in section III help with these unique decisions.

In business, particularly in larger businesses, decisions are not just made by individuals; they are frequently made by a group, a team, or an entire organization. While many of the decision techniques and skills previously introduced apply to groups as well as individuals, there is an added dimension when working together to make decisions. This additional dimension makes it much more difficult to reach a decision, and the result, if mismanaged, can be worse than an individual decision. Personalities differ, people approach the same decision very differently, and the culture of a business has an increasingly evident role in influencing decisions. Organizational decisions also reflect other factors, such as the political, bureaucratic, and cultural aspects of an organization. Section IV explores this added dimension that organizations, groups, and teams bring to decision making.

Projects are essential to all businesses and organizations. Projects are used to create and launch new services and products, build and expand facilities, formulate process improvements, create new advertising or marketing campaigns, make investments, and explore changes in strategic direction, to mention a few examples. While projects are very important to an organization's success, I have found that all too often projects take longer, cost more, and fail to deliver the best results. More often than not, this failure is due to flawed decisions. Section V examines the unique characteristics of project decisions, defining the four aspects of project decisions and the correct way to make these decisions based on the world-recognized PACE process.

By applying the lessons of *Business Decisions!* you will be more decisive and successful. You can lead your business to avoid pitfalls and take advantage of new opportunities. Most important, you will be a winner in this new economy!

SECTION I

Decision Pitfalls

In late 2008, the world economy collapsed in large part due to bad business decisions, particularly by financial institutions. The consequences of these decisions were severe, not only completely destroying some well-established companies, but even reaching beyond these companies to the entire economy. While it is imperative to learn from these mistakes, it is even more important to dig deeper, studying the underlying pitfalls that caused these bad decisions. This approach will provide valuable general lessons that can be applied successfully to a broader range of decisions.

I refer to these major mistakes as "decision pitfalls" because they are decision traps that are not always obvious at the time, but which cause bad — sometimes disastrous — decisions. Decision pitfalls are not unique to this recent period in business history; they have been prevalent in business decisions throughout time. They can be induced by circumstances or by faulty decision-making tendencies. Sometimes decision pitfalls are isolated to individuals, but other times entire organizations fall into the same pitfall.

> Sometimes decision pitfalls are isolated to individuals, but other times entire organizations are swept up by the same pitfall.

In this first section I explore what I believe are some of the most perilous decision pitfalls, starting with looking broadly at decision risk. All decisions have some degree of risk, but some decisions are much riskier than others. In the 1990s and into the 2000s, many businesses made increasingly riskier decisions, some of which led to their ultimate collapse. By and large, these businesses failed to comprehend the magnitude of risk in their decisions. The first chapter examines dramatic examples of failure to understand decision risk, defines the various types of decision risk, and offers ways to better manage decision risk from a practical perspective.

In my many years of studying business decisions, I have found that one of the major pitfalls is not the decisions themselves but the failure to make them. I use the old adage of the frog in boiling water to describe how decisions linger while the frog, or business in our examples, slowly boils. Frequently the failure to make critical decisions happens in slowly deteriorating situations, as opposed to decisions that are made in reaction to an abrupt threat. Other times, companies fail to make opportunistic decisions, letting good possibilities pass them by. The second chapter highlights the pitfall of ignoring critical decisions and provides advice on avoiding it.

Another major, yet common, pitfall occurs when executives and managers disregard the long-term consequences of their decisions. They focus on the immediate impact of a decision and do not consider or care about its long-term consequences. All too frequently, and sadly, the long-term consequences far outweigh the short-term benefits of the decision. And unfortunately this pitfall is not just a problem with businesses; it is also a widespread problem with decisions by governments. Chapter 3 addresses this pitfall in depth with examples and lessons on how to avoid it.

There is a tendency in business (as well as in life) to keep investing in something because you have already invested so much — in other words, throwing good money after bad. This pitfall is common in routine decisions, but also a major pitfall in strategic decisions. In chapter 4, I explain this tendency and how to avoid it.

When you do not know much about something, it can appear to be very simple. The simplicity often is deceptive. Without knowing enough about a decision, it is very easy to make the assumption that doing it or buying it or making the decision to commit to it is going to be much easier than it turns out to be. This common pitfall in the business world is reviewed in chapter 5.

> By studying the underlying pitfalls that cause bad decisions, we can understand more valuable general lessons that can be applied to a broader range of decisions.

The disaster of the space shuttle *Challenger* was a dark day for America. Subsequent investigation revealed that the cause of the explosion was a structural deficiency of which the contractor and NASA officials were both aware. This disaster was a failure of the decision process; specifically those responsible for making the ultimate decision did not have accurate information or chose to ignore it. This decision pitfall is also common in business, and in chapter 6 I look at how information or opinions important for critical decisions are sometimes suppressed within organizations.

Indecision, the topic of chapter 7, can be an extremely debilitating pitfall in business decisions. To put it simply, indecision is the inability to decide or tendency to vacillate between choices, preventing a final decision. It is far too common in business, and is often a problem for some managers at virtually every company. And while indecision is a pitfall that affects small as well as large decisions, it is obviously a much more critical problem when managers are unable to make the most important decisions. Indecision is not just limited to individuals; I have experienced entire companies that are indecisive.

While this section focuses mainly on what I believe are the major pitfalls that businesses face today, other decision pitfalls must be acknowledged. In the final chapter of this section, I highlight additional pitfalls.

CHAPTER 1

Letting Risk Get Out of Control

Failure to manage risk can destroy a company

Uncertainty underlies almost every business decision, but that is not an excuse to take excessive or uncontrolled risk. The economic collapse of 2008 can be traced back to executives who made reckless decisions by taking excessive risk. Their decisions had far-reaching consequences, but they did not understand — or chose to ignore — the risk associated with those consequences. They let decision risk run amok. How did this happen, and what can be learned from these experiences?

Decision risk is not easy to understand; it can be subtle, complex, hidden, and progressive. It can turn what looks initially like a great decision into a disastrous one. As you will see, in some cases, excessive decision risk can even have fatal consequences for a business. Decision risk can be understood and managed, so I have little sympathy for those who claim that they had no idea what would happen. Good decisions can be made in the clear light of the potential risks of those decisions.

> In some cases, excessive decision risk can have fatal consequences.

While elsewhere in this book I write about when to make bold decisions and take measured risk, here I want to focus on the pitfalls of failing to understand and manage risk. Decision risk is not one simple concept. Different types of decision risk depend on the nature and circumstances of the decision. Executives may think they understand the risk of their decisions, only to find out later that they did not consider all types of risk. I define the different types of risk and then look at ways to manage them. But first I want to focus on some dramatic examples in which uncontrolled decision risk had a disastrous impact.

Decision Risk Examples

Unfortunately, the financial collapse of 2008 provided many examples of decision pitfalls. It seemed like many financial executives ignored the risk of their decisions, probably under the delusion that in the heady economy of the times nothing could go wrong. The following case studies illustrate how the failure to understand risk brought down some major corporations and disrupted the entire economy in the process.

Lehman Brothers Commercial Real Estate[1]

Lehman Brothers collapsed in 2008 for several reasons, most of them related to the company's failure to manage the risk of its decisions. One of these risks came from its decision to aggressively finance commercial real estate sales using a financing technique called "equity bridge financing." Lehman decided to put its own cash into real estate deals as equity alongside the debt it raised, making big commissions on the transactions. By taking on this higher risk itself, Lehman facilitated real estate transactions by making it more attractive for buyers to pay higher prices and do the deal with Lehman.

Lehman tried to offload some of these risky investments to others, and while this strategy was initially successful, it eventually failed. For example, in October 2007, Lehman helped finance the purchase of Archstone-Smith Trust, a $22 billion deal that many critics thought was overpriced. Lehman, along with Bank of America, put up $17.1 billion in debt and $4.6 billion in bridge equity financing, but Lehman could not offload its $2.2 billion of bridge equity in this transaction.

> Lehman Brothers collapsed in late 2008 for several reasons, mostly related to its failure to manage the risk of its decisions.

While the financial reward to Lehman for bridge-equity leveraged commercial real estate transactions was appealing, the risk grew progressively greater and greater. As bidding wars between purchasers started for commercial real estate, Lehman's bridge financing helped its clients increase their bids. As long as real estate prices continued to increase, this risk was covered, but the risk began to escalate as deals became harder to finance. Lehman kept trying harder and harder, doing more and larger deals, expanding its risk even more. By the second quarter of 2008, Lehman had accumulated $29 billion in commercial mortgage exposure. The mounting risk exposure helped bring the company down when commercial real estate prices began to drop.

AIG and Credit Default Swaps[2]

Credit default swaps (CDSs) are perhaps the riskiest financial instrument in modern financial history supposedly designed to reduce risk. The CDS market exploded over a decade to more than $45 trillion in mid-2007, according to the International Swaps and Derivatives Association. The massive size of the CDS market was staggering. It was roughly twice the size of the U.S. stock market (which as of March 2008 was valued at about $22 trillion and falling) and far exceeded the $7.1 trillion mortgage market and $4.4 trillion U.S. treasuries market at that time.

Credit default swaps are insurance-like contracts that promise to cover losses on certain securities in the event of a default. They were typically used to insure municipal bonds, corporate debt, and mortgage securities, and they were sold by banks, hedge funds, and others. The buyer of the credit default insurance paid premiums over a period of time to reduce risk by covering a default. It was supposed to work similarly to someone taking out home insurance to protect against losses from fire and theft — except that it did not. Banks and insurance companies are regulated; the credit swaps market was not. As a result, CDSs were traded — or swapped — from investor to investor without anyone overseeing the trades to ensure that the buyer had the resources to cover the losses if the security defaulted. The instruments could be bought and sold by both the insured and the insurer.

AIG, the largest insurer in the world, expanded into the CDS market with its Financial Products group. Using historical data, the company's computer modeling predicted that there was hardly any risk of ever paying out on any CDSs, but its models were flawed. Initially, the CDS business was a small part of the group's total business, so it did not seem like a major decision. Then AIG's credit default swaps evolved into insuring more volatile forms of debt, including mortgage-backed securities, which helped fuel the real estate boom that eventually went bust. The Financial Products group exposed AIG to more than $400 billion in liabilities and entangled dozens of financial institutions on Wall Street and around the world.

> Using historical data, AIG's computer modeling showed almost no risk.

When the housing market collapsed, a chain of events unfolded. Provisions in the contracts kicked in, spurring collateral calls on swaps linked to questionable assets. AIG was required to come up with billions of dollars in cash. It scrambled for almost a year to stave off the collateral calls, but eventually there were too many deals and too much risk exposure to cover. And when its ratings were downgraded, AIG had to post even more collateral, which it did not have. At this point the company went under and was bailed out by the U.S. government.

AIG took on excessive risk when it decided to expand its CDS business. The insurer underestimated the magnitude of this risk, while focusing on the financial gains of these transactions to both AIG and the executives managing its Financial Products group.

Standard & Poor's Rating Escalation[3]

Standard & Poor's (S&P) ran afoul of a different, but related kind of risk. The business provided quality ratings on debt and had a growing market in debt collateralized by mortgages (collateralized debt obligations, known as CDOs). This was a very profitable business, generating $1.4 billion in profit in 2007 and $1 billion in 2008. S&P rated the quality of the debt with 12 different categories, but was paid more when it gave a transaction a triple-A rating. The increased fee unfortunately encouraged higher ratings.

S&P was drawn into higher and higher risk by the temptation to provide top ratings on the growing business of CDOs. It was also swayed by the prevailing opinion that mortgage-backed securities must be secure, because home prices would continue to rise. When these securities collapsed, everyone questioned S&P's ratings and the reasons behind them. The profit of this business was gone, and the company (a subsidiary of McGraw-Hill) faced numerous lawsuits for its aggressive and questionable practices.

S&P's increasing aggressiveness progressively escalated its risk until the company broke. The financial incentives for giving higher ratings encouraged unjustified ratings, masking the decision risk for those relying on those ratings.

Tremont Advisors' Failure to Diversify[4]

Tremont Advisors was a so-called fund-of-funds hedge fund that was supposed to manage the risk of its investors' money by diversifying investments across a range of hedge funds. While somewhat risky, hedge funds could produce superior investment returns, so in theory the diversification offset that risk. Tremont provided superior returns to its investors, making a great profit for itself, but it accomplished that by sacrificing risk management for more concentrated profit. In December 2008, Tremont managed about $6 billion of client assets, but more than half ($3.1 billion) were concentrated with one investment manager: Bernard L. Madoff. His fund turned out to be a Ponzi scheme, and Tremont, through its Rye Investment Management subsidiary, lost $3.3 billion of its clients' money.

Tremont Advisors lost sight of its basic promise to investors to manage risk. Tremont Advisors was not evaluated based on risk, and its investors were pleased with the higher returns. On a regular basis the firm was measured by performance, and concentrating its investment on Madoff seemed the best way to keep its performance strong. Madoff regularly generated higher returns than anyone else — of course because it was all phony. Tremont Advisors compromised risk for return, but few cared because it was making so much money. When Mass Mutual acquired Tremont Advisors, a consultant pointed out the risk of its exposure to one investment, but that warning was ignored because of its high overall performance.

> Tremont put half of its clients' money into the Madoff fund.

Ironically, as a fund-of-funds, Tremont was supposed to reduce risk through diversification, but instead, to use an old adage, it put most of its clients' nest eggs in one basket.

Auto Leasing

For the auto leasing business, risk took the form of estimating residual values for cars when they came off of a lease. In the 1990s, auto leasing was a profitable business. This drew more companies into the business, making it more competitive. To compete more aggressively on lease prices, companies started to increase the estimated residual value of cars they were leasing. They simply made their lease pricing decisions with a more favorable assumption of residual value, lowering lease prices.

From 1990 to 1997, many leasing companies were increasing residual value estimates by more than 50%; obviously, the risk increased simultaneously. As auto leases ended, companies were stuck with big write-offs. Financing companies such as Bank One, Bank of America, GE, and Wachovia wrote off hundreds of millions of dollars, and many of them exited the auto leasing business. This is an example of where just one assumption — the estimated value of a car at the end of the lease — became increasingly aggressive. In order to be competitive, companies needed to match the increasing risk of other auto leasing companies. Eventually, the risk became excessive, causing massive losses throughout the industry.

National Amusements' Debt Obligation[5]

Sumner Redstone, the controlling shareholder of Viacom and CBS through National Amusements Inc., took the risk of borrowing $1.6 billion to fund his various investments. The debt was relatively short term, and he knew that he would have to roll it over or sell some of his investments when it came due. At the time, his substantial investments provided ample collateral, so the risk of borrowing did not seem too high. Much of the money he borrowed went into a risky investment in Midway Games, yet despite his investment of an estimated $500 million to $700 million in Midway, it kept losing money.

His decision to risk taking out so much debt, tied to the value of Viacom and CBS, seemed like a safe decision at the time. When the prices of Viacom and CBS stock dropped almost 50%, Redstone was forced to sell more than $200 million in stock to cover margin calls. (When stock is used as collateral on a loan, some of the loan needs to be paid if the value of the collateral is insufficient because it declines in value.) At the end of 2008, he was forced to sell almost 90% of Midway for $100 million along with the transfer of $70 million in secured debt.

In early 2009, Sumner Redstone's theater chain, National Amusements Inc., reached an agreement to restructure the remaining $1.46 billion of debt, deferring payment to December 31, 2010, with certain repayments due in late 2009 and 2010. The debt was secured by substantially all of National Amusements' assets. The company owned more than 1,500 movie theaters in the United States, the United Kingdom, Latin America, and Russia; the land beneath them; and a large holding of CBS and Viacom shares. The company was likely to sell its movie theaters or its investments in CBS or Viacom to pay off the debt.

At 85 years old, Sumner Redstone made what turned out to be a high-risk decision to borrow $1.6 billion to make further investments, risking a fortune that he worked hard to build his entire life. He is a very smart man who seemed to get caught up in the exuberance that all these investments would continue to grow.

Types of Decision Risk

As these decision risk examples illustrate, risk in business decisions comes in many forms, and the dangers they create are very different. Thus, the best place to start is to understand the different types of decision risk, so that you can better consider the potential risk of your decisions. In many decisions, multiple types of risk are relevant, and you may want to use the checklist at the end of the chapter to help identify the risk of your major decisions.

Types of Decision Risk	
• Unbalanced risk	• Unknown risk
• Incentives for higher risk	• Unconstrained risk
• Compounded risk	• Escalating risk
• Complex risk	• Systemic risk
• All your eggs in one basket	• Running with
• Unanticipated consequences	lemmings

Unbalanced Risk

When a decision balances the expected benefit of the outcome and the risk the company is willing to take, then the decision is said to have a balanced risk. Note that there are two balancing considerations: is the risk of the decision balanced relative to the expected benefit of that decision, and is the risk of the decision within the total risk exposure the company is willing to accept when aggregated with the risks assumed from other decisions?

For example, a company invests $3 million from an annual R&D budget of $50 million into a new product with the potential of generating an incremental profit of $1 million to $3 million per year for up to four years. The risk is balanced with the return for the decision. If the product only generates $1 million a year, it would approximately break even considering the cost of money, and there is significant upside profit opportunity if it generates $3 million per year on the investment of $3 million. The risk is also balanced within the total risk the company can take. Even in the worst case — that the product fails completely — the loss is limited to $3 million, only 6% of the total annual R&D investment.

In the AIG and Lehman examples discussed earlier, the total risk exposure may have been reasonable for an individual deal or even a small portfolio, but the accumulated magnitude of risk jeopardized the entire company. On a total company basis, it was an unbalanced risk.

Unknown Risk

Sometimes the true risk of a decision is unknown, but I divide unknown risk into two categories: risk that could have been known and risk that truly could not have been known. One company I worked with had just released a new product that was a total failure because it could not find a channel of distribution for the product. After investing $6 million in what was a very interesting product, the company found that it just could not sell the product. The company described this as an unknown risk, but I disagreed. I pointed out that this was a knowable risk and could have been managed early in the process, if the company had evaluated the risk instead of assuming that they could find a solution.

> I divide unknown risk into two categories: risk that is knowable and risk that is not.

In contrast, another company invested in a new product line complementary to its existing products, which would help give it an advantage over its primary competitor. A week before launching the product, its competitor announced a merger with a bigger company that already had these products and would quickly integrate them. Even though the first company in this example launched its new products, success was minimal because it could not compete against the new combined competitor. This was truly an unknown risk.

The concept of unknown risk raises an interesting question about the risk that Tremont Investors and others took in investing their money in the Madoff funds. Was this Ponzi scheme a knowable risk or a truly unknown risk?

Incentives for Excessive Risk

One of the underlying causes in some cases where decision risk rises to dangerous levels is the performance incentives that drive management to take higher risks for better performance. There is intense pressure and substantial financial reward for better performance.

> *IN YOUR EXPERIENCE*
>
> *Have you ever experienced a situation where a decision was made without all of the risks considered, and those unconsidered risks caused the decision to fail?*

Corporate organizations and public shareholders increasingly raise the bar for performance, pressuring executives to shift the risk/reward trade-off toward higher risk in their decisions. Some of this pressure comes from comparison with competitors, so if competitors have better performance, even at higher risk, the company is forced to match that performance/risk balance. This approach was seen in the auto leasing example previously discussed.

The executives in turn receive significant bonuses for the increased performance, while there generally are no penalties for the higher risk. The incentive compensation structure drives executives to riskier and riskier decisions, as was seen in the Lehman, Tremont Advisors, and AIG examples. Incentive plans are also skewed in that the executives receive bonuses for higher performance, but the company bears the increased risk later.

These examples show why it is important to understand how incentives influence decision risk. It is easier, and more exciting, to reward performance, but it is more difficult to reward managing risk. Whenever creating performance incentives, you should ask yourself how these rewards may influence decision risk.

Unconstrained Risk

Decision risk can become unconstrained when either there is no boundary to the risk or the amount of the risk extends beyond the boundaries expected. To decide to put an investment at risk is one thing, but putting an entire business at risk is something else entirely. Generally, the probability of an unconstrained risk bringing down an entire company is very low, but the consequences are so severe that the risk needs to be carefully considered. I usually recommend avoiding unconstrained risk in all cases.

> I usually recommend avoiding unconstrained risk in all cases.

Several of the earlier examples illustrated the consequences of unconstrained risk. Sumner Redstone's decision to take on $1.6 billion in debt seemed to be secured by a reasonable value of his assets, but when everything dropped in value, the risk became virtually unconstrained. The Lehman Brothers and AIG examples clearly illustrate the consequences of unconstrained decision risk. The cumulative cost of these individual decisions was greater than the value of the entire business.

Compounded Risk

Decision risk can be compounded through multiple related decisions, or even in some cases what seems like unrelated decisions. When this happens, the cumulative risk can become quite significant. We already looked at how risk was compounded with similar decisions by Lehman as it increasingly did more bridge equity deals and by AIG as its CDS business grew.

AIG not only rapidly increased its risk in CDSs and other risky investments, at the same time it decided to become more leveraged. In the end, the company had a debt-to-equity ratio of 11 to 1, meaning that it owed 11 times more than its equity. The National Amusements example also illustrates the impact of compound risk. Broad declines in the economy lowered the value of CBS and Viacom stock at the same time the Midway business declined.

Compounded decision risk is difficult to measure because it is not created at the point of each decision. Compounded risk is created over time as a cumulative result of multiple decisions, which is why companies need to examine their overall risk profile periodically, at least annually.

Escalating Risk

Decision risk escalates! Failure to realize risk escalation is one of the big mistakes companies make. They estimate the risk at a point in time and then assume it will not change, but it almost always does. What can appear to be a manageable risk in the beginning can become unmanageable over time. If one decision makes sense, the reasoning seems to go, then two or three must also, and if that is the case, then even hundreds of decisions make sense. But this is not always true. As this happens, problems begin to surface and the natural tendency is to take on more risk in hopes that this will make the problem go away.

Decision risk escalates!

We saw how decision risk escalated at AIG as it grew its CDS business and at Lehman as it did more and more bridge equity deals. To avoid escalating risk, you should set some limits for risk escalation when going into new, uncharted business areas.

Complex Risk

Understanding risk can be complicated. Prior to the collapse of the financial system, financial transactions became increasingly complex. Some very smart people worked hard to engineer creative transactions, no matter how complex, where they could make substantial profit. Collateralized debt obligations (CDOs) were an example. Collateralized debt obligations are a type of structured asset-backed security whose value and payments are derived from a portfolio of fixed-income underlying assets, such as residential mortgages. CDOs are assigned different risk classes, or tranches, whereby senior tranches are considered the safest securities. Interest and principal payments are made in order of seniority, so that junior tranches offer higher coupon payments (and interest rates) or lower prices to compensate for additional default risk. A typical CDO was very complex and could involve 15,000 pages of documents.

After a while, complexity can increase geometrically to the point where it is difficult, if not impossible, to measure the real risk. That is what can happen when very smart people work to find money-making opportunities which become so complex that most others cannot understand them. During the collapse of the financial industry, some banks claimed that they had no idea of their exposure to subprime lending because of the complexity of these investments.

Systemic Risk

Systemic risk is the risk of collapse of an entire interrelated network of companies. In finance, systemic risk is the risk of collapse for an entire financial system or entire market, as opposed to risk associated with any one individual entity, group, or component of a system. Systemic risk refers to the risks imposed by interdependencies in a system or market, where the failure of a single entity or cluster of entities can cause a cascading failure, which could potentially bankrupt or bring down the entire system or market.

The creators of CDOs and CDSs unleashed techniques that others on Wall Street rushed to emulate, creating vast, interlocking deals that bound together financial institutions in ways that no one fully understood. This caused the near collapse of the entire financial system. Government regulation is sometimes necessary to manage systemic risk. In the case of these securities, during the Clinton administration, Congress passed the Commodity Futures Modernization Act, which preempted derivatives from oversight under state gaming laws and excluded certain swaps from being considered a "security" under SEC rules, which cleared the opportunity for credit default swaps.

All of Your Eggs in One Basket

There is a wise old saying that "you should not put all of your eggs in one basket," but some business executives seem to have forgotten this. It can be very tempting to put all of your eggs in one basket; it is easier and can be financially more rewarding. Tremont Advisors put most of its clients' eggs in one basket with the Madoff investment. This provided the best return on investment, so the firm was driven by better performance, even though its charter was to be a diversified fund.

One consulting firm put all of its eggs in one basket when two-thirds of its revenue came from a single military contract that renewed annually. Company management did not have to work hard selling new consulting contracts because the business was profitable, grew rapidly, and needed only a few new incremental contracts for growth. Eventually, however, the firm lost the renewal of the military contract and revenue dropped 60%.

When making strategic decisions and considering overall risk, it is good to remember this old adage.

Running with Lemmings

In my first decision book, *Decide Better! For a Better Life*, I discussed the decision concept of running with lemmings. Lemmings are rodents that migrate as a pack by the tens or even hundreds of thousands. As they do, they keep following each other into a body of water or even off of a cliff, and they all die together. It is odd and risky behavior, but one that is seen in business and individual decision risk.

The risk of the financial transactions discussed earlier reflected lemming behavior. "Others are doing it, so we should get in on the action, too." Lemming behavior was observed in the rapid increase in real estate deals. "Real estate prices keep increasing and others are making money, so we should, too." Lemming behavior was also a factor in the financial decisions that individuals made. "Everyone else is taking on big mortgages and credit card debt. Why shouldn't we?"

Be cautious when making a decision just because everyone else is doing it. When this is the case, you should take even more time to understand the decision risk for yourself. Do not be a lemming!

Unanticipated Consequences

All decisions have consequences, but some also have unintended consequences, and frequently these unintended consequences involve significant risks. There can be unintended consequences of individual decisions as well as unintended consequences of collective decisions.

From 2002 until 2005, Intel decided to offer rebates to customers in Europe to gain a competitive advantage over its primary competitor, Advanced Micro Devices (AMD). This decision worked well and helped Intel maintain 80% market share, but Intel then decided to threaten to withhold these rebates from computer makers and retailers who bought more than 5% of their components from AMD. This decision was made informally by pressuring customers in discussions and was not necessarily included in customer contracts. Although I do not know how this decision was made, it is the type of decision that can be initiated by the field sales force rather than at the corporate level. The decision to use this selling technique worked well for Intel, but it had substantial unintended consequences. In May 2009, the European Commission fined Intel almost $1.5 billion for using an illegal monopolistic practice.

> All decisions have consequences, but some also have unintended consequences.

Chances are that Intel never seriously considered this possible consequence of its decision, and if it did consider it at all, did not take it seriously. In fact, this decision could have been made originally by just a few salespeople and then picked up by others without any consideration of the longer-term consequences. This is the classic risk of unintended consequences. Nobody really thought about this, yet it may cost Intel $1.5 billion.

In another example, one company I know decided to lower its prices significantly in order to increase market share. It anticipated the risk that a competitor could follow and decrease its prices, too, and it had a plan to react to that. But it did not anticipate what happened. Instead, the market, with help from its competitor, began to perceive its products as lower quality, and sales volume did not increase with a lower price. Sales actually declined.

Collective decisions also cause unintended consequences. The individual decisions of Wall Street banks would have created only isolated risks, but the collective decisions caused an insurmountable level of risk that resulted in collapse.

In economics, the concept of unintended consequences suggests that the decisions of people and governments always have unanticipated effects. It is one of the building blocks of economic theory. Adam Smith's "invisible hand," one of the most famous writings in social science, is an example of a positive, unintended consequence. Smith maintained that each individual, seeking only his own gain, "is led by an invisible hand to promote an end which was no part of his intention" — that end being in the public interest. "It is not from the benevolence of the butcher, or the baker, that we expect our dinner, but from regard to their own self-interest," wrote Smith.

> It is not from the malevolence of the investment bankers that we expect our financial industry to collapse, but from regard to their own self-interest.

I think Adam Smith's invisible hand backfired in the recent financial collapse. Taking liberty with Smith's theory: "It is not from the malevolence of the investment bankers that we expect our financial industry to collapse, but from regard to their own self-interest."

Managing Decision Risk

Decision risk can and should be managed. Rarely are businesses innocent victims of decision risk. They are their own victims of their failure to manage risk properly. Decision risk can be managed when the decision is made, and as it progresses. Escalating and compounded decision risks can be managed periodically, as part of business strategy decisions.

Understand Risk Up Front

I am continually amazed at how informally companies consider the risks of their decisions. They sometimes identify a few risks, but do not take enough time to look at the full range of potential risks or quantify the potential impact of these risks. Sometimes the identification of risks is incomplete, with critical risks overlooked. Frequently, decision risks are contained in the decision assumptions without adequate assessment to determine the validity of these assumptions.

For major decisions, I recommend a sufficient, up-front evaluation of the risks, including formally answering questions such as these:

- What are the major risks of this decision?
- What is the potential range of cost or damages of each risk?

- What risk is contained in the assumptions?
- Is there a way to eliminate, contain, or reduce major risks?
- If not, how can the major risks be monitored?

I have found, in many cases, that this process helps to identify and quantify risks in a much better fashion. Figure 1-1 at the end of this chapter is a good worksheet that you can use to help you understand your risk better. Once this is done, then you can look at ways to reduce risk or even manage it going forward. Tremont Advisors, for example, in its investment decisions could have put in place a policy with a maximum limit that it would invest in any one investment in order to contain its risk better, even if it was tempting to put half of the investment in one fund that was performing much better than others.

The company that did not know the risk it was taking on distributing its new product into a brand-new market could have invested up front to test the feasibility before spending millions on developing a new product. In some cases, it is not easy to understand the risk of a decision. That was the case with collateralized debt obligations (CDOs) that were sometimes too complex to understand. I think that should be a warning that you need to be cautious in a decision where you cannot understand the risk.

Avoid Unconstrained Risk

Unconstrained risk is risk that has no boundaries. Unconstrained risk exceeds the extent of the entire investment. Typically, unconstrained risk comes from leverage where you are borrowing money to leverage an investment beyond your own money that you are putting into the investment. It could also come from the cumulative effect of decisions like those made by AIG, or it could come from risk that might destroy your reputation, as S&P is facing.

In a later chapter I look at bold-move decisions. I am a big fan of bold-move decisions, but I distinguish between bold moves with constrained risk and unconstrained risk. Basically, you want to avoid unconstrained risk; AIG, Lehman, and Bear Stearns are all examples of the reasons for doing so.

Hedge Risk

If you anticipate risk, you can sometimes find ways to hedge the risk. Ford provides a good example. In November 2006, Ford decided to hedge the risk of a business downturn by mortgaging everything, including its logo, to borrow $23.6 billion. This proved to be a brilliant decision, separating Ford from Chrysler and GM when auto sales collapsed, and the latter two needed to file for bankruptcy. Even better for Ford, in April 2009 it was able to buy back some of the debt for 35 cents on the dollar.

Force Risk Out Early

One of the best ways to manage the risk of a decision is to force it out or test it early. This works especially well with assumptions that you cannot verify. Take the earlier scenario of a company developing a new product assuming that the company would find the distribution channel for selling the new product. Even though creating the distribution channel did not need to be done until after the product was close to completion, I would have tested this sooner by trying to create the distribution channel earlier or perhaps even by doing a feasibility study before investing significantly in the new product.

This technique to force risk out early cannot be used in all decisions, and it is not necessary for all risks, but the technique can be useful in decisions where there is a substantial risk in a decision assumption.

Manage Risk

Companies can manage decision risk in several ways. They can offload some of the risk to others, as Lehman Brothers tried to do initially with some of its risky loans. In this case, a managed risk became an unmanaged risk, which does happen in some cases.

> One of the best ways to manage the risk of a decision is to force it out or test it early.

Another way to manage decision risk is to proceed step-by-step with an investment, being prepared to cut your losses when needed. One pharmaceutical company managed its risk this way when building a manufacturing plant for a new AIDS drug. After considering the low-risk approach of waiting until the drug was approved before building a $1 billion manufacturing plant, the CEO said, "We will not be in a position to have a drug that will save lives, and then say we need 18 months to build a manufacturing facility to make it available." Instead, the company decided to build the plant in parallel with the testing and approval of the AIDS drug. To manage its risk, at any point during the testing and approval if the drug failed, the company would immediately stop building the manufacturing facility. The company took a managed risk, the drug was approved, the plant was completed on time, and an estimated 100,000 lives were saved during those 18 months.

Monitor Risk Continually

The risk of a decision may change over time. In the case of Lehman Brothers Industrial Real Estate, the risk may have been manageable at first because the size of that business was relatively small. Then the business grew rapidly, becoming a bigger part of Lehman's total business, giving the firm more total exposure to the risk. At the same time, real estate prices began to escalate, increasing the risk that prices could decline. Finally, as real estate prices escalated, the deals became harder to close, forcing Lehman Brothers to take bigger and bigger risks on the transactions.

Lehman should have monitored this risk better. It could have measured the risk regularly by putting limits on the total risk of each transaction and the overall risk on industrial bridge loans.

Understand Your Overall Risk Profile

In cases of cumulative and escalating decision risk, the assessment cannot be made with individual decisions. In these cases, I suggest that companies include risk assessment as part of their annual strategic planning. The types of questions to consider include:

- Are we increasing risk as some of our new business areas grow?
- Are external risks changing the overall risks of our decisions?
- Are unrelated decisions in combination increasing our overall risk profile?
- Are our management incentives increasing risk beyond tolerable levels?

- While risk is a part of every business decision, it should not be an excuse for excessive risk.

- The recent collapse of the financial industry was clearly the result of bad business decisions in which executives routinely ignored risk.

- There are several major examples of failure due to inadequate risk management.

- Many types of risk need to be considered with each decision, including unbalanced risk, compounded risk, complex risk, escalating risk, and many others.

- Several mechanisms can be implemented to effectively manage risk, including understanding risk up front, avoiding unconstrained risk, hedging risk, managing or monitoring risk, and forcing risk out early.

Figure 1-1 Decision Risk Assessment

Decision: _____

_____

Risk Estimates:

Risk   Estimated Range of Risk

_____   From $_____ to $_____

_____   From $_____ to $_____

_____   From $_____ to $_____

_____   From $_____ to $_____

Total Estimated Risk: From $_____ to $_____

Risk Evaluation:

1. Is the risk balanced to the benefits of the decision?
   - Relative to the decision?
   - Relative to the business as a whole?

2. Can you think of any currently unknown risks?

3. Is there a possibility of unconstrained risk in the decision?

4. How can the risk of the decision escalate?
   - As the decision unfolds?
   - As similar decisions follow this one?

5. Can the risk of this decision be compounded with other decisions?

6. Does this decision risk putting all of your eggs in one basket?

7. Are you making this decision to follow others who are doing the same thing?

CHAPTER 2

Ignoring Crucial Decisions

*Make crucial decisions; do not
ignore them until it is too late*

There is an old story that if you drop a frog into a pot of boiling water, it will immediately jump out, but if you drop a frog into a pot of room-temperature water and then slowly bring the water to a boil, the frog will remain in the water, boiling to death. While I have never attempted to verify this theory, it is still a useful analogy for many decisions we face in the business world. Just as the frog who sits there as his water boils around him, in business, if you neglect to make crucial decisions, your water will boil away, risking the survival of your business.

The business pitfall of ignoring crucial decisions appears in a variety of ways, but there is a common set of underlying causes. Complacency can play a big part in the tendency to ignore crucial decisions. Keeping business generally as it is becomes a temptation. After all, your methods worked in the past and things will get better again. Related to this is thinking that the problems are short-term only and will stop — just as the frog in boiling water believes. Finally, there is a tendency to delay tough decisions. In business, and sometimes in life, getting out of the boiling water requires difficult change, and human nature likes to avoid difficult change.

Some businesses ignore seriously deteriorating situations that evolve over many years, as much as a decade — just like the water that boils slowly. In others, the deteriorating situation may unfold somewhat faster, over just a few months or a few years, but still slow enough to be able to ignore it. Contrast this with situations where a business faces a major abrupt threat; the business is almost always forced to react quickly.

Examples of Ignoring Crucial Decisions

In this chapter, I use several examples to illustrate cases where crucial decisions were ignored until it was too late. There are also examples where companies finally saw the need to make crucial decisions and jumped out of the boiling water. While most of the examples here are major strategic decisions, this pitfall also applies to smaller operational decisions, too; I provide one example of such a situation.

Deterioration over Time (U.S. Auto Industry)

U.S. auto manufacturers found themselves in a deteriorating situation starting in the 1990s. While the specifics are a little different for each of the Big 3 at the time, the deterioration centered around the inroads of foreign competition. Figure 2-1 shows how foreign competition gained ground on U.S. auto manufacturers in the U.S. market. In a 10-year period from 1996 to 2006, North American car and truck sales by U.S. auto manufacturers dropped by 25%.

Foreign auto manufacturers were able to increasingly capture market share for several reasons. Some companies such as Toyota were able to produce higher-quality cars for less money. Consumers wanted a greater value from reliability, and some of the U.S. manufacturers found it difficult to match the quality and reliability of these foreign competitors.

U.S. car manufacturers also were finding it increasingly difficult to compete on price because their costs were much higher than those of their competitors. Over the previous decades, when there was less competition, the U.S. auto companies made significant concessions to the United Auto Workers (UAW) that raised hourly costs much higher than those of their competitors. When foreign auto companies started manufacturing their cars in the United States, they were able to get a significant labor cost advantage. Even worse, the U.S. auto companies were stuck with extraordinary legacy costs for retiree pension and medical benefits. We examine the reasons behind this in the next chapter on the longer-term consequences of short-term decisions.

The problems with the U.S. auto industry were not all cost related. The industry had a difficult time designing cars that people wanted to buy. They could not seem to anticipate buyer trends in their home market as fast as foreign competitors could, and most disturbing, it took the Big 3 much longer to design new cars. By 1997, Toyota and Honda took over the mid-sized car market. In 1999, Hyundai and Kia overcame their reputations for poor quality by offering 10-year war-

Figure 2-1 Decline in U.S. Auto Manufacturers' U.S. Sales

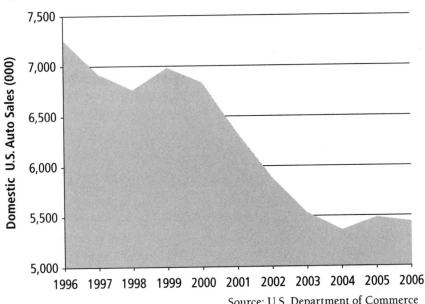

Source: U.S. Department of Commerce

ranties. The U.S. auto companies missed early opportunities to develop fuel-efficient cars. During this period, the U.S. auto manufacturers' focus was on SUVs, which were relatively easy to build and buyers were happy with them. Toward the end of the 1990s, Honda and Toyota began offering SUV-like crossovers. Adapting car designs instead of truck frames, Toyota developed the Highlander, and Honda came up with the Pilot and CRV. The crossovers lacked the off-road capabilities and towing power of traditional SUVs, but they gave smoother rides and achieved higher miles-per-gallon ratings. Ford Explorer sales fell from almost 434,000 units in 2002 to fewer than 240,000 in 2005. During this decade, the U.S. auto companies made some changes but did not react strongly enough to the evolving crisis.

It is helpful to look at how this decline specifically affected one of the U.S. auto companies, General Motors. As you can see in Figure 2-2, since 2001, GM's net income sputtered along at only a couple of billion dollars as it lost market share. In 2005, it lost $10.4 billion, more than its income over the previous four years. It continued to lose money in 2006 and lost almost $40 billion in 2007. Losses in 2008 were much higher still.

Over a 25-year period, GM's share of the domestic automobile and light truck market fell from half to a quarter. From 2002 to 2007, GM's

North American market share dropped from 28% to 23%. Michigan-based GM's toughest competition was not from Japan, but from Ohio, Kentucky, Tennessee, Mississippi, South Carolina, and the other states where foreign-owned auto companies established production facilities. Most foreign-owned auto plants in the United States are nonunionized. Their workers were not as generously compensated as GM's workers, but they were relatively well-paid with good benefits. And because their employers were not saddled with the pension and health-care costs of a UAW contract, the foreign-owned auto plants could produce cars at a more competitive price, creating more opportunity and job security for existing workers.

The reasons for GM's collapse are numerous and complex. Some are internal reasons that evolved over time: outdated designs, long development cycles, brand proliferation, expensive employment, and weak strategic decisions. Others are external reasons that also evolved over time: fuel prices and foreign competition. Combined, they created an untenable situation in which General Motors was no longer profitable or competitive.

Figure 2-2 GM's Net Income Deterioration

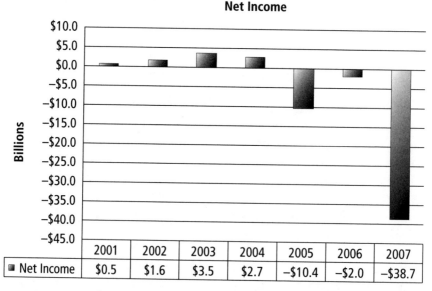

	2001	2002	2003	2004	2005	2006	2007
Net Income	$0.5	$1.6	$3.5	$2.7	−$10.4	−$2.0	−$38.7

GM and the rest of the U.S. auto manufacturers were like the proverbial frog in boiling water. They could see their competitive situation deteriorating, and while they did react to some extent, they did not make the really difficult decisions to change dramatically to get out of the boiling water. To be fair, they were restricted to some degree by union contracts, but they could have taken many other steps, and they could have renegotiated these contracts for everyone's best interest. Finally in late 2008, the U.S. auto market precipitously collapsed, with sales dropping 30% to 50%, and now there was a sufficient crisis to force change — but it was too late. Chrysler and GM were forced into bankruptcy in early 2009.

Boom to Bust (Subprime Mortgages)

Subprime mortgages are loans generally made to home buyers who do not have the income or financial resources to qualify under traditional mortgage lending standards. Subprime and other risky mortgages were relatively rare until the mid-1990s, but then they caught on. By 2001, subprime mortgages, so-called Alt-A loans (generally having incomplete documentation), and second mortgages totaled $330 billion, and grew rapidly to more than $1 trillion in 2004 and $1.4 trillion in 2006.[6]

Many businesses benefited during this subprime boom, which fueled the real estate boom. Real estate firms were able to make more home sales at increasingly higher prices. The number of mortgage brokers increased by an estimated 50%. Banks made money processing loans and then selling them. Appraisers were in demand. Business at Fannie Mae and Freddie Mac grew fantastically as they covered the rapid rise in subprime loans. Investment bankers profited from selling hundreds of billions of dollars worth of new products securitized by these subprime mortgages.

Then the boom went bust, and all of these businesses suffered. Fannie Mae was so devastated that it needed to be bailed out. The lesson here is that all of the businesses involved in the subprime market should have stepped back to think critically about the boom-to-bust cycle. In hindsight it was obvious, but boom-to-bust cycles happen throughout history, and a bust can be anticipated as a consequence of a boom. Most companies were too caught up in the irrational exuberance of the time to step back and make crucial decisions about getting out of the subprime market before it went bust.

Wishful Thinking (i2 Technologies)

One of the most frequent traps for ignoring the need to make crucial decisions is hoping that business will get better. The statement, "This year sales will improve," has been heard in many boardrooms.

Once in a while it is an accurate forecast, but most of the time it is just wishful thinking.

i2 Technologies is a company with which I am very familiar that was stuck in the wishful-thinking pitfall for years. i2 was once a great company with a stock market value of more than $40 billion, but then it discovered that much of its revenue was misstated, and the company had to restate almost $1 billion in revenue. From 1999 to 2004, i2 kept planning that its business would recover, but it was just wishful thinking. During that five-year period, the company accumulated loss after loss — reaching almost $1.5 billion in operating losses.

At the beginning of 2005, the board brought me in as CEO to make the tough decisions to turn around the company. There was no more wishful thinking; costs were reduced to match realistic revenue expectations. i2 was no longer a frog in boiling water; it jumped out. Net income was $98 million in 2005, more than $20 million per year in the next two years, and in 2008 income jumped to $109 million, including settlement of a patent lawsuit filed in 2006 for $83.3 million.

Product Life Cycles (Digital Equipment and Xerox)

All products have a life cycle: their sales grow, peak, and then decline. Product life cycles only vary by the length of the life cycle. In my book *Product Strategy for High-Technology Companies*, I analyze the failure to make crucial decisions on product life cycles, even though for many companies these can be their most important strategic decisions. Product-life-cycle decisions are like the frog in boiling water; you cannot just sit back and watch while the water boils. Here are two contrasting product-life-cycle examples: one company that failed to make the decision and one that did.

Digital Equipment pioneered minicomputers, and by the 1970s many experts believed it would displace IBM as the computer giant of the future. But Digital failed to make crucial decisions about the product life cycle of the minicomputer. During the 1980s, personal computers, made possible by emerging microprocessor technology, began to displace minicomputers in many applications. Digital Equipment failed to make crucial decisions on the decline of the minicomputer. As Figure 2-3 shows, Digital's net income rose during the late 1980s, but then started to decline in 1989. It kept falling for the next four years, as the profitable market for minicomputers was eroded by personal computers. In 1998 Compaq Computer acquired Digital for $9 billion, much less than it was worth in its peak years.

Figure 2-3 Digital Equipment Decline

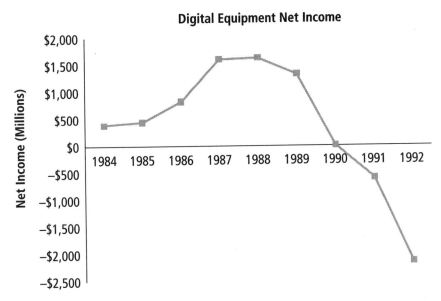

Ironically, Digital actually developed some exciting leading-edge technology in microprocessors, communications equipment, and Internet technology, but failed to exploit these developments because the company did not make crucial repositioning decisions.

In contrast, Xerox faced crucial decisions related to the decline of its proprietary light-lens technology used in its copiers. Xerox was the classic example of a company that would be displaced by new technology. But Xerox faced up to the crucial decision of replacing its most famous technology. The company anticipated the potential impact of digital technology and moved quickly. In 1990, it first applied digital technology in its DocuTech Production Publisher, the first high-resolution digital publishing system. Revenue from DocuTech products was $200 million in 1991. It more than doubled in 1992 to $500 million, continued to increase to $750 million in 1993, $1 billion in 1994, and $1.4 billion in 1995. Xerox continued to develop more digital products. It made the crucial decisions to replace its old technology with new digital technology, and as can be seen in Figure 2-4, by 1998 digital product sales exceeded sales from its old light-lens products.

Having the opportunity to work with Xerox during this transition, I watched it make the difficult decision to shift its R&D investments from traditional technology to digital technology. In this transition,

Figure 2-4 Xerox Shift to Digital Technology

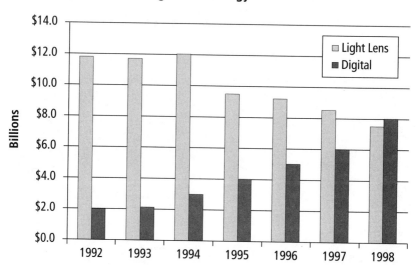

Xerox had the challenge of investing in both at the same time, but it was able to fund this by increasing R&D productivity.

Missed Cost-Reduction Opportunities

This next example is one that many organizations discovered in reacting to the downturn in the economy at the end of 2008. To counteract the threat of the impending impact of an economic downturn, a major company launched a cost-cutting campaign for 2009, reducing expenses by more than $25 million, and increasing profits even with lower-planned revenue. When the CEO reviewed this cost reduction with the board, he was asked how this cost reduction would impact the business. He responded by pointing out that most of the reductions would not significantly impact the business because they were the result of being more productive and cutting marginal expenses. One of the board members was surprised by this and asked why management did not decide to do this previously. The CEO responded by saying that they "just never thought about it." In a closed session of independent directors at the end of the meeting, some of the directors expressed a lack of confidence in the CEO because he did not make these changes earlier.

Numerous companies implemented cost-reduction decisions at the end of 2008 and the beginning of 2009 as the economy declined. Many of these companies then realized they could have achieved much of the savings without the threat of the downturn as the impetus for making business changes. While not as critical as some of these previous examples, such decisions illustrate how important issues are often addressed only when there is a crisis.

Missed Management Opportunity

The chief operating officer (COO) of a major corporation had worked with one of his subordinates, Mark, who he thought had excelled far greater than anyone else who had held the position previously. Whenever he saw Mark doing a good job, the COO thought that Mark deserved a promotion and a raise, but it was never the exact right time to implement it, so he constantly overlooked actually giving him the promotion. The COO kept telling himself that, one of these days, he would bring Mark into his office and talk about where his next move in the company would be. Then one day, Mark approached his boss and asked if they could speak. "Of course," the COO said. But Mark sprung something on him; he informed the COO that he had accepted an offer at another company.

If you do not make an effort to make an intentional decision, you may find that the decision passes you by.

The COO was absolutely taken off guard and tried relentlessly to get Mark to stay. He offered him a major promotion with a generous pay raise. Mark refused to accept the offer. It was not that he did not enjoy the job, and it certainly was not that he did not like the company or his coworkers. He kept refusing the offers from the COO because he had already accepted the offer from the other company and could not bring himself to break his commitment to that company. He had given his word, signed a contract, and there was no changing his mind on it. The COO understood, and he reluctantly let his best employee leave the company almost completely for the reason that the COO had failed to act and make an intentional decision to do what was necessary to keep Mark working for him. He had simply let the decision pass him by.

> **IN YOUR EXPERIENCE**
>
> *Have you ever looked back at a decision that you failed to make and said to yourself, "Why didn't I make that decision when I had the chance? Now I am stuck with the ramifications of inaction, and they are not what I had hoped."*

Avoiding the Pitfall of Ignoring Crucial Decisions

No simple techniques are available to avoid this pitfall of ignoring crucial decisions, but I can give some general advice and guidelines.

Critical Thinking

Critical thinking is purposeful and reflective judgment about what to believe or what to do in response to what is observed or expressed. Critical thinking calls for a persistent effort to examine any belief or knowledge in the light of evidence that supports it. It generally requires the ability to recognize problems, to find workable means for solving those problems, to gather and marshal pertinent information, and to recognize unstated assumptions.

As was seen with some of these examples, there seemed to be an absence of critical thinking. Much of the thinking seemed to be biased, distorted, partial, or uninformed. Crucial assumptions were not challenged. The results were tragic in many cases. I recommend that executives use critical thinking much more often, especially at critical junctures, which typically occur when everything seems to be going great.

Actively Make or Schedule Decisions

Just like the frog in boiling water mentioned at the beginning of this chapter, you will face numerous decisions in the business world that will simply pass you by if you do not make them intentionally before they pass you by. In the example given earlier, the COO's inaction let the decision on how to keep his best employee pass him by. He failed to make the decision a priority, and he lost the employee.

Do not allow your decisions to be made for you because you let them pass you by. Look at a specific decision that you know needs to be made and choose to actively make it. Maybe you have had a certain decision on your desk for months, but you have so far neglected to actively focus on it. Maybe it is not the most important decision you have to make and you have been busy, so you continue to ignore it. And maybe there is no deadline for the decision, while other decisions are more pressing with more serious repercussions for failing to make them. This decision has fallen by the wayside. You know that it needs to be made,

> You also need to make a concerted effort to make intentional decisions about those decisions you do not even know you need to make.

but you simply do not have the time or pressure on you to make it quickly. This is a prime situation for a decision that will pass you by.

In this situation, what you really need to do is to stop one day when the decision catches your eye. Maybe you have left yourself a note somewhere on your desk, occasionally glancing at it in passing. One of these times when you give the decision a glimpse, stop and think about it for a few minutes. When do you need to make the decision? Set a deadline and abide by it. Set an alarm, and when it goes off, make the decision. Better yet, make the decision right then, especially if it is something you have been thinking about for a while. Make it a priority to get this decision off of your desk and stop worrying about it.

Take Stock of Your Decisions

Other decisions may not be so apparent to you. You have seen how to approach a decision that you are aware of and know is hanging over you before it is made for you. How, though, can you make intentional decisions for those decisions that you may not know you should make? This could include decisions about promoting an employee, such as the example earlier in the chapter, or considering the launch of a new product, or whether you should consider restructuring your department. These may not be pressing decisions, and unless you proactively seek them out, you may overlook them. If you fail to take the initiative and take stock of these types of decisions, a time will come when the decisions have been made for you.

> You may want to set aside time every month, or maybe even every week, to take stock of what decisions you need to make.

To ensure that you do not miss these opportunities, schedule time on a regular basis to consider what decisions you should be thinking about but have not had the time to do so. Think about the big and small decisions and the strategic and tactical ones. You may want to set aside a couple of hours each month or 10 minutes every Monday afternoon, for example. Set a time frame with these reflection times built in, and hold firm to your time commitment.

Schedule Strategic Decisions as Part of Annual Planning

If you are trying to institutionalize more proactive intentional decisions in your company, another technique is to incorporate a decision schedule into your annual planning. Figure 2-5 illustrates how

**Figure 2-5 Coordinated Robotics Inc.
Critical Decisions Schedule for 2009**

Strategic Decisions

1. Consider acquisition of competitor X? (Q1)

2. Develop cost reduction program? (Q3)

3. Exit self-cleaning business? (Q2)

4. Reduce product line? (Q2)

5. Increase outsourcing? (Q3)

Financial Decisions

1. Refinance or repay debt? (Q2)

2. Resume dividend? (Q3)

3. Change auditors? (Q3)

Operational Decisions

1. Close or relocate LA office? (Q3)

2. Change assembly supplier? (Q2)

3. Expand capacity for military product line? (Q2)

4. Launch productivity program? (Q3)

Product/Technology

1. Fund advanced technology program? (Q3)

2. Extend industrial product line? (Q2)

3. Consider acquiring advanced optics technology? (Q1)

Marketing/Sales

1. Consider extending leasing program? (Q2)

2. Consider new sales commission plan? (Q3)

3. Reconsider 2010 sales conference to save cost? (Q3)

one company I worked with did this as part of its annual planning. The executives thought through the critical decisions needed in the upcoming year and scheduled them by quarter. For example, the company will consider refinancing or repaying some of its debt in Q2. When the executives meet at the beginning of the quarter, they review their critical decision schedule and determine which decisions will be made in the upcoming quarter. It is fine to delay a decision to a later quarter if it is more logical to do so, but they never overlook the importance of making intentional decisions.

In addition to helping avoid ignoring important strategic decisions, this technique has several other practical advantages. It can help to balance the workload of major decisions throughout the year by scheduling them more evenly. It can also help executives and managers anticipate upcoming strategic decisions and prepare informally for them.

- If you do not make an effort to make an intentional decision about something that is important, you may find that the decision passes you by.
- Sometimes there are decisions that you need to make simply to get them off your desk.
- Other decisions are of the type where you may not know that you are faced with a decision, and unless you stop to consider what decisions have to be made, they will pass you by.
- This problem of letting decisions pass you by can manifest itself in several other ways, including decisions that are ignored and cause deterioration over time, boom-to-bust decisions, wishful thinking, inattention to product life cycles, missed cost reduction opportunities, and missed management opportunities.
- There are effective mechanisms to prevent or stop all of these decision missteps, including critical thinking, actively making or scheduling decisions, routinely taking stock of your decisions, and scheduling strategic decisions as part of annual planning.
- Do not be like the frog in boiling water.

CHAPTER 3

Disregarding Long-Term Consequences

The long-term consequences of short-term decisions are often ignored

Far too often, businesses make decisions with short-term benefits that risk major long-term consequences. There is a lot of pressure on executives to make decisions to solve short-term problems and optimize short-term performance. Under this pressure they tend to ignore or downplay the longer-term consequences. Although it is not usually articulated, the thinking is that the executives will deal with the consequences when they eventually surface, or they will be somebody else's problem by the time that happens. In difficult situations, short-term pressure increases, making it more likely to create longer-term problems in the future. When considered broadly, this pitfall is not limited to business. It is a very big problem with politicians and government leaders who are focused mostly on their own terms in office and re-election is their primary long-term concern. In the future, somebody else will be in office and have to deal with the longer-term consequences of their policy decisions.

> Far too often, businesses make decisions with short-term benefits that risk major long-term consequences.

In this chapter I examine this pitfall and look at the way business practices, such as incentive compensation, are used to force this short-term pressure.

Examples of Short-Term Decisions

Falling into the pitfall of making short-term decisions while ignoring the long-term consequences happens in many different ways. The examples that follow illustrate some of these situations.

Short-Term Labor Concessions (Auto Manufacturers' Mistake)

In 2007, workers at the nation's Big 3 automakers — Ford, Chrysler, and General Motors — decided that they were not receiving sufficient pay and benefits. Acting through the United Auto Workers (UAW), the union that represents workers at the plants operated by the auto manufacturers, the workers went to the management of the companies and demanded that certain additional provisions be added to their contracts. They essentially wanted a complete renegotiation of their contracts. The companies balked, of course, since they did not want to pay these additional costs. As a result, the UAW made a threat: either renegotiate our contracts or we will organize a strike.

The dynamics of the relationship between the automakers and the United Auto Workers are not always pleasant. There is an up-and-down history between workers and the automakers' management, and both sides have learned tricks to use when seeking concessions from the other side. One of these is a strategic strike threat by the union. Workers selected one of the major companies to negotiate with, threatening a strike against that one company. In 2007, General Motors was selected for the strike threat.

The two main issues were job security and retiree health-care costs. General Motors — and the other automakers — preferred to release employees who had a higher pay grade and bring in ones with less experience at lower pay to save money, something that those laid-off workers obviously did not like. In terms of health-care costs, the employees insisted that, upon retirement, the company continue to cover the costs of insurance for the retired workers. The demands were put to GM, and the two sides negotiated for 20 straight days in an effort to come to a compromise. When General Motors refused to budge, the UAW called a strike. On September 24, 2007, 74,000 employees at 82 GM plants nationwide began a strike that shut down the company's production capabilities completely. After only two days, General Motors had largely caved in to the demands of the union. An agreement was reached at 3:05 a.m. on September 26, 2007, and workers returned to work that day.

The new four-year contract incorporated mechanisms that would address the workers' concerns regarding job security and health care. In one of the programs in the negotiations, the jobs bank program, employees who were laid off were allowed to receive 95% of their take-home pay and benefits until they were able to secure another job. As for retiree health-care costs, General Motors agreed to create an independent trust, managed by the UAW, that would cover the costs of health insurance for retired auto workers. General Motors would pay into the fund to establish it and make regular payments to it to sustain the program.

In addition to these concessions, GM also agreed to a moratorium on outsourcing its manufacturing for the entire four years of the contract, as well as committing to build all of its current and future cars and trucks at existing plants. It also transferred 3,000 temporary workers into permanent status with full-time wages. These steps went a long way to assuaging the job-loss fears of the employees.

In November 2008, Andrew Ross Sorkin published an article in the *New York Times*[7] where he laid out his argument that short-term decisions made by the management of General Motors and the other U.S. automobile manufacturers ultimately led to the complete crash of the automobile market in the United States. As he argued in the article, the company's deal with the UAW was the straw that broke the camel's back. Due to the additional details agreed to in the negotiations, the average cost of a single employee, including regular pay and health care, according to Sorkin's estimates, was $74 an hour. In comparison, American workers at plants run by Toyota made only $44 per hour, including benefits — a similar amount to other foreign-owned car manufacturers operating within the United States.

> **IN YOUR EXPERIENCE**
>
> *Have you ever been tempted to make a decision with long-term consequences to solve a short-term crisis because it was easier to do? Did you go through with it? What were the consequences? Was it worth it?*

While it is highly unlikely that the deal reached between GM and the UAW completely caused the crisis in the auto industry in late 2008/2009, it certainly contributed to the financial problems that the industry experienced. The management at GM can be faulted for giving in to the demands of the UAW in an effort to restart the plants and production of cars and trucks, without fully considering the actual longer-term consequences to its financial competitive health. Of course, rising gas prices, competition from abroad, poor strategic decisions, and the precipitous downturn in the economy also made major contributions to the crisis of the auto manufacturing industry. But this decision to pursue short-term benefits at the expense of long-term survival was certainly important to the financial health of the U.S. auto industry.

Dodging Short-Term Taxes (State Pension Funds)

Short-term pressures to push problems out into the future are not just seen in business. Governments are also pushed by the political pressure of the moment to make decisions that benefit the short run by moving the cost into the future for others to worry about after their term in office. At a national level, we see this in unfunded Social Security and Medicare commitments that keep today's taxpayers content but put an extraordinary burden on future taxpayers. The constant increase in national debt that will need to be repaid in the future by tax increases or severe spending cuts is yet another example. Let's look at one specific example of this pitfall at the state government level.

Many states move their pension fund obligations from the immediate term into the future through gimmicks and accounting ploys. Pension plans require that payments are made annually to meet future obligations, and assumptions of the future gains from investments are a key factor in determining the amount of these payments. I use New Jersey as an example.

> If you let current crises get in the way of longer-term strategy, you will be more likely to jeopardize your survivability.

Under political pressure to avoid another tax increase to balance the budget in 1992, New Jersey passed the Pension Revaluation Act. By being more aggressive in the way it recognized investment gains and assuming a long-term average return of 8.75% instead of 7%, New Jersey was able to reduce its pension contributions by more than $1.5 billion in 1992 and 1993. Again in 1993, New Jersey adopted other "reforms" that enabled it to reduce pension fund payments by almost $1.5 billion in 1994 and 1995. Short-term fixes like these tend to be addictive. To avoid a tax increase following the 1993 "savings," another fix was needed.

In 1997, New Jersey turned to risky arbitrage investing by borrowing $2.75 billion of bonds at 7.6% interest so it could invest in the stock market to get higher returns. The state projected this arbitrage would save taxpayers $45 billion, but of course it backfired because the return on its investments was much less than the 7.6% it had to pay. So it cost taxpayers more money in the future. By May 2009, New Jersey's pension plan was underfunded by approximately $60 billion (including a loss of about $26 billion in investments). This will need to be paid by taxpayers in the future — the long-term consequence of short-term decisions.[8]

Performance Pressure (Washington Mutual)

In most companies there is pressure to perform, particularly in the sales functions, but in some cases this pressure becomes so intense that it forces very bad short-term decisions to create revenue, despite future consequences. One example of this is Washington Mutual (WaMu). It aggressively built its mortgage business by increasingly giving mortgages to people who were not qualified.

WaMu was an aggressive lender that showed its eagerness to lend with its "The Power of Yes" campaign to underscore that it would say yes to almost any loan. Performance pressure forced employees to make approval decisions on mortgage loans that should have been turned down. Former employees claimed that WaMu pressed sales agents to pump out loans while disregarding borrower's incomes and assets. Mortgage brokers received big commissions for selling the riskiest loans.

As a result of these mortgage approval decisions, WaMu's home lending business jumped from $707 million in 2002 to almost $2 billion the following year. In September 2008, WaMu had approximately $180 billion in mortgage-related loans when the subprime mortgage market collapsed. Because of its reckless mortgage loans, WaMu was insolvent, and regulators seized the bank and sold it to JP Morgan for $1.9 billion, a small portion of its peak market valuation of $40 billion.

The WaMu example shows how pressure for short-term decisions — approving mortgages — can have dire longer-term consequences. In this case there were also some very unfortunate collateral consequences to these mortgage-approval decisions. Many borrowers who were not qualified to borrow later struggled to pay their mortgages, and some of them lost their homes.

Quarterly Performance Pressure

When I was a management consultant to CEOs of public companies, I used to give them advice to forgo decisions that benefited quarterly results at the risk of future costs. Later when I became CEO of i2 Technologies and had to do my quarterly earnings call and was graded the next day by analysts, I internalized this pressure myself.

The pressure on quarterly performance is intense. Many companies are pressured into making end-of-quarter decisions to increase sales by giving customers discounts or favorable payment terms. For example, one company I ran was considering buying a large printing/reproduction printer, but was not ready to decide for a few weeks. However, on the last day of the quarter, the salesman came into my office about noon and said that he had a deal for me. He offered another 25% discount over the 15% already proposed, but I had to take delivery that day — the last day of the quarter. I was tempted but pointed out that it was already noon, and it was impossible to have it delivered and installed that day. He smiled and told me that he had the printer on a truck circling the office as we spoke and the technician to install it was waiting in the lobby. My company saved 25% since we would have bought it in a few weeks, and the printer company lost 25% because it would have made the sale without the additional discount.

Short-Term Incentive Compensation

For many executives and salespeople, short-term bonuses or commissions are a significant part of their compensation. In some cases, though not all, this incentivizes them to make decisions that have a short-term bias. They try to pull in sales in order to be recognized in the current quarter or year, and it can cause other aberrations. Staying with our WaMu example, here is an outrageous example of biased short-term incentives.

Kerry Killinger reportedly received $88 million in compensation between 2001 and 2007 driving WaMu to short-term decisions with disastrous longer-term consequences. He reportedly pushed people to write mortgages because his incentive compensation was based on revenue and not the longer-term quality of the mortgages they made. He and the executive team were even able to exclude mortgage losses from the computation of their bonuses, giving them the best of both sides.[9] WaMu justified this plan in 2007 by acknowledging the "challenging business environment and the need to evaluate performance across a wide range of factors." Apparently, that "wide range of factors" did not include evaluating management members whose jobs included ensuring the longer-term consequences of the company's loan portfolio in the first place.

Avoiding the Pitfall of Ignoring Long-Term Consequences in Decisions

Remaining aware of the long-term consequences of short-term decisions is probably the best advice I can give. There is no special technique to use to avoid this pitfall, but here are a few considerations that I recommend.

Do Not Get Caught Up in the Moment

Perhaps the most important lesson to learn from the General Motors example is that you cannot get caught up in the moment. This is the largest cause of decisions that will help executives in the short term but have potentially disastrous consequences for the long term. It is easy to see how this could happen. Businesses constantly struggle with increasing profits and reducing expenses. Sometimes events do not go as planned. Expected returns on investment can be threatened, perhaps because of a delay in the release date for a new product, a facility that had to close unexpectedly, a strike such as the one in the UAW/GM example, or even just a key employee leaving the company at a bad time.

Crises happen; this is simply the nature of the beast. But if you let the current crisis take over your rational thought processes, you run the risk of potentially causing much more serious damage to the company in the future.

Evaluate the Short Term vs. the Long Term

The key to making better decisions when you are facing an immediate problem that needs to be addressed is simple. You need to fully evaluate all of the potential consequences within the context of the short-term benefits. Here is an example from a company that provides long-term outsourcing services. The company had an opportunity for a major long-term contract to provide outsourcing of maintenance for a current customer. In proposing the job, the company talked about how it could make productivity improvements over the term of the contract, and in the final negotiations the customer took advantage of this in its pricing.

To get the contract, the company had to guarantee price reduction in the later years of a 10-year contract. The contract was large: $75 million in the first year, and a total of $600 million over the 10-year term. The salesperson and VP of sales argued strenuously for the contract. The CFO was tempted by the increased cash flow it would bring, but was concerned about the long-term consequences.

So the company did an analysis of the potential long-term consequences of the contract. The first cut at this review was based on a constant level of cost; in other words, the company would not be able to realize productivity improvements. This is illustrated in Figure 3-1. While the short-term profits were attractive, the risk of long-term losses was a concern. The salespeople argued that, with productivity improvements, the losses could turn to breakeven or perhaps even profits in the later years.

Figure 3-1 Evaluating Long-Term Consequences

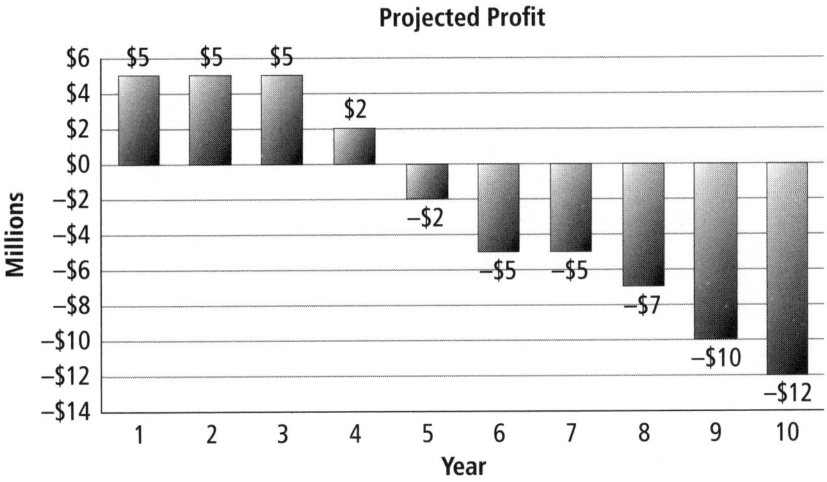

While there was agreement that the longer-term projections would not be this bad, and some productivity improvements were certain, the risk of the longer-term costs was just too much. The company refused the contract and tried to renegotiate it with the customer, but this was unsuccessful. The company could have been tempted to use the boost in profit revenue to improve its stock price. Some even argued that the potential increase in stock price offset the risk of future losses. Short-term pressures were strong, but the company made the right decision for the longer term.

Be Aware of Excessive Short-Term Incentives and Pressure

I doubt that short-term incentives can be balanced with the long-term consequences of the decisions they encourage. The quarterly revenue and earnings performance demanded by Wall Street is unlikely to change. It will continue to emphasize short-term results, and executives and boards of directors will need to have the courage to recognize this emphasis and balance it against the long-term consequences of their decisions.

They can do this in several ways, starting with long-term plans. They need to make the trade-offs that may lower earnings in the upcoming year but will have important long-term benefits. This longer-term focus continues with executive compensation plans. When possible, these plans should balance long-term and short-term performance and certainly not excessively reward short-term performance while ignoring the longer-term consequences.

- Consider the long-term consequences of your short-term decisions.

- A crucial component of your success is how you decide to proceed when you have to balance your short-term and long-term decisions.

- If you proactively examine what the longer-term consequences are of your decisions when you face immediate problems that require your attention, you will be more likely to succeed.

- Do not get caught up in the moment, but rather evaluate both the short-term and long-term consequences of your decisions.

CHAPTER 4

Throwing Good Money after Bad

The perils of not considering sunk money sunk

When I taught in the MBA program at Northeastern University, I used the following technique to teach the students a lesson about decision making: I auctioned a $1 bill. As with any auction, the highest bidder would win the dollar. The only catch was that the second-highest bidder would also have to pay what he or she bid, but would not get the dollar. The bidding would always start out enthusiastically with each student trying to outbid the others, until the bids approached $1, at which point everyone usually dropped out except for the two highest bidders.

When these two bidders realized that they had "invested" almost a dollar and might not get it back, they inevitably continued the bidding over $1. Their logic was generally that "I have already invested $0.95 or $1.05 or $1.25, so why not pay 10 cents more to get the dollar bill?" The bidding continued, often surpassing $3 or even $5, for that $1 bill. Eventually, one of the bidders realized what was going on and stopped bidding, paying several dollars and getting nothing in return. The "winning" bidder got the dollar, but he or she paid many times what it was worth. By the way, I always

IN YOUR EXPERIENCE
Have you ever faced a decision where you had to decide to invest more and more time or money into a project with no guarantee that it would pay off in the end? What did you decide? Was it a good decision?

took their money to teach them a lesson, and then donated it to someone on the street when I left class.

This exercise illustrates the faulty thinking behind a number of bad business decisions, particularly decisions related to investments. The decision to put more money into an endeavor that has already cost too much is often called "throwing good money after bad."

Examples of Throwing Good Money after Bad

When I ask executives about their bad decisions, most of them include one example where they wished they had the wisdom or courage to stop a bad investment instead of continuing to put more into it. Here are a range of examples that illustrate this pitfall.

Throwing the Company into a Bad Endeavor (Bear Stearns)

Bear Stearns created two hedge funds to invest in collateralized debt obligations (CDOs) backed by subprime mortgages. The investment theory was that CDOs paid an interest rate over and above the cost of borrowing, so these hedge funds made a profit on that difference. Thus, every incremental unit of leverage increased the total expected return. These funds used leverage to buy more CDOs than they could pay for with their own capital, so it was very profitable. Originally, Bear had only made a $20 million equity investment in these funds.

Unfortunately, the CDO market began to unravel as delinquencies increased in subprime mortgages, which in turn caused sharp decreases in the market values for CDOs. Because Bear had leveraged its loans substantially, the funds began to experience large losses, which concerned creditors who had taken these subprime mortgage-backed bonds as collateral on the loans. The lenders required the Bear Stearns funds to provide additional cash on these loans because the collateral (subprime mortgages) was rapidly falling in value. Unfortunately the funds had little cash because they were so highly leveraged.

> When you make decisions on continued investments, be careful of justifying these decisions based solely on what you have invested up to that point.

Although initially Bear's risk was limited to its original $20 million, it then invested an additional $25 million as the funds began to fail. In doing this, Bear decided to throw a lot more good money after bad. In June 2008, Bear Stearns committed as much as $3.2 billion to one of the funds, the High-Grade Fund, letting the Enhanced Fund fail. When the High-Grade Fund later failed, too, Bear Stearns had loaned the fund almost $1.5 billion. This additional investment was so large that it brought Bear Stearns itself down. Bear could have limited its loss to $20 million to $45 million, and although its reputation would have been tarnished, it could have survived. Instead, it succumbed to the temptation of throwing good money after bad.[10]

Creeping Investment (Data Communications Company)

Here is an example of how a company can progressively make decisions to throw good money after bad. A data communications company was working on a new switching system for a large market. As a competitive company with a large market share for similar systems, the company was in a good position to take advantage of this opportunity. Figure 4-1 illustrates the progression of decisions.

This appeared to be a good product investment opportunity, and the company approved an investment of $80 million with an expected profit of $150 million. A few months later, the costs were estimated more accurately, and the investment was raised to $100 million, but was still considered a good investment. Then, as problems and delays occurred, the estimated cost increased to $135 million and the expected profit was reduced to $110 million because the product would now be late to market. Here is where sunk costs began to come in. At this

Figure 4-1 Progressions of Decisions

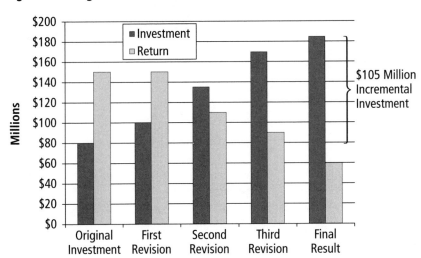

point, the total project was projected to be a loss, but with $100 million already invested, the decision was to go ahead. The justification was that an incremental $35 million would generate a profit of $100 million, as long as these were the last changes — but they were not.

Problems continued, and there was a third revision. The projected cost jumped to $170 million, and the profit was further revised down to $90 million. The management team felt that with $135 million already invested, the company needed to finish this product no matter what. In the end, the product was completed for a cost of $185 million and returned only $60 million, for a loss on the investment of $125 million. The company invested $105 million more than originally projected, and the profit was $90 million less than projected.

The company lost more money than its originally approved investment. It should have decided this was a sunk cost and canceled the project, but the decision turned into a progressive set of decisions, with each increment making some sense. The key decision point was at the second revision where the profit estimate began to erode. At this point, the company should have done a more thorough review of the potential cost to complete the project and the impact on profit of being late to market.

Software Company

A software company that produced specialized accounting and other business software was in the process of developing new medical billing software that could be used to track patients and their billing records. It was truly going to revolutionize the way medical billing and patient tracking were being done at hospitals. The company budgeted $4 million for the development of the complex software, as well as an additional $2 million for an aggressive marketing campaign leading up to the initial software release. The project was thoroughly studied prior to the board of directors approving its development. It was predicted that the prospects for success were extraordinary, but to realize sufficient sales, the software would need to be released within one and a half years.

The developers worked as hard as possible, as much as 75 hours per week, to complete the software on schedule. The head of the development team for the product was hopeful for an on-time completion, but also knew that there would be a lot of long hours and that there could be no kinks in the process to meet the deadline. Six months into the project, the software was on schedule. A year into the project, there were a few issues that concerned the head of development that had the potential to delay the release date. A few months later, the lead software architect was forced to leave his job because of serious health problems. Just one week later, two of the best developers announced they would be leaving the company for a competitor. At the same time, the sales and marketing department notified the CEO that a competitor was extremely close to completing a rival product and that, if its software was not completed on time, the competitor would be able to cut significantly into the product opportunity. Virtually every hospital was tied into a very small network of computer service providers, and each hospital was looking for the new generation of tracking and billing software.

Just a few weeks before the product was slated for release, the head of development submitted his letter of resignation. He had not disclosed all of the costs and pitfalls of the new software. There was essentially no way the product would be ready for delivery to customers, some of which had prepaid large sums of money for it. While a beta version of the software had been presented with many of the features, the actual product still had major security problems and software glitches. When the head of development resigned, the CEO was left with a big crisis, and he faced a major decision with three options:

1. Release the product without some key features and with security problems. It would be only a little over budget, but risked losing a portion of its customers.
2. Completely end the project despite such a big investment.
3. Sink another $4 million investment into the project to release the product in the next six months with all features that were required for full capability.

None of the options seemed attractive to the CEO, but he had to make a decision. He consulted with many people, including key board members, developers, marketers, and others. After these consultations, he determined that the company had spent so much money on the software that, if it did not release the product with all features, it would lose a substantial amount of money. He went to the board of directors with a recommendation to invest an additional $4 million to ensure complete functionality and release of the product in six months. Predictably, the board was visibly upset with the fact that they were not informed in a timely manner about the lack of progress, but they approved the request after serious resistance.

The CEO hired a new head for the project and spent a large amount of money on contractors to write and fix the code for the product, as well as to assure new clients that the product would be available in six months. Ultimately, the product was delayed by six months before the full software was available, and 75% of customers canceled their contracts, requiring $3 million in refunds.

The company lost all of the money it invested the product. In fact, the company almost went out of business because of the failure. The CEO submitted his letter of resignation, which was swiftly accepted by the board of directors.

Consider Sunk Costs Sunk

In economics and business decision making, sunk costs are costs that cannot be recovered once they have been incurred, as opposed to future costs, which are costs that will be incurred if the decision is to invest more. Traditional economic theory assumes that sunk costs should not influence decisions, because doing so would not be rationally assessing a decision exclusively on its own merits. Behavioral economic theory, on the other hand, proposes that sunk costs affect decisions, because humans are inherently averse to losing money and will act irrationally when making sunk-cost decisions. Economists would label this behavior "irrational" and inefficient because it misallocates resources by depending on information that is irrelevant to the decision being made.

The sunk-cost fallacy is also sometimes known as the "Concorde Effect," referring to the British and French governments' continued investment in the joint development of the Concorde even after it became apparent that there was no longer an economic case for the aircraft. The project was regarded privately by the British government as a commercial disaster that should never have been started, and should have been canceled, but political and legal issues ultimately made it impossible for either government to pull out.

Sunk costs apply not only to money, but also to time and emotion. In fact, the tendency to ignore sunk costs in a decision is sometimes greater if there has been a big emotional investment. You may have invested a lot of time

The decision to keep investing in something is not always the wrong decision; sometimes it can even be the best decision. But you should always consider sunk money to be sunk.

and effort into a project and do not want to cancel it because of all that you put into it. Even so, you need to consider this as a sunk cost.

When you make decisions on continued investment, whether it is in time or money, be careful not to justify the decision based on what you have invested up to that point. Look upon your previous investment as a sunk cost, and base your new investment on its own merit. I usually recommend that sunk costs be identified and labeled as "sunk costs" so they are visible to everyone involved in the decision, but not considered strongly in making the decision. You might want to say, "OK, we have a lot invested in this already, but let's set that aside as a sunk cost and make a new rational decision going forward."

Progressively Throwing Good Money after Bad

Frequently, the decision to throw good money after bad is really a series of decisions, which progressively turns out to be a set of bad decisions. As we saw in the creeping investment example of the data communications company, each individual decision to continue to invest more may make some sense, but the situation grew progressively worse. What do you do in these cases?

When you need to increase your investment in a new endeavor, do not just look at justifying the incremental investment. Step back and look at the bigger picture. Reassess the project or endeavor. I have found that once things start to go wrong, they are likely to continue to deteriorate. Just as in the example, one increase leads to another, and the increased investment and time can frequently lead to lower success as the project is delayed.

Look at the possible range of new outcomes, not just a change to the original plan. Understand what caused the problems, because this may lead to similar problems in the near future. In the end, make your decision on this range of consequences.

Should You Invest More?

Of course, the decision to keep investing in something is not always the wrong decision. Often, the investments you have already made can put you in a position where an incremental or additional investment will have a big payoff. This can be particularly true with regard to financial investments and investments in new products.

Here is a useful example: A real estate development company was involved in a number of different types of properties, including houses in need of renovation that they would purchase and proceed to "flip," which is to renovate them quickly, then turn around and sell them for a profit. Time and time again, the company would be required to make decisions about how much renovation and investment in these properties was sufficient to sell them, much of which depended upon current market conditions, the neighborhood, and the price it both paid for the house and sought once it was renovated. Sometimes they made out big.

The company was frequently put into a position of making incremental investments. Sometimes it found that the price it paid for the house was too high, but the incremental investment would increase the resale price by more than the cost. In these cases, it made sense to put additional investment into the project in order to recoup some of the loss.

The company did not make these incremental investments blindly, though. In one case, the company purchased a house in need of moderate renovations for a pretty high price, certain they could still turn a profit with the minimal, mostly cosmetic improvements they deemed necessary. Upon tearing out many of the existing features of the house, however, far more problems than expected surfaced. The company faced a decision: how much money could it invest in the property, knowing that it was likely to sell the house for a loss even after their renovations? After long deliberations, the company decided to invest only enough to return the house to its original condition and sell it quickly, even if it meant selling it for less than the purchase price. Knowing that it should not invest good money after bad, the company decided to cap its losses rather than renovate the property completely.

- In business, you need to make careful decisions about investing more time or money into a project in which you have already invested heavily.
- Investing more time or money could be the best decision, but not necessarily all of the time.
- When making a decision about continued investment, consider your sunk costs as already being sunk, at the risk of falling into the trap of creeping investment.

CHAPTER 5

Underestimating Deceptively Simple Decisions

*Be careful of making decisions that
seem too easy; they probably are*

Have you ever made a decision to undertake something that you thought was relatively simple, only to later find out that it was much harder than you thought originally? Upon reflection, you realize that there was a lot that you did not know when you made your decision, but took for granted. You may not have even known what questions to ask because you "did not know what you did not know." You think something is deceptively simple because you really do not know much about it.

This is a common decision pitfall in business — one that I call deceptively simple decisions. A decision is deceptively simple when the manager or group thinks the decision is easy, but it really just appears easy due to their lack of experience. They look at it superficially and figure that they know enough about it, but are deceived. When they go forward with a major decision on this erroneous assumption that it is simple, they progressively realize that it is much more difficult than they originally thought.

> Something is deceptively simple when you think it is easy because you really do not know much about it.

Generally, the deceptively simple decision pitfall applies to new endeavors, which are likely to have more unknowns. This can include major strategic decisions such as acquisitions, new products, expansion into new markets, and new initiatives or investments where a company is inexperienced. The deceptively simple pitfall can also apply to smaller decisions, such as hiring an employee for a newly created job, buying a new computer system, or reorganizing a department.

Examples of Deceptively Simple Decisions

Deceptively simple decisions occur in many aspects of business when something is new or unknown but appears simple on the surface. You make assumptions that overlook problems or issues that you would know if you were more experienced. Frequently, deceptively simple decisions occur in business decisions when investing in new areas, such as the following examples illustrate.

AIG

AIG was one of the largest and most successful insurance companies in the world. It did business in a broad range of insurance offerings. In 1987, it created a Financial Products group, which was essentially a hedge fund. One of its new products was credit default swaps (CDSs), which were insurance policies against the default of a bond or loan repayment. The CDS business took off when AIG started to insure collateralized debt obligations (CDOs), essentially securities that were backed by subprime mortgages. Companies with CDOs could offset their risk by buying this insurance from AIG. Initially, it was a very profitable business.

In its basic form a CDS was like an insurance policy, so AIG thought this was an easy way to make a lot of money. But this was deceptively simple. What AIG did not understand was that it was not insuring a diversified risk (such as one house burning down); it was insuring a systemic risk, the decline in value of subprime mortgages. In a way this was the opposite of what insurance companies do by diversifying risk.

As subprime mortgages declined in value, AIG had to come up with more assets and credit to cover these losses. Eventually this new product decision, CDS, caused AIG's collapse. AIG was bailed out by the U.S. government with more than $150 billion, and will need to repay that loan by selling its other profitable businesses. AIG's decision to enter the CDS market seemed simple. They were easy insurance policies to sell, but it turned out to be deceptively simple — and fatal.

Google Radio Business

Google was a pioneer in using ad words to get advertisers to bid for selective placement on a pay-per-click program on the Internet. Essentially, Google would auction keyword placement to the highest bidder on an ongoing basis. This strategy and the techniques Google pioneered significantly increased its advertising revenue over the traditional approach of selling ad placement for a set price.

Based on this success, Google thought it could replicate these brilliant techniques in other businesses. In 2006, it decided to enter the business of selling advertising for radio stations. It looked relatively easy to Google. The company would just automate pricing for radio ads as it did with its search engine. Google believed that it could generate increased advertising revenue for radio stations just as it did for itself by holding online advertising auctions. In January 2006, Google acquired dMarc for $102 million and up to $1.1 billion more depending on its success. In October 2006, Eric Schmidt, Google's CEO, was positive about this new business, saying that he "expected more than 1,000 people will ultimately work on Google's efforts in radio advertising, which will someday sell radio ads over a modified version of its current AdWords placement service. The idea: Let a marketer allocate an ad budget across multiple platforms, either in an automated manner or by targeting times and regions."

Developing the technology to auction and track radio advertising proved to be much harder than Google anticipated. It took longer to develop and was much more expensive than planned. On top of that, the radio advertising market was entirely different from Google's search-engine-based ad word business. Google underestimated the uniqueness of this market, particularly the way stations bought advertising. After launching the service, Google sold very little advertising. It encountered resistance in the radio industry, which relied heavily on sales representatives. The hurdle mentioned most often was Google's apparent inability to secure enough air time, or inventory, to make its system attractive to advertisers. Finally, in January 2009, Google decided to kill the entire project, losing an undisclosed, but substantial, investment.[11]

Google made the classic mistake of thinking this new business was easy. It was successful in using auctions for ad words in its search engine business, and the radio advertising business seemed so much easier. Google learned the lesson that things seem simple when "you do not know what you do not know."

Automotive Electronics Company

A major automotive electronics company wanted to expand, and it identified marine electronics as a great opportunity. Even though the company had no experience in this market, the executive team reasoned that marine electronics had to be a lot easier than the automotive market, and there were similarities in terms of technology and distribution. In the end, the company lost more than $20 million over the next two years selling less than $1 million in marine products. After investing so heavily in the expansion, the executive team realized that the company could not make waterproof devices very easily or break into the channels of distribution to sell marine electronics. The company had completely underestimated the demand in the market. Soon after, the CEO was fired, and he knew he learned a lesson that he was deceived by an opportunity that only looked simple. He realized he should have insisted the company investigate its ability to enter the market more carefully before delving into the new venture.

Avoiding the Deceptively Simple Decision Pitfall

This is one decision pitfall that can be easily avoided, and it starts with caution. When something looks simple, step back and ask yourself: could it be because there are things you do not know and should? Here is some other advice for avoiding this pitfall.

Do Your Research

Decisions on major new undertakings are most vulnerable to the deceptively simple syndrome. These include selling a new product ("if others can sell it, so can we"), entering a completely new market ("it has to be easier"), or opening in a new location ("it cannot be any different from our current location"). But do not consider major undertakings lightly. Before deciding to enter into a new endeavor, do your research. Talk with others who have experience. Think about how you would overcome challenges. Read books with tips about this type of project or search the Internet for resources to assist you. Additionally, ask yourself these questions before you delve into a new project that appears to be simple:

- How much do you know about the endeavor already?
- What do you not know about what you will need to do to achieve success?
- Prior to making a large commitment, how can you learn more about the steps to take to be successful?
- What are the risks involved in committing to the endeavor and later being forced to reverse course or end it completely?
- What resources are available for you to explore the unfamiliar components of the endeavor?
- Are you more knowledgeable than others who have tried to accomplish something similar in the past?
- Why do you believe you have everything necessary to be successful at this endeavor?

Do not misunderstand; I am not suggesting that you avoid major new undertakings completely. After all, these provide some of the biggest rewards and opportunities for businesses. You should make bold decisions about doing something new and different, but do so with your eyes wide open to the challenges you are likely to face. Then assess your ability to take on such challenges, again asking pertinent questions:

- Do you have the financial, material, and technical assets to take the risk?
- What is your exit strategy if the venture does not pan out the way you had hoped?
- How will a failure impact the viability of your company?
- Are you able to back out of a failing endeavor without losing everything?

As you approach new and exciting ventures, remember the famous saying, "If something looks too good to be true, it probably is." So before you get too deep into it, find out if that saying applies to what you are seeking to accomplish. Doing so will help you to avoid the deceptively simple syndrome and save you a world of trouble in the end.

Learn from Your Experiences

Even successful corporations make bad decisions based upon faulty assumptions. But some also learn from these mistakes. The automotive

> Make bold decisions to do something new and different, but do so with your eyes wide open to the challenges involved.

electronics company took its lesson to heart when it began to explore entering into a different market than its primary one. Having been burned by previous forays into new markets, it took a very careful approach the next time. The new market it considered entering was the production and distribution of global positioning system (GPS) devices, which were just starting to become very popular and inexpensive enough to stimulate market growth. Before committing to entering the market — one they knew was lucrative and expanding rapidly — the company decided that it would study the opportunity carefully.

The project team talked with designers and engineers. They asked their sales and marketing department to perform a study on what it would take to be competitive with the other companies in the industry. The team looked at the challenges to distribute the products to existing and new retailers. The company spent close to half a million dollars on the project to determine its chances for success — money it deemed well spent — and found that it would be close to impossible for the company to enter the market successfully from scratch.

Learning this, the executive team decided to pursue a different goal: to purchase a small company that already was in the market for manufacturing and distributing GPS devices. The company carefully reviewed its options, negotiated shrewdly with a few companies, and eventually settled on one company with state-of-the-art technology and significant sales potential. The decision turned out to be a big success, and the company grew exponentially upon beginning to sell the new devices.

Seek Outside Advice

If there are components to your decision that you do not know, but should, you probably need to seek outside advice. Hiring a consultant is the easiest way. For most problems there are qualified consulting firms with extensive experience in this new area. Just make sure they have real experience. Some firms may just claim they do, and remember you are at a disadvantage in making this decision because you may not know what experience you are looking for. You can also talk with others already in this area. Do not hesitate to reach out to everyone who can help, including competitors, as I did in one situation.

My management consulting firm was successful in the United States, and now we wanted to expand into Europe. We knew we should start in the United Kingdom because the language barriers were minimal. But I had to make the decision of where to open the first U.K. office. That seemed like a simple decision. We had already opened new offices in the United States, so how hard could it be? But after considering it, I realized it could be deceptively simple.

We already had some projects in Scotland, but most consulting firms were based in London. I just did not have the experience to make this decision. So boldly, I called the U.K. managing directors of all the major consulting firms (our competitors), and surprisingly five out of the six I called agreed to meet with me in person. They were all generous in helping me, educating me on the way the U.K. consulting market worked, how services were sold, what firms were strong in what markets, and even billing rates they charged. By the end of the meetings, I knew a lot more about the U.K. market, and while they all recommended that our first office should be in London, I decided to put it in Scotland. My rationale was that I learned these firms were very strong in London, but weak in Scotland, so we had an easier opportunity to establish a beachhead in Scotland, before expanding from there to London. It was a very successful strategic decision, which I might not have made if I did not seek out experienced advice.

- Many new ventures or projects undertaken in business appear to be simple when they are, in fact, difficult, especially when you do not know enough about the project to make an informed decision.
- When you are considering a new project, be certain to do your research adequately before delving into something in which you have little experience.
- Do not stop making bold decisions or taking justified risks — quite often these are the types of decisions with the highest rewards — but do so only after working to find out what you do not know.
- Remember, if something looks too good to be true, it probably is.
- Avoid falling for deceptively simple decisions by doing your research, learning from your experiences, and seeking outside advice where appropriate.

CHAPTER 6

Dealing with the *"Challenger Syndrome"*

*Information must make it to
the appropriate level*

At 11:59 a.m. on January 28, 1986, 73 seconds after taking off from Kennedy Space Center in Florida, the space shuttle *Challenger* exploded, breaking into millions of pieces over the Atlantic Ocean and killing all seven crew members on board. It was a very dark day for NASA — and the entire country — and one that has had an enormous impact on the space program in the United States.

The cause of the explosion and the loss of the shuttle and its crew was investigated carefully and found to have originated with a failure in the effective functioning of the O-rings on the shuttle's right rocket booster. The O-rings were designed to enable extremely hot gas to pass by the rings and enter the adjacent external tank during the launch, but the investigation ruled that the design of these rings was flawed. Specifically, the flaw was in how the ambient temperature would affect the structural integrity of these O-rings. As the temperature dropped below 53 degrees Fahrenheit, the rings began to fail — a structural deficiency that was fully known by both the contractor who produced them as well as the NASA officials charged with overseeing the launch. But the decision was made to launch the *Challenger*, despite temperatures well below 53 degrees.

Ensuring that the proper information makes it to the correct decision makers is critical for successful business decisions.

The failure to stop the launch has been widely reported as a failure in the decision-making process used to determine whether a launch should proceed or not. As chapter 5 of the official commission report begins, "The decision to launch the *Challenger* was flawed. Those who made that decision were unaware . . . of the initial recommendation of the contractor advising against the launch at temperatures below 53 degrees. . . . If the decision makers had known all of the facts, it is highly unlikely that they would have decided to launch."[12]

In other words, those responsible for making the ultimate decision on proceeding with the launch either did not have accurate information or chose to ignore the engineering advice given by its experts. At the time, there were several layers of managers between the contractors and engineers who built and maintained the shuttle and the top managers who were responsible for the overall shuttle program and launch. In subsequent studies of the process that ultimately led to the decision to launch the *Challenger* on that fateful day, two possible explanations are postulated for why the information did not reach those who needed it.

It is clear that the information existed. Evidence has been gathered that engineers and their managers held a series of meetings — often late into the night — about the effect of low temperatures on the O-rings. The managers who participated in those meetings also had safety meetings with their managers. At some point, the information did not get passed on to the top-level decision makers. The reason for this failure could be that, at some level, someone either deemed that the information was irrelevant or simply decided for one reason or another not to pass it along. Another theory is that there was a large amount of pressure placed by top-level decision makers onto lower-level managers to make the launch happen. In an effort to avoid a launch delay, the managers could have simply chosen to ignore some information that would prevent a timely launch.

Business Examples

The *Challenger* syndrome also happens frequently in large businesses. Unfortunately, just like the *Challenger*, this usually does not surface until after the bad decision is analyzed.

Previous Examples

In some of the examples cited previously, there were people who warned the organizations of the excessive risk of decisions. There were loan officers at WaMu who increasingly saw mortgages being approved without sufficient verification of ability to pay for the mortgage and warned that this would be a problem. There were some at AIG who did not trust the mathematical models that predicted low losses. Throughout the American auto industry there were engineers who expressed concerns about the quality and reliability of the cars that were being designed, as well as the new car product plans. But in these cases, just as in the *Challenger* example, the information did not reach the right people or was ignored.

Hidden Project Information (Major Manufacturer of Complex Systems)

A major manufacturer of complex computer systems decided to enter a new, specialized computer system market. The decision to proceed was made at a meeting of the board of directors. Before making the decision, the CEO assigned an executive to come up with a business plan for the new product, including how long it would take to build the first system, how much it would cost for the research and development, and detailed information about the market for the new product.

While producing this initial product plan, the executive responsible for the product coordinated with each of the departments involved. He held a series of meetings with the directors of each of these departments and got their opinions as well as their research on the creation of the new product. Each department gave him their reports based on the information they gathered from their engineers, marketers, financial experts, and other relevant employees within their departments.

> **IN YOUR EXPERIENCE**
>
> *Have you ever believed that a certain piece of information was not important enough to pass along to your superiors, only to find that the information was absolutely critical?*

When it came time for him to give his presentation to the board of directors about the proposed project, the executive had a very convincing plan based upon all of the information his subordinates provided to him. The presentation went very well, and the board of directors overwhelmingly supported proceeding with the new product. The company spent $14 million to develop and begin to manufacture specialized computer hardware. Well into the project, the executive spoke with some of the developers, and three of them raised some concerns. They requested a meeting with him and told him that they believed the software would prove to be a significant problem for the computer system, because it would take too much of the CPU speed, causing it to run too slowly.

The executive was extremely concerned about this limitation to the computer system, which could pose significant problems for customers. Because of the design of the hardware, the software required to run on the system would have to be so large that it would hinder performance. The executive asked the three developers why they had not spoken up previously, before the project began. They told him they had written a memo to their immediate superior raising the concern and telling him what software they believed would need to be written. The executive called the head developer into his office to ask him why this information from the three developers was not passed along to the executive when he asked the department to provide its advice on the new computer system. The head developer told the executive he did not believe that these concerns were important enough to mention in his report. Unfortunately, this was specifically the type of information that was absolutely necessary for the correct decision. The problem was that one person made a decision that this information was not critical to the decision and unilaterally made the decision not to share that information. The company needed to reengineer the hardware and software for the product, costing an additional $2 million and a nine-month delay.

Limitation of Critical Supplier (Electronic Equipment Manufacturer)

One electronic equipment manufacturer had designed a new product, which it had high hopes would be a big success. Initial sales were terrific. The new product was a hit with customers. But the company had problems producing enough to meet customer demand. It was designed with an advanced electronic component that was scarce (probably one of the reasons customers liked it), and could be produced only in small quantities. Customers eventually became frustrated that they could not get enough of the product and turned to a competitor's product that was not quite as advanced but was more readily available. In the end, the new product was a disappointment, and a postmortem analysis found there were reports and warnings by engineering that the scarcity of the component would severely limit production. Engineering recommended the new product be sold initially only in low-volume specialty segments of the market. Sales executives chose to ignore or overlook this in their exuberance for big sales. Unfortunately, similar stories are not unique in complex businesses.

Invalid Sales Contracts (Software Company)

Sometimes the failure to flow critical information to the right people can border on fraud, which happened in some companies in the late 1990s. Companies with excessive stock market valuations had intense pressure for continued growth to justify their lofty valuations. In one software company the CEO put extreme pressure on the sales force to achieve quarterly sales targets to justify the growth to support its stock price. When it became increasingly difficult for the salespeople to close major sales by the end of the quarter, some resorted to finding ways to record a sale, even though it was not a complete and binding sale.

They used various ways to claim these as sales, such as side letters to customers that were not disclosed, promising customers their money back if they were not satisfied. Under most revenue recognition policies, if the letters were revealed, the sales would not be recognized. Some people in the company were aware of these practices, but did not disclose them to the accounting staff or to management. If they had, the company would not have recognized these deals as revenue. Eventually, these practices accumulated to the level where they were exposed and the company had to restate hundreds of millions of dollars of revenue; its stock price collapsed, and executives were fired.

Now, as a result, at this company and many others, prior to the decision to recognize revenue, there is a formal quarterly disclosure process that requires managers at several levels of the organization to formally sign a disclosure statement that there are no such practices that have not been disclosed. Similar to the preventive practices implemented by NASA after *Challenger*, companies will put in place formal processes to avoid the invalid sales pitfall in the future.

Reasons Underlying the *Challenger* Syndrome

There are several ways the *Challenger* syndrome can occur in an organization. Most are unintentional and due to misunderstandings or system omissions, while others could be deliberate. Here are some that I have seen:

1. *Critical information is stuck in a process.* Business processes move information throughout a business. While these processes work fine most of the time, sometimes critical information gets stuck in the process and does not reach those who make critical decisions. An example of this is an accounting

system that processes customer returns, where there is a pattern of returns, which is critical to decisions on product ordering, but is not identified in the process.

2. *Critical information is disregarded.* Sometimes critical information is known in the organization but is disregarded by decision makers as being unimportant. This was one of the accusations in the decision to launch the *Challenger.*

3. *Incentives or pressure encourage hiding critical information.* As we saw in the software company example where salespeople hid information critical to making decisions on recognizing an order as revenue, pressure or incentives can encourage hiding information.

4. *Information is not identified as critical.* As we saw in the critical supplier example, important information sometimes does not get to the decision maker because the person with the information does not realize its importance.

5. *Critical information is lost in an excess of information.* Sometimes information critical to a decision is mixed with less-critical information and cannot be sorted out. It then gets ignored by the person making the decision or the person providing the data for the decision.

6. *Critical information is suppressed.* For a variety of reasons, information critical to a decision can be suppressed. Some believe this was the case with the *Challenger.* These reasons can be organizational or political. In some organizations, information is considered to be power and is not readily shared. We look more closely at political and organizational aberrations in chapter 27.

Avoiding the *Challenger* Syndrome

Businesses can avoid this pitfall. It starts with awareness of the problem through training and discussion. When making important decisions, executives and managers should try to broadly understand the information that is critical to a decision, without overdoing it. Frequently the mistakes come from making an implicit assumption rather than verifying it. I recommend the use of checklists for all major assumptions of a decision, especially those that are implied. This checklist can then be used to ensure that all of the critical information is available and considered.

Another way to avoid this pitfall is to have an outside review of management processes for major decisions. Typically these management processes include various types of decisions: project, strategic, recruiting, contracting, or purchasing. By taking precautions to avoid the *Challenger* syndrome pitfall, you may avoid a major decision mistake.

- The *Challenger* disaster provides a tragic example of a decision pitfall and a lesson for everyone, especially businesses.

- Ensuring that the right information flows to the decision maker is critical.

- There are many ways that this pitfall affects a business.

- The *Challenger* syndrome can be caused by many sources, including: critical information being stuck in a process, critical information being disregarded, incentives or pressure encouraging the hiding of critical information, information not being identified as critical, critical information being lost in an excess of information, and critical information being suppressed.

- It is important to understand the reasons for the *Challenger* syndrome and how to avoid it.

CHAPTER 7

Suffering from Indecision

The inability to decide can be debilitating

Indecision can be a debilitating business decision pitfall. Indecisive executives and managers are unable to make important decisions when they need to be made. They vacillate on their decisions, second-guessing themselves, even before they make decisions. Leaders who are indecisive continually frustrate those around them to the point where people lose confidence in them as leaders.

Indecision is not limited to individuals. Some businesses, groups, or organizations in general can become what I call decision proof. They just cannot seem to make a decision on anything. Some of this may have to do with organizational decision issues, which I examine in section IV, but here I approach this phenomenon from the perspective of indecision.

Indecision can be extremely debilitating to business decisions. To put it simply, indecision is the inability to decide or tendency to vacillate between choices, unable to arrive at a final decision. It is far too common in business, something that can be seen in varying levels in virtually every company throughout the world. And while indecision affects many people in business as they attempt to make both large and small decisions, it is obviously a much more pressing problem when people are unable to make the most important decisions for their business. Frequently, these people go back and forth on their decisions, second-guessing themselves before making up their minds,

> Indecisive people will go back and forth on their decisions, second-guessing themselves before — and after — they actually make their decisions.

not only during the process of making the decision, but quite often even after it has been made.

Indecision can be particularly debilitating in business leaders when others are relying on them. You may have experienced this before, saying to yourself, *I wish he would just make a decision. I do not even care anymore if he makes a good one or not; I just want him to decide.* You can use a number of techniques to combat indecision, each targeted at a specific indecision syndrome. Of the primary syndromes of indecision, each has a method that can be used to mitigate indecision and lead to a decision. But first, looking at some examples can be helpful.

Indecision Examples

Indecision can manifest in various ways, as seen by these examples.

Indecisive Manager

The events manager for a major company was knee-deep in planning for the company's annual retreat, which was only two months away. The 15,000-employee company took its retreat seriously, sending roughly 500 employees to the retreat every year. Selecting the keynote speaker was among the manager's major responsibilities. He was asked to find a corporate motivational speaker who focused on how groups can work together better to accomplish their projects. The events manager had narrowed the selection to three choices, but was waffling between them. He read and reread their biographies and resumes. He watched samples of their presentations, and he spoke with each of them on the phone. But he was still struggling to arrive at a decision. He spent four weeks in his internal debate, worried that he was going to make an imperfect decision. He agonized over the possibility of making a bad decision and forcing 500 employees to sit through a so-so keynote speech. The retreat director finally came to him one day and told him he had to make a decision by the end of the day.

This threw the events manager into a full panic, but he knew he needed to make the decision. He made one final attempt to analyze all three of the different speakers, and settled on one of them, which he presented to the retreat director at the end of the day. The director agreed and asked the events manager

> **IN YOUR EXPERIENCE**
>
> *Can you recall someone with whom you worked who seems to be consistently indecisive? What impact did this have?*

to book the speaker. But when the manager contacted the agency representing the speaker, he was told the date had already been booked. Moving down the list, he again contacted the agency, and that speaker had been booked already as well. With only one of the three original options remaining, the events manager was finally able to book a keynote speaker. Following the event and the speaker's presentation, the retreat director confronted the events manager and told him that, while the keynote speaker was fine, the one they had settled on initially would have been much better. The events manager's inability to make a simple decision led to a keynote speaker who was selected by default.

Indecisive Board of Directors

Corporate boards of directors can be indecisive when it comes to major — or even minor — decisions. Some of this stems from the diversity of experience and interests on some boards, combined with unclear decision processes. Here is an example.

A large public technology services company was recruiting a new CEO. The board hired a prominent search firm to conduct the search and gave the firm the general requirements the board was seeking. After a couple of months, the search firm came back to the board with 10 qualified candidates. The board discussed this list and narrowed its preference down to five.

Then the board members started interviewing the five candidates, although because of logistics and scheduling constraints, all directors were not able to meet all of the candidates in person. When the board next met to discuss the candidates, there were a wide range of preferences. One director preferred candidate A because of his relevant CEO experience, while another director disliked this same candidate because of his "appearance." Candidate B was preferred by another director because of his potential to grow in the job. Candidate C had a strong sales background, but no experience as CEO, and one of the directors thought sales experience was most important. Finally one director preferred candidate D because of his extensive experience as CEO, although in a different industry. The director claimed the candidate could learn this business.

The directors had a healthy debate about the candidates and decided on follow-up interviews prior to the next board meeting. At that meeting, they cut the candidates down to three but were unable to concur on one, so they scheduled another board meeting, and then another. Before the board got around to making a decision, all three candidates had dropped out, taking other jobs or recommitting to their current companies.

So the board had to declare this a failed search and start all over again. It was not, however, the search that failed; it was the indecision of the board. Each director had different criteria for his or her decision, so they each preferred different candidates. This made it impossible for them to agree on one candidate, and out of respect for each other they just continued to discuss it and not force a decision. By the way, the next search by the board also failed to yield a consensus candidate.

Decision-Proof Company

Entire companies can demonstrate an indecisive culture. I refer to these companies as being "decision proof." Management at one company that I provided consulting for actually referred to its executive management team as decision proof. No matter how hard anyone tried to get them to make a decision, these senior executives resisted. The way this seemed to work was interesting. Since the CEO preferred a consensus from the executive team, he would not make a decision unless all of the members of the executive team concurred. The members of the executive team, however, avoided taking the lead on any decision until the CEO made up his mind, thus ensuring that nothing would be done — at least not quickly. Decision gridlock occurs when everyone is waiting for everyone else to step forward.

As a consultant to this company, I was responsible for getting the executive team to approve the implementation of a plan entailing the sweeping changes the company needed for it to stop losing money and return to profitability. After pondering how to get them to make a decision, I tried reversing the approval process. I presented the plan to the executive team and then asked them if they wanted to make a decision to cancel the program at that point. I did not give them the choice of proceeding with the program. They all looked around the table at each other, and the CEO said that he did not see the need for a decision to stop. So I said, "OK, if there is no decision to stop, then we will go ahead," and they agreed, although with a rather lackadaisical, "I guess so" attitude.

> Decision gridlock occurs when everyone is waiting for everyone else to step forward.

The company implemented the major changes necessary, and the managers were impressed that the executive team could actually make an important decision so quickly. While I did not solve their decision-proof dilemma (I did not set out to do that), I was able to work around their indecision by exploiting it.

This decision-proof problem occurs most often in business situations where multiple people need to make a decision, but nobody wants to take the lead in making or proposing it. Frequently this arises from a culture where anyone venturing to recommend a decision is then criticized for it. Every decision has flaws, risks, and shortcomings, and you cannot be criticized for the decision you do not recommend.

Some companies have corporate indecision to varying degrees, and some incur it with certain types of decisions but not others. In some companies, corporate indecision turns out to be fatal. The correction for this is difficult, requiring extensive retraining and clarification of decision responsibilities, authorities, and processes.

> The best way to combat "decision proof" is to recognize the problems inherent in the decision-making structure and work to make it more viable.

Syndromes of Individual Indecision and How to Correct Them

To best attack the problem of indecision, you need to understand the various indecision syndromes. Once you understand these, you can then work on solving the problem.

Syndrome #1: Trying to Make the "Perfect" Decision

Some people are indecisive in their business decisions, as well as in their life decisions, because they want to make the perfect decision or are afraid to make a decision that is less than completely correct. They struggle with the decision and seem paralyzed by it. They repeatedly put it off, hoping that somehow the perfect answer will come to them. For some, this is a genuine mental disorder that they need to overcome. For others, it is simply sloppy decision making.

To overcome the "perfect" decision syndrome, you need to accept that it is usually better to make a good decision that is timely than a better decision that is too late or takes an inordinate amount of time to make. Theodore Roosevelt once said, "In any moment of decision, the best thing you can do is the right thing, the next best thing is the wrong thing, and the worst thing you can do is nothing." If someone is paralyzed by indecision because of wanting to make that perfect decision, remember this and force that person to make any decision before it is too late.

On a practical level, deadlines are an important remedy for someone who feels the need to make the perfect decision. A decision deadline forces confrontation with those fears of a less-than-perfect decision. This action will need to be done eventually, so why not do it sooner rather than later? I use this technique all the time with someone who is indecisive, even if the deadline is artificial. Actually, I always set an artificial deadline for someone who is indecisive, just to force any decision.

> "In any moment of decision, the best thing you can do is the right thing, the next best thing is the wrong thing, and the worst thing you can do is nothing."
> — Theodore Roosevelt

Syndrome #2: Never Having Enough Information

Some indecisive people need to gather more and more information before making a decision. Do they know everything they need to before they can make the decision, lest they make the wrong decision? Maybe they do and maybe they do not. But do they know enough about the situation to enable them to make a good decision, one that is informed, even if all of the information is not available?

Some people are indecisive because they keep seeking out more information, even past the point of diminishing returns. In these cases, the additional information gathered is less and less significant in terms of its importance for making the decision. To combat this tendency, they must realize how much — and what — information is needed to make a decision. I find it helpful to identify what information is needed to make a decision prior to making the decision. Avoid the tendency to have that information lead to the need for more and more information. Sometimes additional information may be necessary, but most of the time it only satisfies one's curiosity.

When working with someone who is indecisive and keeps gathering more information, I ask, "Is this information really necessary to make a decision? What will it tell you that will influence your decision?"

Syndrome #3: Analysis Paralysis

Some indecisive people just cannot process all of the information they have at hand to make a decision. This is the opposite of the previous problem, where people think they are missing adequate information to make their decision. It is not that these information-overload people are not smart enough to process the information they have. More than likely the actual problem is that they are unable to distinguish the information that is truly important to the decision from the secondary and tertiary information that has little bearing on the decision at hand. This is often referred to as "analysis paralysis."

To prevent analysis paralysis from hindering your decision-making process, you need to get perspective on what information is important to making the decision and what information is not. If the information is not likely to affect your decision, then simply put it aside and stop worrying about it. This will enable you to focus on the information that is actually important to the decision. One approach that can often help in this pursuit is to make a simple list containing all of the available information and then place each piece of information in order of the most important to least important. This will help you to understand better what information should be considered for the basis of the decision and prevent you from being distracted or confused by less important information.

> Some people are indecisive because they believe they do not have all of the information they need to make the decision; others are indecisive because they cannot process the large amount of information they have.

In addition to the use of deadlines, discussed previously, it is helpful for someone with analysis paralysis to budget the time they spend on making the decision. Determine how much time you should take to make this decision. Then follow that as well as possible to create what is essentially a time deadline.

Syndrome #4: Waffling

Waffling is another syndrome of indecision. Some people tend to waffle in their decisions, announcing a decision one day, only to change it the next. This back-and-forth tendency happens because they think about all of the factors that favor one particular decision on one day and then think about the factors that favor the other decision the next. Thus, they are inhibited by their own whiplash style. A variation of this syndrome is when people make a decision and then are uncomfortable with it. A variety of techniques are available to address this syndrome.

You can write down all of the factors that go into a decision. This is essential to a good decision and is discussed in chapter 13 on pros and cons. When all of the factors are written down, you can see them all at one time, instead of going back and forth in the limited capacity of your mind. The try-it-on-for-size technique discussed in chapter 10 can also be helpful for people with this syndrome.

When dealing with indecisive people who waffle, I tend to ignore their decision for a while and wait for it to settle down before I believe it. I tell them good-naturedly that "I have learned that you go back and forth on your decisions, so I am going to ignore it until you settle on one decision for a while."

Dealing with Indecision in Others

Indecisive people need help! If you work with indecisive people, you can apply several techniques to handle them and prevent their indecision from being a hindrance to your company. First, whenever possible, avoid getting these people involved in decisions — especially decisions that are minor. Quite often, indecisive people can spend far too much time and energy waffling on these minor decisions, something that costs them the time they should be spending on other matters. When this is the case, just make the decision for them and tell them the outcome. If they protest strongly and want to change what you decide, then go along with their decision. At least you have now been able to force them to decide. Another method for dealing with others who are indecisive is to simply help them along by explaining to them that some information they are considering is not relevant to the decision, while other information is extremely important to the decision. In other words, help them sort through the information.

Indecisive people need help!

One other technique that can be extremely useful for helping indecisive people make a decision is to create a forcing mechanism. Tell them they need to make a particular decision by a specific time because of some given reason. For example, you can tell them they need to decide by 5 p.m. today if they are going on the business trip next week. Tell them that is when the paperwork needs to be in or that is the reservation deadline for the flight. Regardless of whether these deadlines are actually important, this type of forcing mechanism is useful because it provides a deadline for these indecisive people. While it is usually OK to make up a deadline, it is always better if there is some real rationale for it. It will generally work, however, because indecisive people tend not to question these forcing mechanisms. Such people usually take these mechanisms for granted because they are concerned with the decision at hand, not the deadline. (Or maybe they just cannot decide whether the deadlines are important or not.) A final way to handle indecisive people is to simply let them do their thing. Go away and leave them to work on the decision, but set your expectations accordingly.

Syndromes of Group Indecision and How to Correct Them

Just as with indecision in individuals, groups — such as executive teams, boards, project teams, and entire companies in some cases — can suffer from indecision. Here are some group indecision syndromes.

Syndrome #1: Confusion on Decision Process

Frequently what appears to be indecision in a business is really the lack of a clear decision process. Without a clearly understood process, managers and executives are unsure how a particular decision gets made. They may not be sure who makes the decision, as well as how and when it gets made. I worked extensively helping companies make decisions on new product development and would frequently hear developers and others claiming the company — particularly its executive team — was indecisive about new products.

The fix to this problem is obvious: define and follow a proven decision process for that particular type of decision. In section V, I look at a successful project decision process that addresses this problem.

Syndrome #2: Failure to Reach Consensus

Groups that try to reach a consensus and fail are indecisive. Some groups or teams seem to fail in any decisions and are truly indecisive. The outcome of this syndrome can be debilitating for the company and the people involved. Frequently group indecisiveness comes from personalities in the group. Other times it may come from a lack of training or understanding of how to reach a consensus.

Training is usually the solution to group indecisiveness. I have found that once most groups understand what a consensus really means and they know how to work together in a group decision, then they can overcome group indecision. I discuss team decision making in chapter 24.

Syndrome #3: Indecisive Culture

As we saw in the earlier example of the decision-proof company, sometimes the very culture of a company is indecisive. Everyone is afraid to make a decision, usually because the culture is one where people get criticized for their decisions. This happens more often than you might think. Most business decisions are not always so clear that there are not some problems with them. There are usually cons to the pros in a decision, and there are varying viewpoints to any decision. Criticizing another's decision is easy, and it happens in negative business cultures that feed on criticism. As a result, everyone is afraid to make a decision, lest they be criticized, so they tend to avoid decisions and the entire company culture becomes indecisive.

The solution to this problem is not so easy, because it is much broader. The basic culture in companies like this is toxic. The only solution is to change the culture, which generally requires new leadership and a crisis to shake up the company. It takes a lot of time to establish or change a business's culture.

- Indecision can be debilitating for businesses, not only for the major decisions, but also for the minor decisions.
- There are several symptoms of indecision, each of which can be combated using different techniques.
- Whether you are unable to decide because you are lacking information or because you have too much information, there are steps you can take to help you come to a decision.
- When you confront a coworker who is indecisive, you can implement a number of techniques to help with making a decision.
- Finally, entire businesses can be indecisive, not just individuals; this is commonly known as an indecisive business culture, and it has its own, much more difficult, method for solving the problem.

CHAPTER 8

Considering Other Decision Pitfalls

Other pitfalls you will find in business

In the previous chapters of this section, I covered business decision pitfalls that I felt were the most important in today's economy. However, other decision pitfalls deserve mention. While I would like to list every possible pitfall to give you warning before you make a decision, that is probably impossible. But here are some that deserve at least a brief amount of attention. Some of these pitfalls are also reviewed in later sections of this book.

Incompetence

We have all seen cases of incompetence. Some people simply do not know what they are doing, and this is perhaps most apparent with the decisions they make. Incompetence in decisions can stem from many causes, including insufficient experience, poor decision skills, distraction, and bias. I have found that decision incompetence is not always so broadly based that people are incompetent in all decisions. Rather it most often occurs when people are incompetent with certain types of decisions, while perhaps they are highly capable when it comes to other types of decisions. As an example, someone I used to work with continually made poor hiring decisions. She was typically swayed by initial impressions, neglecting a more thorough evaluation of candidates. More than half of the people she hired did not last more than six months. I have also seen executives who were always enchanted by any new idea and would quickly decide to support it. The associate of one executive said, "He has never seen a new idea he does not like."

IN YOUR EXPERIENCE

Have you ever made a decision that could be classified into one of these decision pitfalls? What did you learn from it? Is it something that you could recognize in advance were you to be put in a similar situation in the future?

Executives with this decision incompetence end up wasting a lot of investment on poor ideas.

Decision incompetence generally can be corrected or avoided with the right training and the right management processes. Training helps managers improve their decision-making skills. Management processes can provide checks and balances to avoid or lessen bad decisions. However, when the CEO or leader of an organization is incompetent in strategic decisions, this situation can have terrible consequences. I knew one CEO who rose to his position through shrewd political maneuvering, but was totally incompetent when it came to strategic decisions. Once he started making strategic decisions, his incompetence began to show and had a detrimental impact on the business.

Politics

In all types of businesses and organizations, office politics can play a big role in a wide range of decisions. Decisions about hiring, firing, promotions, projects, work responsibilities, and who gets corner offices, particular shifts, or certain clients all have the potential to be influenced by office politics. Politics can often cloud an otherwise productive and profitable work environment, forcing decisions for the wrong reasons. Most important, politics can impede successful business decision making.

Some colleges fall prey to this type of political problem, for example. Virtually all colleges and universities in the United States use some type of tenure system when it comes to their professors. While there are differing rules regarding how and when professors are offered full-time, permanent positions, the vast majority of institutions begin by hiring assistant professors or visiting professors who will serve a contract of one or two years, with renewal offered at the pleasure of the department or the college within which they operate. After teaching several classes successfully and publishing the requisite number of articles in reputable journals, professors are required to consider and be considered for a more per-

> Politics can impede successful business decision making.

manent position within the school. These positions — called "tenured positions" — are offered to those whom the college or university deems qualified to be full-time, permanent professors.

While this system works sufficiently in many circumstances, it is often not the ideal mechanism for adequate selection of qualified personnel for the positions that are so crucial to the high-quality instruction of students. While some benchmarks must be met, such as a certain number of publications, courses taught, level of reviews by students, and so forth, what it sometimes comes down to is whether the other professors in the professor's department and key members of the administration get along well with a specific professor. If they do, that professor is likely to be accepted to a tenured position. If they do not, that professor is likely to be fired from the job and replaced with someone else. We look at the broader impact of politics in decisions in chapter 27.

Timing

There is an old saying that "timing is everything." That is especially true when it comes to business decisions. As a business decision maker, you know you need to make your decisions at the right time. If you make them too early, you risk making a poor decision because you do not have enough information. If you make them too late, you risk reducing — or possibly eliminating — all of your options.

Many business decisions require the right timing. Decide to launch a new product too late and you miss the opportunity, but decide to launch it too early and you may exhaust your investment before the market is ready. Decide to terminate a disappointing employee too quickly, and you do not give him or her enough time to improve, but do it too late and it may cost more time and money. Decide to make a cost reduction too quickly, and you may take away business opportunities, but do it too late and you will lose money.

> As a business decision maker, you need to make your decisions at the right time.

Some decision timing requires assumptions about what may happen in the intervening time if you delay your decision. Investing in another company, for example, requires timing assumptions. Even after deciding on a company to invest in, you need to decide when to make the investment. Will the price go down after you buy it, or will it continue to go up? You need to make an assumption.

Organizational Compromises

Compromise can often lead to some of the best business decisions, but it can also lead to bad decision making if not done appropriately. A major software company desired to launch an updated version of its most popular software product. Its current version was very good, but there were many features that clients had requested for inclusion in the next version. The top executives met to go over the plan for the new version, and it was clear that each person had a different idea of what the new version should look like. The marketing and sales executives were adamant that the product include all of the features that the clients had been requesting, since it would enable them to sell even more copies of the software and branch out to new industries. The software development team was excited to include more features as well, but warned that they would have to hire more staff to do it correctly. The finance team, on the other hand, warned that the immediate costs that would be required for the new developers would cause major financial problems for the company in the near term, even if it would lead to greater sales and higher revenues in the long run.

> If not done appropriately, compromise can lead to severely deficient decision making.

With all of the different views represented, the sales and marketing team worked with the development team to figure out a way to include the vast majority of the most important features into the new product, but doing so without having to hire too many new developers. The finance team was happy with this compromise, because it meant that the company would not face the short-term financial shortfall it predicted under the full development option. After creating the new version, the company initially saw its sales boom, with all customers purchasing upgrades and new customers flocking to the software because of its extended features. A few months later, however, it was clear that the developers had to cut some corners to be able to produce the number of features the sales and marketing team had wanted, while doing so within the budget that the finance team required. There were hundreds of bugs in the software — so many, and so severe, that the company finally had to pull the product completely, refunding hundreds of thousands of dollars in software purchases, not to mention helping customers re-install the previous versions of the software. Looking back at this failure, it was clear that it was simply a bad compromise that had led to a bad decision about what to include in the new version of the software.

Conflicts of Interest

We have all faced times when we can see that a conflict of interest can feasibly alter the success of a business decision. One example of this can be seen in the case of one investor in a major publicly traded company. This particular investor, Andrew, owned $100 million in convertible preferred stock in the company. (Preferred stock is different than common stock because it is always paid out first, prior to paying out to common shareholders.) While he was not a majority shareholder in the company, his $100 million in preferred stock made him one of the most powerful investors in the company.

The company had been in negotiations to be acquired by another, larger competitor. Under the contract terms of his preferred stock investment, should the company be acquired, Andrew would receive his $100 million investment plus 10% of his investment. If the company was sold for more than $500 million, he would get an even higher payout because of the increase in the value of the common shares. The company had initially been in discussions to be acquired for $600 million, but that changed suddenly. The economic problems that affected the entire world and a rapid, unforeseen change in the CEO of the company precipitously dropped the company's net worth from $600 million to only $350 million. Eager to get out of the investment, Andrew teamed up with another major preferred stockholder to push for the sale of the company, virtually at any price. Due to the terms of their investment, the two of them would receive their original investment plus 10%, regardless of the sale price. Since it was highly unlikely the company would be acquired above the $500 million threshold that would kick in their increased payouts, they used their influence to push for the sale. In addition to receiving the first $110 million of any sale, Andrew was also slated to be offered the ability to fill two seats on the board of directors of the larger company that bought out the company in which Andrew had invested so much money.

It was a clear-cut case of a conflict of interest. While the board was supposed to be looking out for the good of the company, the sale of the company meant more to these two large shareholders than the actual price paid for the sale. In this case, a flaw in the design of the preferred stock contract created the conflict of interest whereby two of the largest

> Conflicts of interest in business not only bring ethical dilemmas, they also bring faulty decision making.

shareholders would rather the company be sold at a low price than hold off on being sold. Their plan succeeded, and the company was sold for just under $330 million, plus the retention of several seats on the board of the larger company.

Inadequate Time Spent on Decisions

A common pitfall is the failure to spend enough time actually making important decisions. As a rule, you should think long and hard about all major decisions, which is usually worth your time investment. Here is a way to calculate the value of your time to make a decision. Let's say that your time is worth $25 per hour to you (this is the equivalent of making $50,000 per year). You are facing a major decision, say to invest in a new product, and you invest 100 hours thinking about your decision. In this case, your opportunity cost would be $2,500 (100 hours times $25 per hour). Do you value a good decision in this case at $2,500? If someone offered to sell you a certificate good for "one better decision," would you pay $2,500 for it? Would you pay $5,000?

Business examples abound where not spending enough time on decisions ultimately leads to extreme failure. A good one involves a department manager who was responsible for more than 35 employees. He not only served as the director of all of the activities and responsibilities of the department, he was also essentially the administrative director charged with all staff, including hiring and firing decisions. Recently, this department had seen significant turnover among key staff members, and the manager had been particularly overwhelmed with interviewing potential candidates for a number of positions, in addition to ensuring that his "regular" day-to-day job was being done with enough attention and accuracy.

> Not spending adequate time on an important decision is simply reckless and will almost certainly lead to poor outcomes.

One week, the manager was interviewing for four positions that he needed to fill immediately. At the same time, he was working on some of the most important initiatives in the company's history. The manager's time was compromised by the multiple responsibilities demanded simultaneously. This particular week, he did more than 20 interviews, each lasting roughly 45 minutes. He also reviewed several resumes, writing samples, and recommendations. Throughout this time, he let some of the ongoing projects he was responsible for fall behind — something that led to performance reductions in his department. He even let his primary project — the changeover of one system to another — fall sufficiently behind that it began to show signs of not meeting the specifications for its performance. It was pretty clear that he was making decisions based upon the fact that he had less time than he actually needed to make these decisions correctly.

Spending enough time on major decisions requires prioritization. You need to allocate more time to the most important decisions. Successful executives realize this and give priority to the most important decisions. If they do not have enough time themselves to spend a sufficient amount of time on the decision, they will bring in an expert to help them with the decision. They know that it is worth spending $100,000, or even a lot more, to make better strategic decisions. The cost of a bad decision can be hundreds of times more expensive.

Rash Decisions

There is something to be said for intuition. It can often be a great skill, but it can also quite often be a terrible weakness. When you make a decision based upon your gut feeling, you have little idea of why you are actually making the decision that way. You simply believe instinctively that your decision is right. Some people believe gut feeling is an internal spiritual, mystical, or psychic source that guides a decision without any thought or logic. Since there are no logical or rational explanations for how these decisions are made, these people believe there must be some greater force at work that is imparting wisdom to make the correct decision.

> Sometimes it is difficult to discern between a gut-feel decision and a simple guess.

But gut-feel decisions can often be wrong, and it is difficult to discern between a gut feel and a guess. You might just be guessing when you think you have some great intuition about some decision. Sometimes gut-feel decisions can actually just be an excuse for sloppy decision making. You do not want to do the hard work involved in making a decision correctly, so you just leave it up to intuition. I discuss intuitive decision making in chapter 11.

Calculation Errors

Many times I have seen simple calculation errors lead to flawed decisions. The most common of these are calculation errors made with spreadsheet software, which can be used to create very sophisticated modeling and calculations. While spreadsheets make planning and analysis much easier by providing simple mathematical equations, you need to be careful that the calculations are correct.

Here is just one example. A company I consulted for was working on a plan to create a new product that had the potential to garner a significant portion of the market. Development was still in the early stages, but initial reviews of the plans were promising. The projections for the profit margins seemed to be incredible, and this created a lot of excitement. The return on investment (ROI) was 200% within the first year alone. How could the company not proceed with the project? The company quickly decided to move forward based upon these projections. After a significant amount of time and money was already invested in the product and it came up for another review, the projections were much lower; in fact, they were not very good.

When asked what changed, the project manager was very embarrassed to admit that there was a calculation error in the initial projections. As it turned out, the initial spreadsheet summed up the profit by month for each quarter to show how the profit would unfold throughout the year. When it summed up the information for the entire year, the person doing the original spreadsheet forgot to remove the quarterly figures from the equation, which meant that the total yearly profit was actually double what it should have been. Because the detailed data was not displayed in the projection, this error was not obvious. Ultimately the project did not succeed in the manner the company initially expected.

Like-Minded Decision Makers

Some executives surround themselves by like-minded people. This can be very supportive and comforting, but when faced with a difficult decision, this group may not have the diversity of viewpoints. They fall victim to group-think. A wrongheaded view on a decision can be perpetuated. An example of this was a finance and accounting department that over time recruited people of similar views. When faced with decisions where they should have looked openly at several alternatives, they refused to do so. They all had the same view, so that was the only alternative. This eventually stifled and hurt the company.

This like-minded decision pitfall generally occurs in groups or departments within a company. It can also occur with the executive leadership team, but this is less likely because of the varying responsibilities of executives.

One solution to this pitfall is for leaders to integrate more humility and openness into decisions. They should seek out other viewpoints and listen. Another solution is to make sure that every group or team has diverse experiences and backgrounds, as well as an openness to work together. When you work with a group within a company that is like-minded, be careful of their decisions. Take the time to examine the decision for this pitfall.

- There are a wide range of other pitfalls that you may face in business decisions.
- There is no excuse for incompetence in business, but it can quite often infect the process by which important decisions need to be made.
- Bad decisions can often be made for political reasons, simply because of the relationships and politics at work within a company.
- Many times decisions are not made correctly because they are not made at the right time.
- Compromises within organizational structures can lead to faulty decisions.
- Conflicts of interest in business not only bring ethical dilemmas, they also bring poor decision making.
- Clearly, rushing decisions and not spending enough time on them can lead to making the wrong decision.
- Intuition can be good, but if it is just an excuse for sloppy decision making or guessing, you will quickly find out the perils of not doing your research.
- If you make a decision based upon faulty calculations, you will end up costing your company much more than a simple spreadsheet.
- When a decision maker surrounds him- or herself with others who are like-minded without any diversity of opinion, bad decisions often result.

SECTION II

Successful Decision Techniques

In my many years of working with executives and managers it is clear that one characteristic separates those who are successful from those who are not as successful: those who are successful are more skilled at making decisions. They have studied decision techniques, learned them from others, and learned from their own mistakes. They are keenly aware that the decisions they make will shape the success of their business, and they work at constantly developing their decision-making skills.

Executives, managers, supervisors, and all workers within a business face a range of decisions every day. These decisions can be routine, critical, easy (or seemingly easy), or difficult. Decisions can be made individually or by teams, groups, or committees. And all of these decisions, big and small, are important. They take time, thought, and resources. These decisions have results: expected results and results that are less than expected; intended results and those that are unintended.

A wide range of techniques permeates business decision making; no one technique fits all situations. In this section, I have included a selection of business decision techniques that I believe are particularly useful in today's economy. You will find that some of these traditional techniques have been used successfully for a long time, while others are new techniques that you may not have heard of before.

The first technique deals with complex decisions. When decision makers face complex decisions, all too often they fall into two opposite traps. The first is that they try to make a complex decision at once, resulting in oversimplified or rushed decisions that usually are not the best decisions and sometimes can be quite costly. At the other extreme, they waste time in wandering meetings and discussions, never arriving at a decision, or eventually making any decision just to get it over with. The first chapter of this section introduces what I call the two-step decision process that achieves the right balance for making complex decisions efficiently and effectively.

Frequently managers or executives make decisions they soon regret, often the result of seeing something they did not notice when they considered their decision. One of the most successful techniques to avoid this problem is one I call "see if it fits." In other words, take the opportunity to "try on" a decision tentatively before you make a final decision. Chapter 10 explains this decision-making tool.

Intuitive decisions can be powerful! They happen quickly and relatively easily. Making intuitive decisions can be seductive. They give you a sense of confidence that you made a good decision, even if you do not know why. Intuitive decisions can also be very dangerous for the same seductive reasons. Sometimes it is difficult to discern between an intuitive decision and a guess — except the results can be very different. Chapter 11 will help you understand when you are good at intuitive decisions and when you are not. In fact, most people who make good intuitive decisions in some areas can make terrible intuitive decisions in others. This chapter explores intuitive decisions as a technique, showing when to rely on intuition and when to reject it.

Decision deadlines are a fundamental technique for successful and timely business decisions. Yet often even successful business people forget to apply this technique. Chapter 12 describes different types of decision deadlines, how and when to apply them, and what happens when you fail to use them.

One of the most successful techniques for making business decisions is evaluating the pros and cons of several alternatives. This provides a rigorous analysis leading to a better decision. However, many executives overlook this simple technique, frequently using less successful informal techniques instead. Building on the wisdom of Ben Franklin, chapter 13 describes an effective way to apply this simple, but powerful, technique.

Sometimes you want to convince others to make a particular decision. Decision framing is one of the most effective techniques to do this. It is also helpful on the defensive side — knowing when others are trying to "frame" you into making the decision they want you to make. Chapter 14 introduces various decision framing techniques and describes how and when to apply them.

Getting advice can help you make better decisions, but it can also steer you into a poor decision. Some people can share their invaluable experience with you and help expand your thinking. Other times, however, people provide biased input for their own benefit or are eager to provide you advice on your decision even though they do not have applicable experience. In chapter 15, I examine how to distinguish between good, bad, and biased advice.

Finally, flipping a coin to make a decision is underrated as a decision technique. I find that it works well, but not for the reason you may think. In fact, I think more people end up going with the alternative not selected by the coin. The reason it works, as I explain in chapter 16, is that it forces you to confront how you really feel about the decision the coin made for you.

CHAPTER 9

Using a Two-Step Decision Process

Avoiding endless wandering
meetings or hasty decisions

Complex decision making often falls prey to two opposite traps. The first trap involves trying to make a complex decision in a single meeting. This tends to happen when the decision is mistakenly oversimplified or rushed due to unchecked enthusiasm. The result all too frequently is a hasty or ill-conceived decision with severe consequences. The other trap is the opposite: wandering meetings that seem endless and never result in a decision. Following are examples of these two extremes and an explanation of the two-step decision process to achieve the right balance.

Overly Simplified Rash Decisions

In 2004, a small local bank had a growing business opportunity for vacation home mortgages. It hired an aggressive young loan officer who became very popular in the community and was generating a lot of new mortgage business. The problem was finding the money to fund these mortgages because the increase in loan activity was outstripping growth in customer deposits and savings. The president of the bank called a meeting with the executive team to discuss this problem, and they were all pleased when the young loan officer had a solution.

The solution was to borrow short-term funds from large corporations that were looking for opportunities to invest their cash for short-term periods of 60 to 90 days at favorable interest rates. All the bank had to do was offer to pay slightly higher competitive rates than the market, and the bank could then get as much cash as needed. The CFO was excited that the interest that the bank paid on these short-term loans was much less than the interest generated by the mortgages. They discussed the issue of continually borrowing short-term funds, but did not think that would be a problem since they were such a small bank. If necessary they could always resell their mortgages on the mortgage market. They also were excited by the executive bonuses that came from this new business. So in one short meeting they made the decision.

Over the next few years, the bank grew rapidly, and was in fact recognized as one of the 10 fastest-growing companies in the state. When interviewed about the bank's key to success, the bank president said, "We are very decisive. When we see an opportunity, we make a quick decision and take advantage of it."

You can guess what happened, of course. Toward the end of 2007, it became more difficult for the bank to continually refinance short-term borrowings from corporations, and it had to offer higher interest rates. By the first half of 2008, borrowing dried up almost completely and the bank was forced

> Complex decisions cannot be made in a single step or at a single meeting.

to resell much of its mortgage portfolio, but it was unable to do that because the secondary mortgage market for vacation homes almost disappeared. The bank quickly became illiquid because it could not pay back the short-term loans when they became due, and nobody would lend them additional money. It became insolvent and closed.

The bank's problem was rooted in that hasty, oversimplified complex decision. It turned out that the bank's executive team was not decisive; they were reckless. If the bank executives had only taken more time to understand the problem, evaluate the alternatives, understand the risks, and then make a more careful decision, they could have averted disaster.

Wandering Decisions

At the other extreme of complex decision making is what I call the wandering decision. Here is one of my favorite examples. The executive team of a growing software company was trying to decide on a new bonus program for software developers. The employees had been working hard for the last several years designing and refining several successful software products, all while having a bonus plan that was widely perceived to be outdated and unworkable as the company grew. The executive team, which comprised the CEO, the CFO, the CTO, the VP of human resources, and the three heads of each software division, held a special meeting to decide on changes to the bonus plan. They discussed problems with the existing program. The three software division heads discussed the frustrations of the developers, especially the higher performers. The CFO discussed the problems with the cost of the program and issues with timely accounting for bonuses.

The group shared recommendations on how the program should be changed, including the timing of the bonuses, what incentive metrics should be considered, how a bonus should vary by position, how large bonuses should be, whether they should be capped, and many more issues. Changes were also proposed in the combination of stock options, base compensation, and vacation time in conjunction with changes to the bonus plan. The VP of HR presented her recommendations based on the bonus program where she previously worked. The CFO was concerned about the overall cost of that program.

> **IN YOUR EXPERIENCE**
>
> *Have you ever been involved in a decision that seemed to wander endlessly?*

At the meeting, discussions went around and around as opinions varied on how the new program should look. After three hours passed, nothing had been resolved. The team decided to schedule a second meeting for a week later. Unfortunately, that second meeting ended the same way — in gridlock and frustration. A third meeting was scheduled, and then a fourth. This went on for two months, with no decision. In the end, the executive team simply tired of the discussion and turned to other problems without making any decision on the bonus program.

The executive team inadvertently created a wandering decision process with no structure and no end. Figure 9-1 illustrates this wandering process showing the meetings (boxes) over time compared to progress toward the decision. Progress was slow, then stalled, then they backtracked for a couple of meetings, then appeared to make some progress, and so on. Eventually, the team gave up on the decision because there was no conclusion in sight.

Their first mistake was that they did not first agree on the objectives of the new bonus program. They jumped right into solutions without defining the problem. So they got into a dysfunctional wandering process: discussing alternatives, running into disagreements and problems, failing to agree on what decision to make, and then restarting again at the next meeting. Typically, when this happens, either no decision gets made or the person who has the stamina to outlast the others prevails. Neither outcome is acceptable.

Figure 9-1 Wandering Decision Process

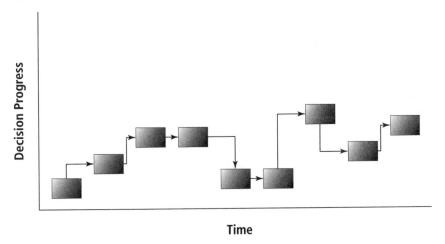

While these two examples are certainly distinct from one another, they both prove a similar point: complex decisions cannot be made in a single step, nor can they be made in an indefinite series of steps. Rushing into decisions without first understanding what decision needs to be made and its end goal can lead to the type of problems illustrated in these two examples. Approaches and techniques for making complex decisions are reviewed in later chapters; here the focus is on simply structuring the process for making complex decisions into two (or more) steps. If you do not start out by breaking the process into two steps, then specific techniques will not help make the decision successful.

Making Complex Decisions in Two Steps

For complex business decisions, particularly those made by a group, it is often best to employ the following two-step approach. The way this process works is illustrated in Figure 9-2. In step 1, the group meets to arrive at a common understanding about the decision that needs to be made, including clearly defining the objective, specifying the alternatives, and agreeing to the time frame and approach. Make it clear up front that a decision will not be made at the first meeting. Step 2, the second meeting, is when the decision is actually made. In between these two meetings, group members have time to think about the problem, conduct research, and talk it over with others who provide additional insights. When the group meets the second time, it will usually make a much better decision than it would have made if it had tried to make the decision at its first meeting.

Figure 9-2 Two-Step Decision Process

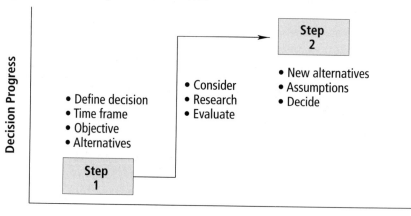

I have successfully used this two-step approach many times to make complex decisions. I always start the first meeting by saying, "It's not our intention to make a decision at this meeting; we first need to understand the problem we are trying to solve." When initially introduced to this two-step process, the group is intrigued, and soon it becomes the normal way to make complex decisions.

Step 1: The Setup

In the first step of the two-step process, the majority of the work needs to be done. This is the time when the decision needs to be defined. The following questions should be posed — and answered — by the group during this meeting:

- What is the decision that needs to be made?
- What type of decision needs to be made (a yes or no decision;

a decision to make a change or maintain the status quo; a full decision; a partial decision, etc.)?

- When does the decision need to be made?
- What is the overall objective of the decision?
- What will the outcome look like?
- Who will have input into the decision?
- Who will ultimately have the final say in the decision?
- What are the alternatives available for consideration?
- What risks need to be considered?

In other words, the decision needs to be set up in this first step. If you are not clear on exactly what decision needs to be made and its underlying framework, the decision-making process will be flawed. Moreover, if the participants do not all agree about these things, there will never be consensus and the likelihood of the best decision arising out of the process is decreased significantly. Participants will challenge each other in a nonconstructive manner, and a decision will be made with less than the full complement of facts. Agreeing on the parameters of the decision process and the components of the decision ahead of time will prevent these pitfalls.

In the example of the software company discussed above, the group should have used the first scheduled meeting to agree on the objectives for changing the bonus program. Was the objective to reduce the overall cost of the program? Was the objective to improve the benefits of the bonus program to the software designers? Was the objective to streamline the program to make it more efficient? Was the objective to increase the bonus for higher performers? The group should also have discussed the problems with the existing program and the various alternatives available to alter the program. The group should have also used the first meeting to determine who was ultimately going to be responsible for making the decision — whether it was going to be made by a unanimous vote of the group, by a majority vote, or by the CEO alone. Finally, the group should have determined a time frame within which the decision would be made. This could have included a simple deadline for the final decision or deadlines for each part of the process, including one for suggestions, another for deliberations, and a deadline for the decision itself.

> Step 1 defines the decision to be made.

In the initial example of the bank, the executive team should have used the first meeting to more clearly define the problem and consider alternatives instead of jumping to what appeared to be an all-too-easy solution.

Inter-Step Time

At the end of the first meeting, the participants in the group should be directed to use their time between the first and second meetings to think about the decision at hand. Now that they are all aware of the process and the desired objectives of the decision, as well as some of the likely alternatives and options available for the decision, they will be able to gather information more effectively. Participants should use this inter-meeting time to speak among themselves as well as with others who are not involved in the decision group, mull over the decision on their own, and research alternatives. They should write down their ideas and reconsider them, continually reworking their thoughts in an organized manner. They should be directed to use this time to come to a basic position on the issue, ready to ask all necessary questions, bring up any relevant additional information, provide their opinion, and ultimately make a decision during the second meeting.

In the case of the software company, the time spent between the two meetings should have included discussions between the CEO and the CFO about what the company could afford, what would best save the company money, and how to efficiently structure the bonus program. It should have also included discussions between the CTO and the directors of each of the three software development teams about what the software programmers believed would be the best bonus structure, as well as what type of combination of available bonus options would spur the best work and highest productivity levels among the developers. Time between meetings should also have included discussions with the software programmers themselves, in an effort to bring their opinions directly to the table, since they did not have a say in the decision itself. Finally, it should have provided each of the participants time to reflect on the options and form an opinion about how to make the decision.

> The time between the first and second meetings is used to think about the decision at hand.

In the bank example, following the first meeting, the CFO should have done some mathematical modeling of the alternatives, which would have shown how quickly the bank would have become dependent on short-term borrowing. This would have enabled them to more thoughtfully assess the risks of this alternative. The bank president could have also talked with some of his peers at other banks to get their opinions.

Step 2: Making the Decision

If the first meeting of this process is conducted successfully, and if the time between meetings is used in the best possible way, the second meeting of the decision group should be much easier. This meeting should be used to actually make the decision. But before making the decision, the participants should use the beginning of the meeting to ask any more questions they have that will help them to clarify the situation. What are the nuances of each of the options? Are there more options that have been identified by the participants since the first meeting? What other information has been made available in the time between the two meetings?

If major new alternatives are defined, assumptions challenged, or new problems introduced, then it is acceptable to use the second meeting to redefine the decision and alternatives, and make the decision at a third meeting. This is different than wandering in an endless process, since the team is still narrowing in on making the decision even though it is taking another step.

Once this information is considered and all opinions are shared between the meeting participants, they can evaluate the alternatives and reach a decision. While very few decisions are perfect, there is a much higher probability that a group determination made under these circumstances will be superior to one made using either a wandering method or a rushed single-meeting decision.

> Step 2 is to make the decision.

In our bank example, if the executive team had followed the two-step process, perhaps they would have chosen another alternative such as reselling the mortgages right away to manage the risk, instead of holding them to make a higher profit. They might have considered putting limits on short-term borrowing in order to limit the bank's risk. Maybe a hybrid alternative would have been preferred if they had taken the time to make a more responsible decision.

Variations to Two-Step Decisions

There is no magic about the two-step process, and sometimes a complex decision will take several steps. For example, the first step could be to agree to the objectives, the second step could be to define the alternatives, and a third step could be to evaluate the alternatives and reach a decision. Section V shows how project management decisions are made in multiple, clearly defined steps (phases).

The point is that complex decisions should be made in clearly defined steps. The first step meeting should define the process for the decision, including how many steps and the purpose of each step. Some decisions, such as product development decisions and project decisions in general, lend themselves to multiple steps that are clearly defined up front and possibly even defined as a standard process, as explained in section V.

Two-step decision processes do not only apply to group decisions. It can be a very successful technique for an individual making a complex decision. Define your decision process and break it into steps. Stop at each step and write down your results. Schedule the next step for yourself, but think about the decision in between those steps.

- Complex decisions should not be made in a single step; otherwise they can be oversimplified and made rashly or become a wandering process without conclusion.
- The first step is to define the decision, then spend some time thinking about it before the second step of actually making the decision.
- Two-step decisions work for individuals and even better for groups.

CHAPTER 10

Trying It On for Size

*Tentative decisions can help
make better final decisions*

Frequently managers or executives make business decisions they later regret. Within weeks, they realize that the decision just does not seem right. They see something they perhaps neglected, underestimated, or overestimated in their deliberations. In most cases, such mistakes can be avoided by using a technique that I call "try it on for size." Here is an example where it would have helped avoid a mistake.

A partner at a major law firm was approached by a large corporation about representing it in a lawsuit against a competitor charging patent infringement on a software product. The partner had to decide whether to accept the case or pass it along to another firm and was given several days to do so. While he was widely known as an expert in this type of patent infringement case and knew he would be able to represent the company well, the attorney was also aware that the leadership of the company and its in-house counsel were reputed to be pigheaded and did not listen to the recommendations of the attorneys they hired. This particular partner had a very high success rate in these suits, but he knew that his success came as a result of his clients taking his advice. He was unsure this would work with regard to this new client. When he met with the executives and counsel of the company, he discussed his reservations about taking the case. The executives assured him that they would offer their opinion, but accept his advice unchallenged. After the meeting, he considered the situation for an hour or so, and decided that he would take the case.

> Just as you would try on clothes before buying them, it makes sense to try on a major business decision before you "buy" it.

About a month into the trial preparations, the attorney was already having reservations. He was getting fed up with being constantly undermined by company executives. Already, he had been forced to implement a number of procedural measures that he believed hurt their chances of victory. While he was not happy with the situation, he decided to stick with it through the end because he did not want to abandon any of his clients during the process of representing them. When the case finished up a year and a half later, they had lost their patent fight.

> **IN YOUR EXPERIENCE**
>
> *Have you ever looked at a decision you made and said to yourself that if you had only tried it out a little you would have made a different decision?*

The attorney, however, remained convinced that he would have succeeded if company leadership had not forced him to make several legal maneuvers that hurt their overall chances of prevailing in court. After performing a decision postmortem, he determined that his fault had not been that he did not stand up to the company leadership enough — he believed he had made his case strongly throughout the process — but rather that he had taken the case to begin with. So, how could he have known that the company leadership was not going to follow his advice? By discussing the case with them over the course of several meetings and "trying on" his relationship with them. Talking openly about the various options for how to proceed in bringing the suit to trial likely would have revealed the company's proclivities and better forewarned the attorney. The partner learned from this experience, however, and whenever he encounters a similar company looking to retain him for his services, he attempts to mentally construct how his relationship with the representatives of the company will unfold. If he notes any red flags, he initiates a "trying-it-on-for-size" scenario.

Try It On

When you are inclined to make a particular decision, but are still hesitant, use this technique and try your tentative decision on for size for awhile to see if it fits. Just as you would test drive a car or try on clothes before making a purchase, it only makes sense to try on a major business decision before you "buy" it. As illustrated in Figure 10-1, you can continue to ponder your decision, or you can try it on to assess your comfort level with it. While this cannot be applied to all decisions, there are some where it works well.

Figure 10-1 Try It On For Size

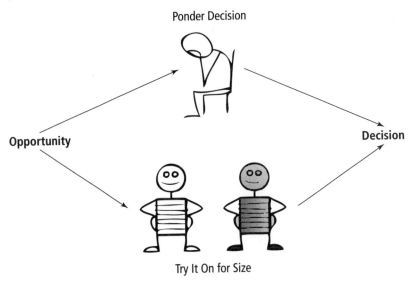

Try It On for Size

When using this decision technique, you are only trying on the decision tentatively, so it is important to keep it to yourself or to the other decision makers if it is not your decision alone. You can test situations and simulate the results in your mind. Watch your reactions to see if you want to keep the decision or throw it out as you would anything that does not fit well. If you feel comfortable with your decision, you can metaphorically cut off the tags and throw away the receipt. This means you will make the decision official by announcing it publicly and acting on it. Just as you would not buy expensive clothes from a store with a strict "no returns" policy without first trying them on, why would you make a major business decision that is going to have indelible consequences without checking to see if it fits first? If the fit is wrong, the style does not become you, or if you decide that you just plain do not like the decision that you have tried on, then no harm has been done. You were only imagining it for a short time. If this is the case, then you can proceed to try on a different decision. In fact, you can try on as many decisions as time permits. But what exactly does it mean to try something on by imagining it? You can imagine you have decided to hire someone or you have decided to take on a new project and then study your feelings about what you have decided.

Trying On Promotion Decisions

I have used the try-it-on technique very successfully in promotion decisions. You may have an employee whom you are thinking of promoting, or possibly two candidates competing for a position. With try-it-on-for-size, you select that candidate in your own mind without telling anyone. Then, over the course of a few weeks, as you see situations that person would encounter in the new position, you simulate in your mind how he or she might handle them in order to understand if you are comfortable with it.

An even better way to try on your decision is to put the person into actual situations that he or she would encounter in a new position. I would regularly try out executives being considered for promotion by putting them in situations where they would lead a similar meeting, make a customer presentation, or resolve a problem that would be typical of the position I am considering. More than once this enabled me to avoid making the wrong decision.

Trying On Employment Decisions

If you are considering hiring a new employee, you should consider how well the person would fit into the culture of your office and how well that person's skills would meld with those of the existing employees. Typically, candidates are very different, offering different skills, experience, and cultural fit. Would the personality of the new employee be well accepted by others? Would the new employee bring new skills?

Select the top candidate in your own mind and then think about how he or she would handle a situation that comes up, or fit in with others in different circumstances. By simulating this in your own mind, you can get a better feel for this candidate. If you are satisfied, then make an offer; if not, then consider another candidate.

Here is a good example. John was responsible for making a hiring decision for an open management position. He had two candidates, both outwardly qualified, but both also very different from one another. From his interviews and reference checks, John had a fairly good sense of the strengths and weaknesses of both of the candidates, as well as their personalities. He understood how they react and how they operate. So he made a tentative decision, but kept it to himself. In the ensuing weeks, he extrapolated his pick's performance in the context of the situations that arose.

> The bigger the decision, the more important it is to try it on before you commit to it.

After less than two weeks, John realized problems with his tentative candidate. While the tentative candidate had strong credentials, he did not have great interpersonal skills. When John imagined how the candidate might handle controversial situations in the department, he became worried that the man would cause more problems. It gave John a better appreciation of how important this weakness could be. So he tried on the other candidate for a short period, and hired him. By trying it on for size, John avoided a major mistake.

Trying Out Business Relationships

I have frequently recommended to clients interested in making a strategic acquisition that they try it out first before making an acquisition decision. Acquisitions are irrevocable decisions, with many turning out to be bad choices. If you can try the business relationship out in some way before making the decision, you could avoid a big mistake. One way I recommend doing this is to try working with the company in some form of partnership first. This gives you an opportunity to test the strategic benefits and the potential combined working relationship. After trying it on, you will be able to have a much better idea of whether it would work before pulling the trigger on the final decision.

If you are considering entering into a joint venture with another firm, you can also try that on for size first. Pick a common business opportunity and first try to see how you can work together on it. Was it as you expected? Was it beneficial for both parties? If so, formalize the joint venture.

Trying Out Products

This try-it-on technique can also be applied to new products. Software companies do this all of the time when they create "beta" versions of their software. These versions are designed to serve as a test to determine if a particular change in existing software will work correctly or if a new type of software can be successful. One software company, for example, decided it wanted to consider adding a major component to its functionality — one that would cost a lot of money but had the

---

The try-it-on technique works best for individuals and for small groups of people.

---

possibility of adding significant benefit for software users. In one new software package version, the company rolled out a beta version to some of the top customers who volunteered to try out the new features, including the one that would cost a lot of money to implement. As it turned out, the clients were not enthusiastic about the new feature, and many noted they would rarely use it. The software company saved a lot of money by trying it out before committing to an expensive new feature.

Beware of the Limitations

Just like other decision-making techniques, the try-it-on-for-size method has its limitations. Extrapolation will obviously not give you clairvoyance. The technique works best for an individual, and perhaps for a small group. Otherwise, it is nearly impossible to keep the dry run a secret, and before you know it, it becomes a fait accompli — you will find you have bought something that you may not have wanted. There is a big difference between a private decision that you have changed your mind about before anyone else knew about it and a public decision that people think you changed your mind about after you made it. So be careful about how you use this technique.

A tight decision deadline can also limit the usefulness of the try-it-on-for-size technique. In order to get the most out of trying something on, you need enough time to simulate, so you may want to begin thinking about your upcoming decision earlier than you normally would. But it is important to remember that insufficient time is rarely a good reason for making a critical decision badly. More often than not, the mistake was buying your decision before trying it on.

- If you are facing a major business decision and are uncertain how to proceed, your best option may be to tentatively make the decision and see how you feel about it.

- Just as you would try on clothes before buying them, you should try on a major decision before "buying" it.

- This technique takes time, so be sure to dedicate an adequate amount of time to do it right, and start the process early.

- This method can be helpful when considering promotion decisions, employment decisions, product decisions, and business relationship decisions.

- Trying it on works best when it is implemented on decisions you are making by yourself, or with a small, select group of other decision makers.

- Also important, however, is to realize that there are many limitations on this method that you should take into consideration when making your decision.

CHAPTER 11

Relying on Intuition

Sometimes you just need to follow your gut

Intuitive decisions can be powerful. They happen quickly and relatively easily. They usually instill a sense of confidence that you made a good decision, even if others or the facts advise against it. You do not know how you got there, but you like your decision. In a famous story of relying on intuition or instinct for a decision, in 1960 Ray Kroc was advised against paying $2.7 million to purchase the McDonald's franchise from the McDonald brothers. He claimed that he relied on his instinct to make the decision to purchase McDonald's.

Intuitive decisions can also be dangerous. They can be wrong because you did not spend enough time on your decision, yet they give you a false sense of confidence. Few people admit to relying on their intuition when making a bad decision, but it happens at least as frequently, if not much more so, than correct intuitive decisions. Sometimes intuitive decisions are successful by chance, reinforcing a mistaken belief in intuitive decisions. I worked with one CEO who insisted on making an acquisition despite paying a much higher price than a detailed financial analysis showed that it was worth. He claimed that his intuition told him that this would be a great acquisition with many additional benefits. After two years, the financial analysis proved to be correct, and the company wasted a lot of precious cash on a poor intuitive decision. The board of directors later fired the CEO for his poor decision making.

The challenge with intuitive decisions comes from knowing when to rely on them. Let's start with a more complete example.

Rebecca, a division general manager at a large food distribution company, was responsible for the hiring decisions in her division. During all of the interviews she conducted, she asked a series of questions to understand how well the potential employees would fit into the company and how well they would be able to fulfill the requirements of the specific positions. After reviewing the resumes of each of the applicants and listening to their responses, she would take a step back and then say, "I have a good feeling (or not) about this candidate. We seemed to click very well (or not), and I think he understands (or not) what is involved in this position." And the decision would be made. Rebecca used her intuition to make her hiring decisions. When asked why she hired a particular candidate over another, she would respond, "I don't really know, I just had a feeling that one was a good fit and the other just didn't seem right for the job. Not sure why."

Over time Rebecca's hiring decisions proved to be excellent. The people she hired worked hard, stayed with the company, and progressed rapidly. Rarely were any of them problems, and they were all dedicated to the company. Rebecca was eventually promoted to general manager of a much larger division, in part because of her talent for hiring excellent people. Claude took over as general manager of Rebecca's previous division and asked Rebecca for advice on hiring decisions. She told Claude to just go with his gut, and it would all work out. But it did not. Intuition is not transferable to another; you cannot teach someone else how to be intuitive.

> **IN YOUR EXPERIENCE**
>
> *Have you ever made a good decision based on your intuition? How do you think you made this decision?*

Claude made a number of bad decisions. After seven of those hired were either fired for nonperformance or quit because they could not fit in with the other employees in the division, Claude's boss decided to look at how Claude hired his employees. The boss sat in on the interviews for one position and listened to the discussions about the candidates that followed. After Claude made his decision, his boss understood the problem. Claude was relying on his intuition about who to hire, and his intuition was flawed. In some cases, his intuition was based on the wrong characteristics, such as "the person had a great smile" and in others it was no more than a guess.

Why was it that Rebecca could make great intuitive hiring decisions and Claude used his intuition to make such bad decisions? Intuitive decision making is not a skill that everyone has, and it cannot be easily learned. As illustrated in these two examples, intuitive decisions can be powerful and they can be dreadful. How can you tell the difference?

What Are Intuitive Decisions?

When you make an intuitive decision, you have little idea of why you are making the decision the way you are. You instinctively know what to decide without obvious reasoning or deduction.

How do we make intuitive decisions? Some people believe intuition is a spiritual, mystical, or psychic source within us that guides us to make a decision without any thought or logic. Since there are no logical or rational explanations for how these decisions are made, these people believe there must be some greater force at work that is imparting the decision.

It is more likely we make intuitive decisions when our minds rapidly process a great deal of information, mostly small, unrelated bits of information, to arrive at a decision. It all happens so quickly that we do not know how we got there. The brain rapidly draws on past experiences and external cues and then processes this information at a subconscious level, so we are not aware of any rational thought process taking place. All we are aware of is a feeling that our decision is either right or wrong. Physicians, for example, make intuitive decisions when they diagnose their patients' problems. Clinical intuition is a skill that is created and refined over many years through experience with thousands of patients. The physician processes information on the patient's problems from medical history, physical examination, diagnostics, blood tests, and many other factors. Intuitively these form a pattern, which the physician may recognize to make a diagnostic decision. This can occur quickly, without any conscious analysis or step-by-step determination. There are many cases where physicians decide on a correct diagnosis, but do not have a good idea about why they have made that particular diagnosis. In some cases, these intuitive decisions are life-saving.

> When you make an intuitive decision, you make it instinctively without knowing why you have decided the way you did.

Intuitive decisions can be made based on rules of thumb or pattern recognition. Skill in making intuitive decisions can be refined over time through successes and mistakes. Though it is a powerful decision technique and can often lead to highly accurate and successful outcomes, relying too heavily on intuition has its perils. Physicians also make bad intuitive diagnostic decisions. They may jump to a decision prematurely without collecting all of the necessary information. Their instinctive decision may be unduly influenced by recent cases that were somewhat similar. They may apply some mental templates or rules of thumb and fail to consider other possibilities.

What Enables Intuitive Decisions?

- *Experience* — The more experience you have, the more you can instinctively compare similar situations to the past. For example, in hiring decisions you may have made a mistake hiring people before who appeared not to be sufficiently committed. When you see this trait in a candidate again, your intuition may throw up a red flag.
- *Pattern recognition* — Intuition is essentially pattern recognition that takes place subconsciously. You combine a number of factors in your mind that just give you a certain feeling. For example, you may feel that a decision is too risky and that those risks outweigh the benefits, even though you cannot articulate these clearly.
- *Intelligence* — Although there is disagreement to this, I think that more-intelligent people tend to make better intuitive decisions, while less-intelligent people tend to make poorer intuitive decisions. To be sure, this may be a combination of mental intelligence and emotional intelligence.
- *Personality type* — We explore personality types and decision making later in this book, but I believe certain people have a personality that is more disposed to make intuitive decisions (good and bad) than others.

Gut Feel or Guess

Sometimes it may be difficult to discern between a gut feeling and a guess. You might just be guessing when you think you have some great intuition about a decision. You may call it intuition, but it may be no more than a guess. That was Claude's problem; he was simply guessing at who was the best candidate.

When you ask gamblers why they picked a particular number in roulette or craps, they will frequently answer that they had a good feeling or intuition that it was the "right" number. They feel good about their number decision, at least until it is played out. Not many of us believe these are good intuitive decisions in any way, yet the decision has the same feel as an intuitive decision.

Sometimes intuition is just an excuse for sloppy decision making. You want to avoid the hard work to make a decision correctly, so you just leave it up to intuition. For example, in reviewing why many banks made poor mortgage decisions that later turned into bad loans, a lot of the blame was due to intuitive decisions. On paper the person did not really qualify for the mortgage and would have trouble repaying it, especially when interest rates increased after a couple of years. But the mortgage underwriter just had a good feeling about it. The person would probably make more money every year, and the value of the house would increase, so it would work out OK.

Calibrating Intuition

Here is one of the major points I learned about intuition. While some people may make great intuitive decisions on some types of decisions, that does not mean they make great intuitive decisions on all types of decisions. For example, I have learned that I make great intuitive decisions when hiring people, but I make poor — no, actually bad — intuitive investment decisions. I have actually calibrated my intuitive decision abilities, so I know what decisions to make intuitively and which ones to make through deductive reasoning and more formal evaluation. Over time, you can calibrate your intuitive decisions to understand how well you should trust your intuition for each type of decision that you make.

Some people continually make poor intuitive decisions. This is the way it was for Claude at the food distribution company described at the beginning of this chapter. He made decisions based on his intuition time and again, only these decisions seemed to be flawed. His boss noticed this after deciding to examine the seemingly poor decisions about hiring that Claude had made on a number of occasions. Seeing this,

> **IN YOUR EXPERIENCE**
>
> *Have you ever watched someone make what they called an intuitive decision, and you knew they were just guessing?*

his boss decided that Claude would no longer be responsible for these decisions. He decided the company needed to institute a more formal hiring procedure and someone else in Claude's division would take the ultimate responsibility for all hiring decisions. Claude would still have input, but not the final say. While it was clear to his boss that Claude made certain intuitive decisions very well, hiring decisions were definitely not one of them. The new process was designed to counter his bad intuition.

I instituted a similar procedure at the consulting firm I founded and ran for 25 years. While I initially made most of the hiring decisions, I noticed when others started making these decisions they also tried to make them intuitively, but were not as good at it. So I instituted a more formal hiring decision process to fix the problem. Each candidate for a consulting position was required to meet with five people in separate interviews, including with two partners, and the decision would be made based upon what each of the five thought, not based upon the intuition of one single interviewer. This solution brought us the best, most highly qualified individuals who were critical to the firm's growth.

> Some people continually make poor intuitive decisions; others make bad intuitive decisions only for specific types of decisions.

The same goes for decisions that are made by your coworkers. They, too, will likely have very good intuition about some specific types of decisions but be bad at other decisions. When working with others who have these symptoms, the best thing you can do for them, the company, and yourself is to calibrate their intuitive decision capabilities. If they make good intuitive decisions, then support it with more opportunities to use their intuition. If they make bad intuitive decisions on certain types of decisions, then you need to actively work to manage their ability to make these decisions. This can be done either by putting the decision-making authority in the hands of a different person or by instituting a specific process for getting around these deficiencies.

As a manager or executive, you need to calibrate the intuitive decision-making skills of your employees. You need to learn what intuitive decisions they make successfully and what decisions you should not let them make. This may take a little time and effort to do the calibration, but it is worth it since you can avoid mistakes. After I have done this, I know which people make great intuitive decisions, and when they recommend a decision, I just tell them OK, do it. Other times, I ask them to do a more formal analysis of the decision and review it with me in more detail. Frequently they revise their decision after spending more time analyzing it. That proves the point.

The worksheet in Figure 11-1 can help you identify the areas where you and others make good intuitive decisions.

Intuition as a Validation

Intuition can be invaluable in validating a decision you reach in rational ways. At times you may make a rational decision, but feel that it intuitively does not make sense for some reason that you cannot explain. Perhaps your intuition is right. Intuition can strongly validate a decision. If your decision "just does not feel right," then stop. Look at the decision again. For myself, I have found that when intuitively a decision just does not feel right, that it is usually wrong.

If this occurs, you should consider reviewing your rational decision to see if there was something missing that you did not consider. You may just find you overlooked something crucial to making the best decision and your intuition was right all along.

- We can all use our intuition to help us make better decisions.
- Sometimes our intuition can be very helpful, but other times it can be detrimental.
- Quite often, people can make very good intuitive decisions for certain types of decisions, and very bad intuitive decisions for other types.
- Several factors enable intuitive decisions: experience, pattern recognition, intelligence, and personality type.
- If you or others make bad decisions when it comes to certain types of decisions, you can either task someone else with making these decisions or institute a process for avoiding these problems.

Figure 11-1 Are You Intuitive?

Type of Decisions	How Often Do You Make Intuitive Decisions?			How Often Is Your Decision Correct?	Comments on Why You Make Intuitive Decisions in This Category
	Most of the Time	Some of the Time	Rarely or Never		
Hiring decisions	☐	☐	☐	___ %	_____
Promotion decisions	☐	☐	☐	___ %	_____
Project selection decisions	☐	☐	☐	___ %	_____
Strategic decisions	☐	☐	☐	___ %	_____
Marketing decisions	☐	☐	☐	___ %	_____
Financial decisions	☐	☐	☐	___ %	_____
Technical decisions	☐	☐	☐	___ %	_____
Budget decisions	☐	☐	☐	___ %	_____
_____	☐	☐	☐	___ %	_____
_____	☐	☐	☐	___ %	_____
_____	☐	☐	☐	___ %	_____
_____	☐	☐	☐	___ %	_____

Conclusions: _____

_____

_____

_____

_____

CHAPTER 12

Using Decision Deadlines

Don't let decisions pass you by

It is a mysterious (or maybe not so mysterious) business phenomenon that decisions tend to get made right before the deadline, even though they could have been made much earlier. The opposite situation is that decisions tend to drift without resolution when there are no deadlines. Deadlines are an integral part of any successful business. Sometimes they are preset for us by a procedure or statutory provision. Other times we have to determine them for ourselves, not doing so at our own peril. Some deadlines are rigid and cannot be changed; others are artificial and set so we can simply get something off our desk. Sometimes the deadlines we set are designed as steps on our way to achieving a larger project, and other times they help ensure we do not miss opportunities. In some cases, you need to set decision deadlines for others in order for them to make a decision. Whatever the type, deadlines should be viewed as our friends, not our enemies. Whether set by ourselves or someone else, deadlines are useful to help us achieve desired business goals.

> Deadlines are not our enemies; they are our friends.

Roger was responsible for facilities at a company that produced chairs and desks. The company leased its factory in an area outside the city that had grown to be an increasingly popular manufacturing location since the company started manufacturing during the last 10 years. Roger knew that the company's 10-year lease needed to be extended in the upcoming year, so he began to consider alternatives, including staying there or moving to a larger facility that would provide additional capacity.

He was also busy installing new manufacturing equipment to automate some of the chair assembly process, and that project was not going very well. That project consumed Roger's attention, and he held off working on the lease renewal. When he got back to it, he had a big problem. The company that owned the building had an offer to sell it now that the lease was up. Another manufacturing company wanted the building and was willing to purchase it.

Figue 12-1 Progress is Faster with a Deadline

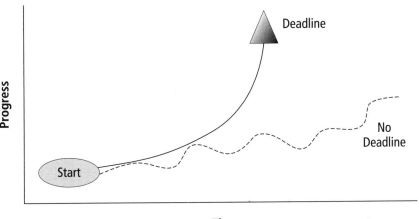

Roger frantically looked at other alternative manufacturing facilities. Unfortunately, the available ones were much farther away, which would cause many production workers to quit. There were opportunities to contract to build and lease a new building, but that would take more than a year to complete. Roger failed to set a deadline for himself. Had he done so, he would have addressed the problem in time to line up other viable options. Unfortunately, when the president of the company asked Roger about the lease renewal six months earlier, he said, "Don't worry, it's under control." Now he had to break the bad news to the president. After listening to Roger, the president furiously fired him on the spot. Roger learned a very costly lesson on the importance of deadlines.

If decision deadlines cause you anxieties or even lead to mental blocks, it is time to change your relationship with them. Deadlines are not our opponents. They can be good masters, and are even better servants. Either way, you need to know how to use them to help you make decisions.

Types of Deadlines

In my experience, I have found there are different types of deadlines, each with a different purpose:

- *Project Decision Deadlines* — These are intermediate deadlines at key points throughout a project that enable you to complete the entire project on schedule. Without these deadlines along the way, projects will almost always be late.
- *Process Decision Deadlines* — Companies establish deadlines within common business processes in order to coordinate completion of specific tasks. Examples of this type of deadline include completing employee reviews, selecting 401(k) withholdings, and completing expense reports.
- *Decision-Forcing Deadlines* — These are deadlines you set for someone else or someone else sets for you in order to get a decision made. I look upon these as forcing mechanisms and use them all the time as a technique to prompt others to make a decision.
- *Negotiating Decision Deadlines* — These are a variation of decision-forcing deadlines that are used in negotiations. Typically with a negotiating deadline, someone makes an offer conditioned upon accepting or rejecting the offer within a limited time frame.
- *Artificial Decision Deadlines* — These are deadlines you set for yourself just so you can make a decision and stop procrastinating. Artificial decision deadlines are efficient ways to get on with a decision and not let it linger. I call these "artificial" because there is not any particular reason for setting a specific deadline. I sometimes make up artificial deadlines for others to use them as decision-forcing deadlines.
- *Opportunity Decision Deadlines* — These deadlines are ones you set that are designed to help you take advantage of opportunities that you may otherwise miss. If too much time goes by without making a decision, then it may be too late to take advantage of a particular opportunity.

Project Decision Deadlines

Project deadlines are those deadlines that are individual steps leading to a larger project outcome. You may set 5 or 15 deadlines that are all part of one specific project you are trying to bring to completion. Maybe you have set a deadline of 10 days before a board meeting to allow yourself time to decide on the agenda or finalize a recommendation to the board. Maybe you set a deadline regarding the scope of work created for a potential client five days prior to the date of your client presentation. Perhaps you set a deadline of the end of the week to select which prospective new employees to consider in the first round of interviews, a deadline of two weeks to have completed the first-round interviews, a deadline of another week to decide on the final-round applicants, a deadline of a week to interview them, and a final deadline of another week to decide to which candidate you will offer the job.

Project decision deadlines are best set by milestones or project phases, which are covered in detail in section V.

Process Decision Deadlines

Process decision deadlines are used to run businesses more efficiently. Examples of these types of decisions abound. A college has an annual deadline to decide on tuition increases. A marketing organization has a deadline to set price increases. A manufacturing organization has a deadline to decide on production plans. A company needs to determine its recruiting goals prior to initiating its recruiting campaign. An executive team has an annual deadline to formulate its financial plan for the next year. Process decision deadlines are reduced to practice through organizational policies and processes.

These process decision deadlines are critical to a smoothly running organization. Without following the right deadlines, an organization can become dysfunctional and lack a coordinated business effort. On the other hand, poorly set decision deadlines can make an organization less flexible and inefficient. I have seen this happen when one part of a business sets early, unrealistic deadlines for another part of the business. For example, the manufacturing organization in one company set a deadline for the next year's sales forecasts from the sales organization by June. This gave the manufacturing organization leisurely time to study the numbers and plan for the next year. Of course, it was virtually impossible for the sales organization to make these decisions so early, and they were always grossly inaccurate, which caused arguing and blaming within the company. I solved this by setting two decision deadlines: one for a rough-cut planning decision in July and the other for final forecasts in November.

Rigid deadlines are those that are extremely difficult — or even impossible — to change. They are usually set by someone external, or even by an existing procedure or process that cannot be altered. A good example of a rigid deadline is one that all public companies have to face: the filing deadlines imposed by the Securities and Exchange Commission for quarterly or annual reports. While you may or may not want to meet these deadlines, you do not have any choice. And they cannot be extended. The deadlines are set far in advance and are the same for every company in the same situation, regardless of conflicts that come up within the company or within your personal life. These can also be process deadlines — ones that are instituted by your company, its board of directors, or by a client or consultant.

> Process decision deadlines are reduced to practice through organizational policies and processes.

Decision-Forcing Deadlines

Decision-forcing deadlines do just that: force a decision. Many times in business we use these deadlines to compel someone else to make a decision that favors our own timetable. One common business example is during a job offer decision. If you are responsible for hiring someone and you have honed your decision down to three finalists, you may take the top option and make that person an offer. But, since it is unlikely that person is going to accept your offer right away, you want to give the person adequate time to assess the offer and make a decision. However, you want to be sure not to give the person enough time to play your offer off other offers in the similar time frame. Thus, you assign a decision-forcing deadline for accepting or rejecting your offer. If the deadline is missed, you move on to the next candidate on your list.

Decision-forcing deadlines are useful in sales. For example, a copier company maximizes its quarterly sales every quarter. When you, as a potential customer looking for a new copier, call the company to inquire about prices, you will likely be given a quote for full price. On occasion, you may be told that you qualify for a small discount. But if you call at the most opportune time of the sales quarter, you may qualify for such a deep discount that you may actually be paying less for the copier than it costs the company to produce and distribute. The reason is that the company needs to hit its quarterly sales goals, and by calling two days prior to the end of the quarter, you may be offered these deep discounts if you make your purchase before the end of this artificial deadline.

Similarly, quite often other people will set decision-forcing deadlines on you, so you should be aware of how they are set and how you can deal with them. These deadlines can be imposed by your boss, coworker, client, or an outside entity. An example is a specific due date for a simple report evaluating a project for a client. If you miss the deadline, you are likely to lose that client. Or if you are going to bid on a project and you miss the deadline set by the potential client, you will certainly not win the contract.

> Decision-forcing deadlines help get decisions made.

Negotiating Decision Deadlines

Decision deadlines are essential in negotiations. Without them the potential exists for negotiating parties to sit tight waiting to see if a better offer comes along. I have been involved in the merger and acquisition of several companies, and negotiating decisions were essential in all cases. You have to set a deadline — usually a short one — for the other company to respond to the offer. Negotiating decision deadlines can be extended if it makes sense, but eventually one of the parties gets fed up and sets a drop-dead deadline — and this is usually when the serious negotiation begins.

At the end of March 2009, U.S. President Barack Obama set a deadline for GM and Chrysler to reach agreements that required concessions from various parties. When both companies missed the March 30 deadline they were previously given to reorganize, the president gave them both new deadlines of June 1 with more serious consequences: that they would both face controlled bankruptcy if they were unable to reach the concessions needed. By that deadline, both companies declared bankruptcy. The deadline forced all the parties involved — the UAW, banks, and so on — to come to an agreement by that date that was then legally enforced through bankruptcy. Without that deadline, negotiations would have gone on indefinitely, with the U.S. government expected to provide more loans.

You see the same process invoked with legal disputes. One party makes an offer to another with a specific decision deadline. Then there is a counteroffer with a deadline. This activity continues until there is some material deadline such as the case actually starting in court, which is where legal fees rapidly increase for both parties. Most disputes are settled at this point.

When you are involved in negotiations, be sure to use decision deadlines wisely. Deadlines offer one of the most important tools you have in making negotiation decisions.

Artificial Decision Deadlines

Sometimes you may set artificial decision deadlines for yourself, perhaps just to stay on top of your workload. Maybe you are responsible for hiring someone for a position in your department. Even though you have no real need to make a decision about it by any specific deadline, you know that you need to fulfill this responsibility, so you set a deadline of two weeks to create the position description, or Thursday morning to decide who you are going to ask in to interview for the position, or Monday afternoon to make an offer to your top candidate. You have no need to make a decision by these specific deadlines, but you know that setting deadlines for these or other steps will help you complete the process.

Perhaps you set an artificial decision deadline for someone else simply because you know they need to make a decision, and you want them to do it in a timely way. You may tell someone who works for you to decide whether to attend the sales conference by Wednesday afternoon, or to make a decision about which consulting firm to hire for the project within a week, or to decide on what the following month's advertising budget is going to be by the fifteenth of this month.

In my years as a management consultant, I have often found that people make better decisions when they believe they are forced to make them. In a number of circumstances, I have invented decision deadlines for boards, CEOs, and project managers in an effort to help them to make decisions. Every time, I would tell them the decisions had to be made by a specific time or day, although I offered no particular reason. For the most part they simply accepted the decision deadline without challenging it, not because I had any particular authority to set the deadline, but I think because they intuitively un-

> People at all levels in an organization are more comfortable working with reasonable decision deadlines.

derstood there needed to be a deadline and the one I gave them was reasonable. People at all levels in an organization are more comfortable working with reasonable decision deadlines.

Opportunity Decision Deadlines

Opportunity decision deadlines are easiest to overlook because you need to anticipate opportunities, which is different from being confronted with the need for a decision. You need to make an intentional decision to avail yourself of opportunities, which starts with setting the deadline to consider an opportunity. These types of deadlines quite often do not have a specific time frame, but if you fail to act by a certain time, you may needlessly miss an opportunity, and quite often an important opportunity.

I saw a good example of this with a client whose executives periodically talked about acquiring a small company that had some terrific technology, superior to their own company's in some important ways. Some executives considered that the technology had the potential to create a new generation of products if combined with their own company's capabilities and distribution. The CEO would say, "I like that company. Someday I think we

> Deciding to set deadlines and to abide by these deadlines will help you to achieve your goals and be successful in business.

should acquire them, but right now our plates are full with other challenges." They never set an opportunity decision deadline because they somehow assumed the opportunity would always be there for them when they wanted to make a decision. It was not. Their major competitor acquired the company. Not too long after the acquisition, the competitor had already taken away a lot of market share with this new technology. This lack of a deadline to initiate follow-through turned out to be both a major missed opportunity and a major strategic error.

Applying Decision Deadlines

Setting decision deadlines and abiding by them, whether they are imposed by someone else, internal ones you set for yourself, or external ones you impose on other people, help you make better and more efficient business decisions. Some deadlines may already be set for you, but to get the most out of decision deadlines, try creating some for yourself. Self-imposed deadlines can serve you well. When you set deadlines for yourself, there will be occasions when you need to give yourself an extension. On rare occasions you may want to give yourself multiple extensions, though it is unwise to do this too often or you simply diffuse the advantages of using deadlines. Providing yourself with deadlines helps you create mental focus and a sense of urgency about the decision at hand. Using deadlines to your advantage is a skill in business that cannot be understated.

Deadlines are not our enemies, but our friends. They can serve as great masters, but even better servants.

* Deadlines are an integral part of any successful business.

* There are six different types of decision deadlines that can be applied, depending on the situation: project decision deadlines, process decision deadlines, decision-forcing deadlines, negotiating decision deadlines, artificial decision deadlines, and opportunity decision deadlines.

* Deciding to set deadlines and to abide by these decisions will help you achieve your goals and be successful in business.

* Deadlines are not our enemies, but our friends; they can serve as great masters, but even better servants.

CHAPTER 13

Applying Pros and Cons

*A very simple method to save
you time and money*

One of the most commonly known methods for making a decision in business is simply to make a pros and cons list. Write down all of the benefits of proceeding in one direction and then all of the drawbacks. Whether selling or buying; promoting, hiring, or firing someone; endorsing or abandoning a new product; or with any other decision scenarios that require a yes-or-no decision, a pros and cons list can truly be a formidable tool in your decision toolbox.

Detached Thinking

The CEO of a medium-sized commercial construction company that had dozens of subcontracts building industrial facilities was struggling for a new way to increase sales. Looking into various options, he realized that there were hundreds of city and state road construction and maintenance projects that they had the equipment and personnel to bid on, and which could prove to be extremely lucrative for the company. He knew that there would be a lot of work involved in proving that his company could fulfill the contract requirements and complete the projects should they win the business. In the end, the CEO decided to pursue the option. While the company lost the first three contracts it bid on, it won the fourth — a substantial contract for the maintenance of the major highway that ran through one of the largest counties in the state. The company labored hard to fulfill the terms of the contract. Unfortunately, the cost structure was far off, and the engineers quickly realized that the company lacked the needed experience and skilled laborers to actually complete the contract according to the proposal specs. In order to fulfill the contractual terms, the company ultimately had to make a sizeable increase in staff and incur substantial extra costs.

In reviewing his decision, the CEO saw that in not wanting to rush into the decision, he instead racked his brain about it whenever he had time to consider it. He sought the advice of his friends, other executives of his company, chief engineers, those responsible for submitting proposals for new contracts, and truly anyone he believed would have any advice for him. One day he would realize he had all of the required equipment, the engineers with experience in all types of construction projects, the manpower to physically implement the projects, and other requirements he believed he needed. The next day he would realize he really did not have senior engineers with enough detailed experience in the very specific requisites involved with road and highway construction and maintenance. He would ask the director of special projects whether she believed the company could begin this as a new division, and she advised that this would certainly be possible. It would simply be a matter of time and money. Then he would ask the senior engineer whether he thought that the company could actually implement the programs, and, based on the engineer's response, the CEO would realize that it was certainly a challenge. While there was a possibility of success, there were many major roadblocks in the way. To borrow a phrase now popular in the political realm, he flip-flopped.

> There are many types of decisions where writing down your thoughts proves very useful.

The CEO realized he had failed. He had failed to adequately assess all of the pros and cons, and particularly to assess all of the pros and cons at the same time, alongside each other, to enable him to determine how well they weighed against each other. Had he done so, this combined pros and cons list would have allowed him to make a more informed, well-rounded decision based on all of the facts.

Ben Franklin's Letter

On September 19, 1772, Benjamin Franklin posted a letter to a good friend, Joseph Priestly, advising him on a major decision Priestly was having trouble making. The letter provided Priestly with useful advice, not on which decision should be made, but on how he should approach making the decision. The entire text of the letter is as follows:

In the affair of so much importance to you, wherein you ask my advice, I cannot, for want of sufficient premises, advise you what to determine, but if you please I will tell you how. When those difficult cases occur, they are difficult, chiefly because while we have them under consideration, all the reasons pro and con are not present to the mind at the same time: but sometimes one set present themselves, and at other times another, the first being out of sight. Hence the various purposes or inclinations that alternatively prevail, and the uncertainty that perplexes us.

To get over this, my way is to divide half a sheet of paper by a line into two columns; writing over the one Pro, and over the other Con. Then, during the three or four days consideration, I put down under the different heads short hints of the different motives, that at different times occur to me, for or against the measure. When I have thus got them all together in one view, I endeavor to estimate their respective weights; and where I find two, one on each side, that seem equal, I strike them both out. If I find a reason pro equal to some two reasons con, I strike out the three. If I judge some two reasons con, equal to three reasons pro, I strike out the five; and thus proceeding I find at length where the balance lies; and if, after a day or two of further consideration, nothing new that is of importance occurs on either side, I come to a determination accordingly.

And, though the weight of reasons cannot be taken with the precision of algebraic quantities, yet when each is thus considered, separately and comparatively, and the whole lies before me, I think I can judge better, and am less liable to make a rash step, and in fact I have found great advantage from this kind of equation, in what may be called moral or prudential algebra.

Wishing sincerely that you may determine for the best, I am ever, my dear friend, yours affectionately,

B. Franklin

Write It Down

What Benjamin Franklin defined here was essentially one of the first uses of the pros and cons list, a method of helping to approach a decision where you have to choose between selecting one of two options. While a great number of useful lessons can be drawn from this letter that Franklin wrote to his friend Priestly — who is most notably known for his discovery of oxygen — I want to emphasize one in particular: the importance of writing down the implications of a decision.

Franklin states that all the reasons, pros and cons, cannot be present in the mind at the same time. Sometimes you think of a particular set of reasons and lean toward one alternative, but other times you think of a different set of reasons and lean another way. What causes you to go back and forth is the different set of reasons in your mind at a particular time. To correct this problem, you should write down all of the reasons, pro and con, and, when completed, you see them all at the same time. Once you see them all together, you can better weigh one set against the other. Many times the preferred alternative becomes clear as soon as you see them all, but sometimes you need to weigh the factors more closely.

> Franklin states that all the reasons, pros and cons, cannot be present in the mind at the same time.

For many types of decisions, writing down your thoughts proves very useful, and I have used this technique frequently when facing major business decisions. Should I promote my assistant? Should I move forward on the new project? Should I advertise on this website? I would not recommend doing a pro and con list for all of the small decisions you face in business because it would simply take too much time. I do, however, recommend using it for major decisions.

Putting It to the Test

It is helpful to look at an example when considering how to use pros and cons to take action, make a purchase, sell belongings, or make other types of yes or no decisions. A relatively small but successful software company — Watson Software, named after its founder — was considering whether to agree to a buyout offer from a larger company looking to expand its business into the collaborative software industry. The board of directors spent several months considering the positives and the negatives of agreeing to the sale. The largest shareholders in the company were not all on board with the sale, not to mention several of the key employees who either stood to lose their jobs or lose much of the value of their stock options. The company, while not publicly traded, offered employee ownership options to its top employees, as well as having put out several rounds of private equity by selling stock in the company.

After many dissentious discussions the board put together the pros and cons list illustrated in Figure 13-1. The members put together their own personal lists and then shared them. The figure is a simplification of the combined list. The board members spent a meeting discussing the list and then held another meeting to evaluate it. After lengthy discussion, they agreed not to sell the company because the risk of the sale was too high and they did not want to give away the potential future gain.

Several of the board members commented later they would not have reached a decision they were comfortable with without using this pros and cons technique. As Ben Franklin said, it really put in front of them at the same time all of the matters to be considered.

Evaluating Pros and Cons

I have found Benjamin Franklin's way of writing a pros and cons list very useful on a number of occasions. Taking it at its simplest, Franklin's decision-making pros and cons list works in the following way: Draw a line down the center of a piece of paper, labeling the top of one side "pros" and the top of the other "cons." Then proceed to place the factors you would feel to be beneficial on the pros side of the sheet and place the factors you feel would be detrimental on the cons side of the sheet. Then compare all of the factors and make your decision.

There are various techniques for easily evaluating the pros and cons on your list:

- Some people just count the pros and cons as if they were votes. I highly discourage this because all items are not of equal weight, and sometimes a factor could be expressed in multiple items or consolidated into one.
- You can use the method Ben Franklin recommends of offsetting equal items or crossing off one item on a side if it equals two on the other side.
- In Figure 13-1, the pros and cons are separated by category, and you can make a determination in each category. Then consider the decision based on the category assessments.

Figure 13-1   Watson Software Acquisition Evaluation

	Pros	Cons
Price/Value For Shareholders	• $25 million is above the current value. • The investment banker's opinion is that this is within the fairness range. • One of the largest shareholders wants to sell the company to gain liquidity. • It's not likely that the company will be able to go public for many years.	• $25 million is well below most expectations for future value. • The price is not acceptable to all shareholders. At this price, later investors make a quick profit while early shareholders have a loss. • More than $25 million has been invested in the company.
Timing Sell Company Now or Wait	• The largest shareholder wants to sell now. • We have talked with many potential buyers, and this is the only offer. • The company may be too small to go public and eventually needs to be acquired. • The economy is down, and it's not clear how long it will take to improve.	• The stock market is down, and this is lowering the market price for acquisitions as well. • We have strong cash flow and no need to sell now. • The economy and company markets may improve, and we could be selling at the bottom.
Risks Of Selling the Company	• The economy and company markets may continue to decline, and the company could require more cash. • There could be shareholder lawsuits and unrest if we don't sell.	• There will be lawsuits if we sell the company. • The deal may not close, and the company may be irreparably harmed. • After the sale is announced, customer orders could diminish or stop entirely.
Management Miscellaneous Considerations	• Some executives will realize at least some gain on their options.	• Most of the management team will lose their positions in the acquiring company. • Some executives will not get much of a gain on their options.

- Sometimes, I circle the items that stand out as the most important and then step back and look at the balance of the circles to make a decision.
- Another method is to put an approximate value next to each item, such as a + or ++, and then add up the approximate values.

While this is the simplistic way of looking at this method, some more accurate and detailed options are based on this approach, including how to assign a value or a weight to each of your pros and cons.

Using a Pros and Cons List in a Group

A pros and cons list can be a powerful technique for group decisions. This can be done in two ways. The first is to have the group create a combined list. The group can create the list together. Typically one person stands at a board and writes down the items as people in the group shout them out. While this gets everything on paper, it frequently results in redundant items just stated differently. Another step, editing and combining the list, thus needs to be included. This can take some time but is necessary. In Figure 13-1, many comments were made on the economy, but they were combined into the ones illustrated.

Another technique is to have each member of the group do one's own pros and cons sheet. Then everyone shares them with the others and talks through how they would arrive at a decision. If this works right, then some members of the group will revise their own pros and cons sheet based on what they learned from others.

In the End

When I personally reflect on some of the bad decisions I have made in business, I realize that I failed to consider what turned out to be an important factor when I made the decision. It was not that I had not considered that factor prior to making the decision; I did. The problem was that I did not bring that factor sufficiently into my mind when making the decision. If only I had written everything down, I may have avoided making a bad decision.

Weighing the pros and cons of a decision in your head can often lead to mistakes. Follow the advice of one of the smartest people in history, Benjamin Franklin, and take the time and care to write them down. This step can make all the difference and lead to better results from your decisions.

- Ben Franklin's idea of a pros and cons list is still one of the most valuable decision techniques today.

- Too often managers will try to make complex decisions informally in their heads, and then get frustrated because they think of one set of factors at a time.

- Several ways exist to evaluate a pros and cons list, including counting pros and cons, offsetting equal items, separating them by category and then evaluating them, or circling items that are the most important and evaluating them from there.

- There are special considerations for a team doing a pros and cons list.

CHAPTER 14

Framing Decisions

*Sometimes you frame; other
times you get framed*

I have been framed. You have been framed. We have all been framed. I have even successfully framed others. But why am I bragging about something that sounds reprehensible? What I am talking about is not illegal, unethical, or immoral. It is decision framing.

Decision framing is an extremely effective technique used to get others to make the decision you want them to make. It puts you into control of the decision you want. There are several decision framing techniques you can apply. We look in this chapter at several of these techniques and also discuss what to do if you are being framed.

Being Framed and Framing Others

What does decision framing mean? The decisions we make in business are framed by the choices that are offered to us and by how those choices are presented. Moreover, the way you present decisions to others creates their range of options from which to choose, as well as affects the way they will go about making their decision among those options. There are several varieties of framing, and you can often direct decisions by how you frame them. But the same can be done to you, so be on the lookout for decision framing.

I learned a long time ago from selling management consulting projects that how you frame a project proposal usually determines what the client ends up buying. For example, suppose a client is given a $500,000 project proposal. The

> The decisions we make in business are framed by the choices that are offered to us and how those choices are presented.

135

client may well think that is an awful lot of money and balk at hiring you. So instead of presenting only one proposal, I found it was more effective to give the client three alternative proposals at different price points — say, at $250,000, $500,000, and $750,000. I can tell you from experience that the client will immediately focus on the value of the services each figure represents, rather than on the amount of money you are charging. I can further tell you that the client will choose the $500,000 project proposal and feel good about it.

> How you frame a project largely determines which option a client will choose.

Why am I so confident about this? I have learned that, given three graduated options, people will gravitate toward the middle option, so it is just a matter of placing the option you want the customer to choose between a cheaper and a costlier option. Happily, I can report the middle option was almost always the best value for both my company and its clients.

Why do people gravitate toward the middle option? Perhaps they do not want to seem cheap by selecting the lowest-cost alternative. Maybe they feel one of the lower-end options will not meet their needs. The highest-priced option is usually rejected as not being a good value or as being overly extravagant. It may have some nice extras, but the customer reasons that those extras are probably not worth the additional money.

Three Bears Framing Technique

IN YOUR EXPERIENCE

Have you ever tried to figure out the best way to persuade someone to make a business decision that you wanted them to make or thought they should make?

We are all familiar with the story of Goldilocks and the three bears. When faced with a choice among three alternatives, Goldilocks always chose the middle alternative — the porridge that was neither too hot nor too cold, the chair that was neither too small nor too big, and the bed that was neither too hard nor too soft. This story demonstrates how people are drawn to the middle choice, or perhaps many people were taught this story when they were children, and are now drawn instinctively to the middle choice.

Here is an example of how to frame alternatives using the "three bears" technique I found was successful time and time again. This is illustrated in Figure 14-1. If you start with the middle-priced alternative you are trying to get the customer to select, give it 80% of the total possible value. Give the highest-priced alternative 100% of the value, but price it 50% higher than the middle alternative. Price the lowest-priced alternative at half of the middle alternative, but include a much lower value, say 25%. The middle alternative offers the best value because the alternatives were framed with that objective in mind. Customers will perceive the highest-priced alternative as overpriced and the lowest-priced alternative as undervalued.

Figure 14-1 Framing Alternatives

Price	Value	
150%	100%	Overpriced
100%	80%	"Just Right"
50%	25%	Undervalued

A carefully framed range of alternatives is a potent tool for inducing decisions in others. In addition to getting customers to select the alternative you want, they usually start to focus on which alternative to select instead of the decision to buy or not buy. This helps to induce them to make a decision faster.

To test this theory, for example, go to any major-chain hardware store and look at the rakes or the shovels or any other simple piece of hardware. You are likely to see three models labeled "Good," "Better," and "Best." You were just looking, but all of a sudden you are saying to yourself, *Hmm. Which one should I get? One of them has to be right for me.* Whether you realize it or not, you have been framed, albeit in a minor way. This "Three Bears" framing technique is used by purveyors of everything from management consulting services to vacation cruises to caskets. By knowing how framing works, you can put this knowledge to work for you.

Fast Framing

Some of the most successful framers in business are fast-food companies, who continually make a large amount of their profit from getting you to buy what they want you to, instead of what you intended to buy. Here is an example you are likely very familiar with: You go to lunch at a chain sandwich shop down the street from your office, knowing that you are going to get a turkey sandwich with lettuce, tomato, and mayonnaise. You order your sandwich, take it to the register, and the cashier turns to you and says, "For only $1.50 more, you can have a bag of chips and a 16-ounce soda." You did not want a soda, nor chips, but for some reason you find yourself walking out of the sandwich shop with cheese curls and a Pepsi. You have been framed in a simple way, but one that proves to be very lucrative over the course of hundreds of thousands of customers for this — and other — fast-food restaurant chains.

The Discount Game

Another familiar form of framing you can use to your own advantage in selling products is the discount game. Here is an example. People feel infinitely better about buying a piece of furniture that has been marked down by 25% to, let's say, $600, than they do about buying the same item for a list price of $600. The discount shifts the decision maker's focus from the $600 cost to the $200 "savings." (Stage magicians call this tactic "misdirection.") This framing technique works so well that shoppers often think they are saving money rather than spending it. You, too, can do this when you are selling consulting projects or other services to business or consumer clients.

Even colleges and universities use this form of framing to recruit the highest-level students, while maintaining sufficient tuition income. They use inflated list prices to frame students, few of whom end up paying the list price for a college education. Here is an example: A young man decides to attend College A because it has offered him a $10,000 scholarship — that is, a $10,000 discount — from the list-price tuition of $30,000. College B, which is equal to College A in every educational respect, offered him only a $5,000 scholarship from its list-price tuition of $25,000. Although the net cost of attending both institutions is the same, the student thinks he is getting a better savings at College A.

Sometimes, It Is Emotional

Look at the psychology of the emotions that go into certain framed decisions to understand how to best frame the decisions that you pose to others. In this regard, recognize that some framing uses emotional aversion as an advantage. In other words, people are likely to reject decision options that contain an explicitly negative consequence (losing money, losing business, etc.), but will select that same alternative if it is framed in positive terms (less cost, higher value, etc.). This principle has been proven through decision-making exercises such as the following. One hundred people are stranded and at imminent risk of dying. There are two possible plans for saving them. Under Plan A, half of the victims will live and half will die with 100% certainty. Under Plan B, there is a 50% chance of saving them all but a 50% chance of saving none. Leaving aside the moral agony intentionally built into this decision exercise, let's focus on how the framing of the two options affects the study subjects' decisions.

> People are likely to reject decision options that contain an explicitly negative consequence, but will select that same alternative if it is framed in positive terms.

Cognitive experiments have repeatedly shown most people will choose Plan A because of its positive framing (50 people will live). The all-or-nothing alternative of Plan B is not so attractive. When Plan A is worded as "under Plan A, 50 people will die," however, then most people will select Plan B. The outcome of Plan A is the same either way, but how it is framed profoundly changes the likelihood it will be selected.

Two Sides to Every Story

There are two sides to the framing game: either someone is trying to frame you, or you are trying to frame someone else. There are some offensive and defensive techniques that can help you get what you want when faced with either situation. If you are the one framing, frame the decision in positive terms and present multiple options, even if you have only one option in mind. Hold out a few carrots, or positive benefits of the options, not only the one you want to sell.

If you are the one being framed, on the other hand, ignore the frame and focus on the picture. Take the decision out of the context of the framed alternatives and re-

> If you are the one being framed, ignore the frame and focus on the picture.

frame it around your own objectives. If the framer is offering you A, B, or C, your best choice might well be D, or none of the above. Learn to manipulate the outcome so it meets your objectives. If you are purchasing consulting, for example, determine which services you actually need and which ones are just bells and whistles. If a consultant presents you with an option A that includes less than what you need, an Option B that includes almost all of what you need as well as some things you do not really need, and an Option C that includes everything you need and much more, consider your needs — not the options presented to you. Ask for a proposal for Option D, containing only those services you need. Maybe they will come back with a better price option, or perhaps you need to cut your losses and select A, B, or C. But at least you attempted to break free from the frame to get the best value for the services you need.

It is also important to consider alternative ways to frame a decision before you make it. Sometimes, the best decision is not to make one at all. When you are being framed, make sure you realize it. For best results, when you are the one doing the framing, make sure the person you are framing is not aware of it. As long as you are offering real value at reasonable prices, you can rest assured you are playing fair.

- In business, sometimes you frame other people and sometimes you are framed.
- There are several framing techniques you will encounter in business, including fast framing, being framed and framing others, three bears framing, the discount game, and emotional framing.
- Decision framing allows you to present various options to a potential customer that gives both you and the customer the highest value for the money.
- Emotions can often come into play when it comes to decision framing.
- Be sure to understand both the offensive end and the defensive end of decision framing, lest you be tricked into something you do not actually want.

CHAPTER 15

Getting Good Advice

Not all advice should be considered equal

One of the questions I am often asked is when to listen to advice regarding a decision. Advice can be helpful, but it can also be misguided and biased. There is a definite skill to soliciting and filtering advice on decisions.

On October 16, 2003, the Boston Red Sox held a three-run lead over the New York Yankees with just five outs needed in the seventh and deciding game of the American League Championship Series. Pedro Martinez, Boston's ace pitcher, was still on the mound after more than seven innings, but he had clearly lost his edge. Red Sox manager Grady Little went to the mound and asked Pedro if he wanted to keep pitching. Of course he said he did. What else would you expect?

The coach let Pedro make the decision, and the rest is history. Pedro gave up the tying runs, and the Yankees won the game in the eleventh inning. The Yankees went to the World Series, and the Red Sox ended their season prematurely, yet again. (The following year, the Red Sox won the World Series for the first time in 86 years.) Grady Little made the mistake of letting someone else make a decision he should have made for himself. Everyone, except for Grady Little, apparently, knew Pedro Martinez's opinion was partial. Like any good athlete, he did not want to give up. He wanted to continue pitching. That is why the manager, not the players, is supposed to make these decisions.

Grady Little was fired by the Red Sox owners because of his poor

> **IN YOUR EXPERIENCE**
>
> *Have you ever asked someone for advice only to realize that they may, in fact, have a personal stake in the outcome of your decision? Have you ever given someone advice on a decision when you had a stake in the outcome?*

Be careful when listening to someone's advice when that opinion is clearly colored by his or her unique position.

judgment. I bet if they asked him for his opinion on whether he should be fired or not, he would have said no. But unlike Grady Little, the owners knew the decision was theirs to make, not their employee's. For his part, Grady Little said, "A guy in my position makes 1,000 decisions a week. Sometimes the results are good; sometimes they're not. A lot of friends have said to me, 'Would you have done it differently?' Well, sure, if I knew the results ahead of time." But it is not about one decision out of 1,000 or knowing the results ahead of time. There is a lesson to be learned from this example: Do not listen to someone's opinion on a decision when that opinion is obviously colored by that person's unique position.

When Should You Listen to Advice?

If you think about this from a business perspective, it becomes even clearer how biased others can be. If you ask your subordinate if you should give him a raise, what would he say? If you asked your boss whether you should work extra hours on the weekend, what do you expect the answer would be? If you asked the CEO whether she would be interested in having you implement a project that would save the company $1 million per year, what do you think she would say? If you ask consultants to your company whether they think you should renew their contract, would they ever say no? Beware of the opinions of those who have a bias toward their own benefit.

Remember that the same bias holds for you when you are asked to give your advice to someone else who is making a decision.

This opinion bias takes different forms. If you go to your boss and ask whether he or she thinks you should consider taking a job with a competitor because it pays better and involves increased responsibilities, do you think your boss will provide you with an unbiased opinion? Your boss may even tell you that you will be in line for the next promotion that comes along and you will be provided with additional responsibility as soon as possible. He or she may tell you how much you are appreciated at the company and how your good work is not going unnoticed. I will not go as far as saying you should never listen to the advice of coworkers, but you should look at their advice as helpful reasoning and not always as a recommendation for a specific decision. You can apply guidelines, however, that will help you to determine whether people are giving you advice for your own good or advice for their own good.

Is There a Personal Stake in Your Decision?

One software company was looking into the possibility of being acquired by one of its larger competitors or another company that would possibly be interested in expanding into its market segment. The CEO wanted advice from different people with different points of view. One of the places he went for some baseline advice about the feasibility for being acquired was the investment bank the company had used for a transaction in the past. The company asked the investment bank for information about the likely financial value of the acquisition and then proceeded to ask the representative from the investment bank for his advice about whether this was a good financial move for the company at this time. The investment bank representative not only had the standing to provide accurate advice, but he also stood to gain substantially from the sale, and therefore had a personal incentive to promote an acquisition. The investment bank would charge a significant fee for completing the acquisition, and the representative would receive a big bonus. Of course the representative indicated to the executives that this was a fair price and that the time was right for selling the company. But the board of directors needed to determine if the advice given by the investment banker was in the company's best interests. They decided to make their decision based upon the raw information provided by the investment bank, ignoring the actual advice from the representative about whether to sell.

Another good example is a company that had been losing revenue because of the combination of an economic recession and a loss of market share due to a range of competing products. The CEO was responsible for making decisions on what to do about the situation and had to present his plan to the board of directors. In an effort to produce the most responsible and effective plan, the CEO solicited advice from his top executives. Going first to the finance VP, he was advised that the best way to solve the financial problems of the company was to cut costs. Moving on to the sales VP, he was told that, in order to successfully stop losing money, the most effective action was to beef up the sales force, thereby increasing sales. Next, he asked the marketing VP, who told the CEO that increasing the advertising budget and getting in front of more people would lead to more prospects, which would ultimately lead to higher sales. Meeting with the engineering VP, he was told that the company should invest more in new product development because new products would increase revenue. Finally, he went to the manufacturing VP, who told the CEO the company needed more production volume so it could lower manufacturing costs per item produced. Each of these executives advised the CEO of a different solution to the problem, and each of them told him a solution that benefited them and their departments, not necessarily the best advice for the company.

When you ask for someone's advice on making a decision, first understand that person's interests. Could those personal interests bias the advice given? If someone is going to be affected in some way by your decision, then the opinions offered are most likely shaped by these biases. Sometimes, however, a person may provide advice that is counter to those personal interests and truly based on what is best for you. When this happens, usually it is good advice. (Either that or maybe they have other personal interests that you do not understand or had not considered!)

> When you ask for someone's advice on making a decision, first understand where that person's interests may be coming from.

Do They Have Relevant Experience?

Sometimes I am asked to advise an executive on a decision that I am very familiar with and in which I can add value to the conversation. Other times I am asked for advice on a decision that I do not know much about. Here I have learned to avoid the temptation to conjure up advice; instead I provide advice only on how to make the decision and avoid advice on the decision itself. However, some people do not hesitate to give advice even if they have no experience or particular skill in the topic area. They just have an opinion.

Martin was the CEO of a successful clothing company who was considering cutting prices across all products to increase revenue. Over drinks one night he asked a close friend, who was a renowned engineer, what to do. His advice: to absolutely cut prices. It was mathematical: more sales volume at lower prices. He said, "This has been proven over and over again in many industries, and you just need to look at personal computers to see an example."

Martin decided to lower prices across all products, not on his friend's advice alone, but it played a major role in Martin's decision.

After cutting prices, three problems quickly became apparent. First, since the clothing was sold in premium stores, lower prices did not bring substantially more customers into the stores, so volume only increased slightly. Second, some competitors cut their prices in response, lowering profit for everyone. Finally, since profit margins were already slim, the price cuts caused the company to lose money. Martin's company never recovered. After losing millions of dollars, the company was acquired by a competitor at a loss for Martin.

Why Listen to Someone Who Has Not Worked on It?

When I face a major decision, I work hard at it. I take time to clarify the objectives, consider alternatives, weigh the risks, and evaluate the options. By that time I know more about that decision than anybody else. When I ask for input or test the decision with others, it is frustrating. They make recommendations I have already considered and discarded. They raise issues I have already taken into consideration. It is frustrating for them and for me: for me, it sets me back because I have to explain the work I already did; for them, because I dispose of their suggestions too abruptly.

Yet every once in a while, someone brings up something I totally overlooked, and it changes the way I approach the decision. That is invaluable, but how do you get at that nugget? One way is to take the time to explain the entire process you have been through, then let the person take some time to consider it, and then that person can provide advice. This approach requires a lot more work for you and the other person, but it may be worth it.

Another method is to ask for advice on specific steps along the way. For example, ask for advice on defining the problem and clarifying the objectives. Do not let the person jump to a recommendation at that point. Take the person through the process with you as an advisor at each step.

How to Solicit Useful Advice

Getting the right advice can be critical to any important decisions. Some of the best decisions I have made were improved by advice from others, and some of the worst decisions I have made could have been avoided if I asked for advice from the right people. But, as we have seen, getting the right advice can be tricky. Here are some guidelines for getting good advice and filtering out poor advice:

- Think through someone's personal interests and biases before you ask for advice, and reassess these interests and biases after receiving the advice.

- Seek out people who have experience in this type of decision. They may be difficult to approach, but their advice could be invaluable. If it is an important decision, do not hesitate to pay them for their time.

- Be skeptical of advice someone gives you from the "seat of their pants" when you have spent many hours working on the decision.

- Consider asking for advice at different steps along the way, not just when you are done.

- Recognize that you may need to vet a decision or sell it to someone whose support you need, but do this differently than really asking for advice. Take the time to walk the person through your decision process in detail, then allow the person time to think about it, and then come back and discuss each other's views.

- Good advice can be tremendously helpful in making a good decision, but bad advice can be disastrous.
- Understand bias and personal interests before accepting advice.
- The best advice comes from someone with experience.
- Be careful of "seat of the pants" advice when you have been working on the decision for many hours.
- Consider asking for advice on steps along the way, not just at the end of the process.

CHAPTER 16

Flipping a Coin

You possess a powerful decision
tool you may not know about

Sometimes your choice between two alternatives appears to be a tie. For example, you many need to decide between hiring one of two candidates, purchasing one of two items, or attending a conference or skipping it. In those cases, you can apply a simple and proven technique: flip a coin. But you may find that this works differently than it may seem on the surface. Let's look first at a straightforward example.

A marine supply company in Los Angeles did business all over the world. It manufactured, distributed, and maintained mechanized hardware for loading and unloading cargo ships at major ports. While the company employed a number of local technicians who were routinely on call, occasionally it was required to send maintenance technicians from L.A. who were specialists in fixing more difficult problems with the hardware. One day, the division manager was asked to send a technician from the L.A. office to Hawaii to fix a major equipment malfunction that the local technician was unable to fix. It was highly likely the problem would take several days — if not an entire week — to fix properly.

Upon hearing of the assignment, two of the top technicians began lobbying the division manager to send them. After all, it was a trip to Hawaii, something that would allow them to enjoy their down time immensely while also doing their job. Both technicians were capable of doing the job, and sending either of them would not disrupt ongo-

> **IN YOUR EXPERIENCE**
>
> *Have you ever found yourself unable to decide between two options when a simple flip of a coin could have made your decision much easier than the painful process you put yourself through?*

ing operations in Los Angeles. Of course, only one of them was needed to fix the broken machine, and the division manager had to decide which one to send.

The division manager knew that not only did he not want to play favorites — he liked them both equally — he did not even want to give *the impression* that he preferred one more than the other. Having been lobbied enough by both of the technicians, each of whom were constantly asking him if he had made his decision and telling him why they would be a better person for the assignment, he simply called them both into his office and sat them down. He told them they were both equally qualified, but he could only send one. Thus, he told them, the only fair way to choose was to leave it to chance. He took out a quarter and said one of them was "heads" and the other was "tails," and he proceeded to flip the coin. The coin landed with tails up, and the decision was made — a decision that disappointed the other technician because he lost, but one he accepted as fair.

Believe it or not, if you have a coin in your pocket, you are in possession of a powerful decision-making device. Flipping a coin is a vastly underrated method for making decisions. It can work extremely well in many circumstances, and not always for the reason that you would imagine. Consider any decision you make at work that is a choice between two options. If you are having a difficult time choosing, your best decision may be made by simply flipping the coin: heads for one choice, tails for the other. We already looked at a simple example in which the coin flip *determines* the decision. Now let's look at an example in which the coin flip *influences* the decision.

> The most powerful part of using a coin is that you do not have to accept the results.

You Do Not Have to Accept the Results

While you can always use the coin flip technique to help you make your decision, are you really going to let chance determine your decision? The most powerful aspect of using a coin to help you decide is that you do not have to accept the results, but you can learn from this exercise. Consider your reaction once you flip a coin to help make a decision. After it lands, you will immediately have a sense of having "won" or "lost" the coin toss, even though you had been prepared to accept its results. Once you flip the coin, if you do not like the result, you can simply void the decision. In such a scenario, your dissatisfaction with the results of the coin toss is pointing you straight to the decision you actually prefer.

The pocket decision-maker works so well because it forces you to confront your true feelings about the two decision options. The coin gives you an answer and directly confronts you with the decision it made for you. Immediately, you will either feel comfortable with the outcome or uncomfortable with it. If you feel comfortable with the coin toss result, then go with it. If you think the coin gave you the wrong decision, and you begin to argue with yourself for the other outcome, then you know what to do: go with the other outcome. Either way, the exercise will help you to confront your feelings. If, after the coin flip, you are still dissatisfied, you can still proceed to implement a more thorough examination of the two options by using one of the other decision-making techniques presented in this book. On the other hand, if you have already im-

> The objective is to make the decision, not to let the coin toss tell you which option to choose.

plemented one of those techniques and come up with the conclusion that each option is exactly equal in terms of its costs and benefits, then you can return to the coin flip and know that you have exhausted your more detailed analysis. The coin can make your final decision.

Here is another example that illustrates this decision dynamic. Joan had intended to attend a major medical industry conference in San Francisco. She had attended every year and always learned a lot from it. She also had made many friends and contacts who became resources she used throughout the year. However, this year she was busier than usual and it would be difficult to take the time off, and she thought it might be good to save the travel expenses. So she was hesitant to make her final decision, and her associates kept bugging her to make up her mind so they could plan meetings.

So Joan took out a coin and flipped it to make her decision. It came up tails, "Not Go." She accepted this briefly but then started to feel regret at missing the learning experience and the opportunities to catch up with her peers from other companies. And the keynote speaker was an expert in making decisions, which she knew she would learn from. Joan decided to attend the conference because the coin flip had simulated the regret she would feel if she did not go.

The decision maker in your pocket works by summoning your intuitive powers in the service of good judgment. Toss a coin, and the decision alternatives are suddenly vivid. Sometimes the trick can work very well because it helps you to test what you have already considered to be your decision.

If you examine the technique analytically, you can see the decision device (the coin) is programmed specifically to select either alternative with an equal probability. But what happens quite often is that people tend to override the coin's selection and go with the opposite alternative. This could be because the coin flipper actually prefers the other outcome, but another possibility is that the flipper is not yet ready to make the decision. In this case, the flipper's refusal to accept the outcome of the coin toss may reveal a reverse bias to the coin's selection. If this happens to you, you might decide to keep flipping the coin until it comes up with the decision you like the best. "I think I will do the best of three flips of the coin . . . or maybe I will do the best of five." Or maybe you will decide that the first flip, or the first three flips, were really just "practice." These techniques work, because they are part of the learning process about how you really feel about a decision. Remember that the objective is to make the right decision, not to let the coin toss determine which option you will choose.

Delegating the Coin Flip

You may find it helpful to flip the coin in the presence of others, or have someone else flip the coin for you. If you choose to do this, it often forces you to verbalize your reaction to the result. Articulating your reaction to others often helps you make the better decision or to better understand which option you actually prefer. Some people choose to use a lucky coin because they have used it successfully before to provide a good outcome. "This coin has been tested by other decision-making tosses that I agreed with." The point is that the coin toss facilitates a process of finding out how and why you feel a particular way about one or the other option.

Another powerful method of using the coin toss technique is to help push someone else to make a decision when they are struggling. If coworkers or employees come into your office and ask you to make a decision they could make, and you can tell they just need a little push to help them make it, try taking out a coin. Tell them they can make the decision by asking them to determine which option is heads and which option is tails. Then flip the coin and watch their reaction.

I have used this technique many times, but I do it with a smile and sense of humor to teach them a lesson that they should not be afraid to make decisions, especially simple decisions that can waste time. By the way, I always let them keep the coin, and tell them it must be a lucky coin.

This exercise helps in two ways. First, it helps your coworkers to better understand their true feelings about the decision at hand. But in addition to the immediate implications of the coin's result, by flipping the coin you are also making a point that they could have easily made this decision without you. It serves to show them you are not necessarily able to make the decision any better than they could have.

- Flipping a coin is a vastly underrated method of helping to make a decision.

- By flipping a coin when making a decision, it will help you get in touch with your true intuition about which option to take; you immediately have an emotional response about whether you "won" or "lost" the coin toss.

- The best part about flipping a coin is that you do not have to accept the result.

- Flipping a coin can be used to help you make a decision as well as to help push someone else into making one.

SECTION III

Special Situations

Some of the most important business decisions are not routine, but are the type where there is a lot more at stake than with routine decisions. These are strategic decisions, crisis decisions, or other types of nonroutine decisions. Frequently, executives and managers are inexperienced with making these decisions. This section is designed to help you face critical decisions, whether for the first time or the 20th time.

I love bold-move decisions! Bold moves are aggressive, game-changing strategic decisions with extraordinary impact — and high risk. There are two parts to a bold-move decision: identifying the bold move and then weighing the risk. This risk can either be constrained or unconstrained, which is critical to evaluating bold-move decisions. In the first chapter of this section, we examine a variety of bold-move decisions and apply an evaluation framework.

During an unexpected crisis, a company can fall on its face or show courage and weather the storm. Crises, especially major ones, rarely happen, but when they do, the decisions made in response are critical. Chapter 18 explores examples of crisis decisions, illustrates what to do and what to avoid in a crisis, and provides guidelines for dealing with these decisions.

There will be times when you will not have control over the outcome of your choice; you just make your decision and await the result. In some cases like this, you may want to hedge your bet by not casting your fate immediately to one choice. In chapter 19, I will show you when and how to hedge your bet.

Some businesses seem to make decisions to seize opportunities while others overlook them. Chapter 20 introduces a decision technique I call "crossing your path." It applies when there is something in the future — a strategic opportunity or operational move — that you

153

might like to do if you have the opportunity. You identify the vision, define a potential path, and watch for appropriate opportunities.

Tough decisions are those in which none of the alternatives are attractive, but the decision still needs to be made. Chapter 21 provides examples and guidelines for making these tough decisions and explains why many companies tend to avoid them and suffer even more drastic consequences.

Executives who continue to improve their decision-making skills evaluate their decisions through a decision autopsy. They determine what they could have done better and learn from their experience. In some companies, decision autopsies are done after all major decisions take place and can be done for self-evaluation or employee development. The final chapter of this section presents evaluation techniques and includes a decision evaluation worksheet.

CHAPTER 17

Taking Bold Moves

*Bold-move decisions are the most exciting
business decisions; they can have a
big impact but carry a high risk*

Business success sometimes requires strategic decisions that can catapult a company to a new level. I call these "bold moves." Bold moves are game-changing strategic decisions that can have an extraordinary impact, but come with a high risk. The following two examples illustrate the success and risk of bold moves.

On October 1, 2005, his first day as CEO of Disney, Bob Iger made a bold move. He recommended to the board of directors that the company acquire Pixar in order to fix Disney's slumping animation business.[13] The board approved his bold move and acquired Pixar for $7 billion. The bold move was very successful for Disney.

New animated features such as *Bolt* revitalized the Disney animation franchise. The value of these films was extended into new revenue sources for Disney as well. Three years after it released the film *Cars*, merchandise sales were $2 billion a year. New ventures such as Car Land promised even more revenue. And Disney broadly benefited by applying the considerable talent of Steve Jobs and John Lassiter across all of Disney's businesses.

The Royal Bank of Scotland (RBS) is the second-largest bank in Britain and a 282-year-old institution. Historically it was a conservative, stable British institution. Then it started to grow rapidly by making bold-move decisions. In 1998, RBS made a $34 billion hostile takeover of NatWest, which was twice the size of RBS at the time. Continuing bold-move decisions, RBS made more than 20 other acquisitions in quick succession, including Mellon Financial's retail banking and Charter One Financial in the United States. As a result of these bold-move decisions, *Forbes* magazine named CEO Sir Fred Goodwin as Global Businessman of the Year in 2002.

Then in 2007, RBS went one bold-move decision too far with its hostile takeover of Dutch bank ABN Amro for $100 billion. Many skeptics thought the acquisition was well above the price it was worth. Additionally, because this was a hostile takeover, RBS did not have a clear understanding of what it was actually buying. After the deal closed, RBS and its partners were unable to get the funding they expected when the global financial markets began to collapse. RBS reported a loss of $35 billion in February 2009, the largest in British corporate history. As RBS failed, the government was forced to nationalize the company. RBS demonstrated many good bold-move decisions, but it only took one very large, bad bold-move decision to bring it down.[14]

What Are Bold Moves?

Sometimes, but not frequently, you need to make a bold business move. These are strategic decisions that have the potential for either great returns or big failures. Businesses take bold moves when they believe they need or want to seek a major change or opportunity. A bold move is a big, company-changing decision. While they have the potential to achieve wonderful results for your company, bold moves also have the potential to result in disappointing — or even disastrous — outcomes. Bold moves are, therefore, inherently risky decisions.

> Bold moves require enormous and dramatic changes in your business, but require a lot of research ahead of time.

When making a bold move, you need to deeply understand the opportunity it presents and the full range of risks that accompany it. While this is true of most decisions, the substantial strategic impact of a bold move necessitates a very deep understanding of the trade-off between the opportunity and the risks associated with it, especially knowing the limits of risk you are willing to take. There are no simple techniques for making bold-move decisions, but there are guiding principles. The first is to understand the type of bold move, since the decision process depends on the type. The second is to understand the extent of risk, especially identifying that some risks are constrained while others are not.

Types of Bold Moves

Businesses make different types of bold moves, each having unique characteristics that, when understood, are the starting point for approaching a bold-move decision. Here are three major types of bold moves.

Major Investment or Acquisition

In business, a bold move is frequently characterized by a major acquisition or investment decision, with the company expecting a big return on this investment. We looked at two contrasting bold-move acquisition examples at the beginning of this chapter.

These decisions require a lot of analysis and preparation before the bold-move decision is made. The analysis undertaken for an investment decision is much different from an acquisition. In an acquisition the majority of the data is available from the company to be acquired, while in a major investment much of the information is based on estimates. In both, however, it is critical that the evaluation be thorough and the risks measured. Against all these alternatives is the base one of not making a bold move.

In my book *Product Strategy for High-Technology Companies,* I discuss the range of objectives for acquisitions. Some are more like investments, where the objective is a pure return on investment. Others are more strategic, where major benefits come from the combination of two companies. It is important to understand what the specific objectives are in assessing this type of bold move. In particular, know the answers. Is the investment or acquisition primarily intended to be an investment? If so, then the criteria for making the decision is the return on that investment. If it is more strategic, then it may be a hybrid bold move that also initiates a change in direction.

Success in this type of bold-move decision comes from deeply understanding the potential return on investment and balancing potential risk. The Disney acquisition of Pixar discussed earlier is a good example of how thoroughly the acquisition opportunity was understood. Failure with this type of bold move generally stems from underestimating the potential risk or overvaluing the asset acquired. The RBS example illustrates some of these bold-move cautions.

Change in Strategic Direction

A second type of bold-move decision is a major shift in strategic direction. A good example of a bold move was the decision made by Porsche when they were considering producing a completely new line of vehicles. The car manufacturer, widely known for its fast sports cars, was considering whether to design and manufacture a sport utility vehicle (SUV). Extensive market research indicated that there was a new market for its cars that need not achieve top speeds of up to 190 miles per hour. This was certainly a daring move for the company whose cars, for the most part, had no more than two doors. Eventually the SUV model, called the Cayenne, accounted for a full 45% of the company's new car sales. Porsche made a big decision to make a bold move, and it also paid off big. But it was Porsche's extensive market research that enabled it to determine if a successful market existed for these new cars.

One of the most successful bold moves to change direction was Microsoft's decision to develop its first operating system, PC-DOS for IBM (MS-DOS for the Microsoft version). Microsoft did not have the experience or resources to develop this operating system, so it licensed 86-DOS from Seattle Computer to form the core of its new operating system. Bill Gates saw this exciting opportunity and decided to shift the company from programming languages to operating systems, a decision that led to the creation of one of the most successful companies in history.

A bold-move change in strategic direction can also come from a change in business model. An example of this is a software company that alters its strategy from selling perpetual software licenses to an on-demand model. This changes the entire business model and requires significant financial resources to make the transition.

Success in this type of bold move depends on a deep understanding of what is required to make the shift in strategic direction. Failure of this type of bold move often comes from not understanding what is needed to make the change or from making faulty assumptions.

Reaction to a Threat

Sometimes a bold-move decision needs to be made in reaction to a threat to the business. In 2007, Ford Motor Company sold Jaguar and Land Rover for $2.3 billion, less than half of what it had paid for the two brands. Ford had acquired Jaguar in 1987 with grand ambitions of getting a position in luxury cars. That decision was a bold-move acquisition, but it did not work out. Some estimate Ford invested another $10 billion in Jaguar following the acquisition. With the bold move to sell Jaguar, Ford successfully cut its losses and helped its own chances of surviving, putting it in a stronger financial position than GM or Chrysler.

Here is a personal example of a bold-move decision. In February 2005 I took over as CEO of i2 Technologies, a once great company that was on the verge of collapsing. The company had not made a profit in years and had $217 million of debt coming due that exceeded its cash. It also had other legal and securities problems. The situation was clear: a bold move was mandatory. In the first 30 days, I cut more than $100 million of expenses, enabling the company to be profitable in the next quarter and every quarter after that.

In situations such as the one at i2 when I took over as CEO, it is clear that a bold move is needed. The risk of not making a bold move far outweighs the risk of the bold move. It is not a question of "if," but of "how" and "when," so in a way, it is easier to decide upon a bold move while under a business threat. When presented with this threat scenario, a bold-move decision must be made quickly. Do not worry about making the perfect decision in this case, since taking longer to make the decision is riskier. President Obama made the case for this in promoting his economic stimulus program. He acknowledged that the program was not perfect, but the risk of doing nothing was so great that this bold-move decision had to be approved quickly.

In these cases, understand the objective very clearly and keep it in constant focus while defining the bold move to undertake. Avoid making it too complex. Usually the initial bold move stands out from other decisions. At i2, for example, there were other threats the company faced, but it was clear that it needed to cut costs quickly in any case, so that was the first priority. It did not fix all of the other problems, but it enabled their resolution later. Failure with this type of bold-move decision sometimes comes from taking the wrong actions, but usually comes from not deciding to do enough.

Understanding the Extent of Risk

Since bold-move decisions are big, they require sound judgment of the expected benefit versus the potential risk. Many bold moves fail because they do not consider the extent of risk.

Figure 17-1 illustrates a framework for differentiating bold-move decisions, primarily by risk. For a decision to be considered a bold move, the impact needs to be more than strategic; it needs to be game changing. But it also needs to balance risk. Risk is on the horizontal axis of this framework. A balanced risk essentially balances the risk of a decision with its benefits. When the risk is unconstrained as it was in the RBS example, it becomes more of a gamble than a bold move. An unconstrained risk can get out of control and outweigh the strategic benefits of the bold move.

When I was CEO of i2 Technologies I considered the bold move of suing a much larger software company, SAP, for patent infringement. The potential cost of this was as much as $5 million in legal fees, and there was a risk that SAP could countersue for violation of its patents. The benefit could be very high if i2 won the suit. A bold-move decision requires an in-depth understanding of the opportunity and risk, so I spent a lot of time on weekends and nights going through the patents with the R&D staff to see how significant the violations were. I also spent some time reviewing SAP's patents to see if they had anything to use against us. And I spent time understanding how we could get advantages in the legal process by filing the suit in friendly territory, East Texas.

Figure 17-1   Bold-Move Decision Classification

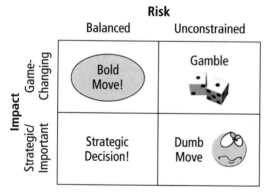

I decided on the bold move to file the patent suit against SAP, but decided not to file a similar suit against another software company that had also violated the patents because they had a large patent portfolio to use against us, and it would also raise the risk of fighting two large companies at once. A characteristic of bold-move decisions is that they can be complex. In this case, it was difficult to explain the confidence I had about this bold move to the i2 board of directors because they could not expend the hours that I did gathering enough facts to get comfortable. They grumbled a little about the potential cost of the legal action, but I went ahead with it. This is one of the characteristics of bold-move decisions: because they tend to be complex, they are difficult to explain.

The cost of the lawsuit was approximately $3 million. Less than two years later SAP paid $83.3 million to settle the patent infringement, one of the largest ever in the history of software patents. Because of the size of this payment to i2, it was considered to be a bold move.

In this example, the risk was contained to the cost of the litigation. I was confident that at any time, SAP would agree to settle the suit for more than it cost us, so I did not evaluate the risk as great. And the benefit was well worth it. So this bold move was not a gamble; it was a shrewd investment.

> The complexity of a bold move makes it difficult to get everyone on board supporting it.

Here is another personal example of understanding the risk limits of a bold-move decision. When I was president of consulting firm Pittiglio Rabin Todd & McGrath (PRTM), we considered acquiring ADL, one of the most prestigious consulting firms. ADL had made some poor decisions, risking the entire company on expanding into telecom consulting, and went bankrupt. Here again, this is also an example of a bold move gone badly for ADL.

We stepped in to acquire ADL. I was very excited about this opportunity because it would catapult PRTM/ADL into the ranks of premier firms, and the synergies between the two companies were significant. In the end, however, the risk became too high. ADL had hundreds of subsidiary corporations throughout the world, and it was impossible to assess the contingent liabilities PRTM would inherit in the acquisition. We reached the limit of balanced risk and withdrew from the acquisition. We did not want to risk our own firm as part of this bold move.

Bold Moves in Steps

Sometimes bold-move decisions are made as a series of steps, with one bold step leading to another. One of my favorite bold move examples is the bold move Apple made into the music market with the iPod and the iTunes store, followed then by another even bolder move with the iPhone. Figure 17-2 illustrates these steps. Apples's first step was not particularly bold, but it set up the next bold move. iTunes is a proprietary digital media player application, introduced by Apple on January 9, 2001, at the Macworld Expo in San Francisco. It was adopted from another software product and was relatively common to other software music players.

Apple then made a bold move into portable music players with the iPod. First announced on October 23, 2001, the original iPod cost $399 with a 5 GB hard drive. The iPod connected to the product Apple introduced in the previous step, iTunes. Critics panned the unit's price, and declared that a computer company had no business going into consumer electronic products, such as music players. But the iPod proved an instant hit in the marketplace, quickly overtaking earlier hard drive MP3 players. Apple designed a mechanical scroll wheel and outsourced the implementation and development to Synaptics, a firm that also developed the trackpad used by many laptops, including Apple's PowerBooks. The first generation iPod featured four buttons (Menu, Play/Pause, Back, and Forward) surrounding the circumference of the scroll wheel. Although superseded by nonmechanical "touch" and "click" wheels, this circular controller design has become a prominent iPod motif. Critics lambasted the $400 price tag, the unconventional scroll wheel and the lack of Windows compatibility. Despite all this, the iPod sold beyond everyone's expectations, went on to revolutionize the entire music industry, and the rest is history.

Apple's next bold move was to tackle the controversial issue of music downloads, which were then being downloaded for free, costing the music industry hundreds of millions of dollars. With shrewd nego-

Figure 17-2 Apple's Bold-Move Decisions Over Time

iPhone
2007

iPod
2001

iTunes
2001

iPhone
Apps
2008

iTunes Stores 2003

tiation, brilliant positioning, and promotion, Apple launched the iTunes Store on April 28, 2003. Apple's idea was simple – provide a virtual store where people can buy and download digital music on-demand. Initially, the store only hosted 200,000 tracks and only Mac users were able to buy and transfer music to the iPod. PC users had to wait until October 2003 for the release of the Windows version of iTunes. Today, the iTunes Store is the second largest seller of digital music in the U.S. and has sold over 4 billion songs. Again, there were many critics of this bold move. How could Apple be successful selling songs at $0.99 when they were available from other services for free? The iTunes store sold 70 million songs in its first year and by 2008 had sold more than 4 billion songs.

When Apple first launched its iTunes digital music service it had already signed deals with major record labels. Big names such as Universal Music Group (UMG), EMI, Warner, Sony, and BMG all signed up. With the iTunes Store, Apple created the legal music-download industry and implemented a clever way to control the portable hardware compatible with its iTunes Store.

Apple's next bold move in this progression was the introduction of the iPhone, another market where Apple had little or no experience, but felt it had something revolutionary to offer. Introduced January 9, 2007, the iPhone combined three products: a revolutionary mobile phone, a widescreen iPod with touch controls, and a breakthrough Internet communications device with email and other functions. The iPhone was also met with criticism:

> *"There is no likelihood that Apple can be successful in a business this competitive. Even in the business where it is a clear pioneer, the personal computer, it had to compete with Microsoft and can only sustain a 5% market share... And its survival in the computer business relies on good margins. Those margins cannot exist in the mobile handset business for more than 15 minutes... What Apple risks here is its reputation as a hot company that can do no wrong. If it's smart it will call the iPhone a 'reference design' and pass it to some suckers to build with someone else's marketing budget... Otherwise I'd advise you to cover your eyes. You're not going to like what you'll see."*
> —John C. Dvorak, Market Watch, March 28, 2007.

We all know by now the tremendous success of the iPhone. It went on to become a powerful handheld computer that can do almost anything you need. (It is my all-time favorite product.) One million iPhones were sold in the first 74 days on the market, and Apple was selling more than five million per quarter in 2009.

Apple then followed this in 2008 with expansion into applications for the iPhone, again another bold-move decision that some dismissed as something not suitable for a device like the iPhone. In its first year, people downloaded 1.5 billion apps from the more than 65,000 apps in Apple's store.

- Sometimes in business, you have to make bold moves.
- Bold moves are high-risk, high-reward pursuits.
- Bold moves are moves that you instigate; they are not decisions about options that are presented to you.
- Some types of bold moves include major investments or acquisitions, change in strategic direction, and reaction to threats.
- Be certain that you understand the extent of the risk that you are facing before jumping into making a bold move.
- Be careful, because bold moves do not always pay off.

CHAPTER 18

Dealing with Crisis Decisions

*How you make decisions in a crisis
can mean survival or failure*

Companies can fail or thrive during unexpected times of crisis. While strong, successful companies are prepared for crises when they occur, other companies may take a large financial hit and even possibly go completely out of business. The very word "crisis" indicates something that is unexpected, something that poses a unique challenge to a business that is not a traditional challenge faced on a regular basis. Some crises are caused by outside forces beyond the control of executives. Others result from failures in actions or decisions by executives, managers, or other employees. And some are caused by a combination of external and internal factors. How a company and its leaders react during these times of crisis is crucial, and good business leaders can manage crises and come out on the other end intact — and possibly even in a better situation.

> What a company and its leaders do during times of crisis is crucial, and good business leaders can come out on the other end of the crisis intact.

Failing to Act Is Acting to Fail

On March 24, 1989, the tanker ship *Exxon Valdez* struck a reef in Prince William Sound, spilling 10.8 million gallons of crude oil into the sea, an amount that eventually covered 11,000 square miles of the ocean. The spill was the result of several factors, including an uncertified third mate at the helm of the giant ship, insufficient rest between shifts for key employees, and excessive alcohol consumption by some of those working at the time aboard the ship. The spill quickly represented a major crisis for Exxon. Many consumers saw the company response as a major failure to address the resulting damage, act quickly to contain the problem, and begin to clean up the spilled oil. It was perceived as a failure to care about the fact that the company had just been responsible for the largest oil spill in the sea to date.

To begin with, the company's efforts to contain the spill were deemed slow. More important, perhaps, was the failure of Exxon's public relations campaign. Many sources believe this was due to the fact that the chairman of Exxon at the time, Lawrence Rawl, was suspicious of the media and did not believe it was important to address this crisis from a public relations point of view. While the media immediately jumped on the story and began round-the-clock coverage of the crisis, Exxon repeatedly refused requests for interviews. Company spokespeople rebuffed requests to interview Rawl by stating that the chairman of the company had no time for that type of thing. The spill continued to get worse as the cleanup operation faced setbacks from the weather and other factors. Eventually, more than a week after the spill, Rawl decided it was time to go on TV. In a live interview, he was asked about the most recent plans for the cleanup, but had neglected to read the plans, stating that it was not his job as chairman to read the detailed reports of a cleanup operation.

Blaming the media for negative coverage, mismanaging a public relations campaign, and responding slowly to the oil spill in general are clear examples of a failed response to a major crisis. In addition to the costs Exxon incurred with the cleanup operation and the lawsuits that ensued, the public relations damage was also massive. The company slipped from the top oil company in the world to third. "Exxon Valdez" remains a common term to describe corporate arrogance and inaction in the face of a major crisis.

> **IN YOUR EXPERIENCE**
>
> *Looking back at some of the decisions you have made, if you had to make them again, would you make them differently? Was there something inherently wrong with how you approached the decision that might have prevented you from ending up with better results?*

Move Quickly

As the *Exxon Valdez* example shows, perhaps the most important step to take when a company is facing a crisis is to act quickly. Without making that decision, you could find yourself doing nothing, which can often end up being worse than doing the wrong thing.

In another example of a crisis, a company's actions served to reassure the public that the company was looking out for the best interests of the consumers, even taking a financial risk to solve a crisis that was not its own creation. Johnson & Johnson, the company that produces the most popular analgesic drug on the market, Tylenol, faced a crisis of catastrophic proportions. Commanding 37% of the market share, Tylenol was far and away the most successful and highly used drug of its kind. In the fall of 1982, however, all of that had the potential to come to a sudden end. One or more individuals, acting for reasons unknown, replaced the Tylenol within several bottles with cyanide-laced capsules and subsequently placed these bottles back onto the shelves of several drugstores and grocery stores throughout the greater Chicago area. As a result of these actions, seven individuals died from cyanide poisoning.

> In any time of crisis, the most important thing to do is to respond quickly.

Immediately upon hearing of the incident, James Burke, the CEO of Johnson & Johnson, established a seven-member strategy team to which he provided the following guidance: First, do what needs to be done to protect the American public; second, do what needs to be done to salvage the popular Tylenol brand. The first action taken was to tell all consumers throughout the nation, via the media, to immediately cease taking Tylenol until the company had time to assess the problem and reassure its consumers about the product's safety. Concurrently, the company recalled all Tylenol from stores in the Chicago area to determine the extent of the tampering. Upon finding two more bottles that had been tampered with, the company issued a nationwide recall of the product, costing it millions of dollars.

Over the ensuing days and weeks, the company provided regular public updates through the media, using both the news media and other PR strategies, including regular press conferences that could be viewed nationally. James Burke even went on *60 Minutes* and *The Phil Donahue Show* to discuss the crisis and the company's response. It proved to be a successful strategy. Consumers widely viewed Johnson & Johnson as a victim of this event, not an unwitting conspirator. Through one of these press conferences, the company became the first to introduce tamper-resistant packaging for its product, something that is now used industry-wide. This response is considered one of the most successfully implemented strategies for managing an outside crisis, and Johnson & Johnson was able to regain the lion's share of its market for the drug. There were even reports of consumers switching from other brands to Tylenol because of the resulting increased confidence in the brand. Quick action and direct, visible involvement by the CEO worked to ensure continued confidence and proved to be the foundation of this successful strategy.

Filter Up

In crisis decisions, it is extremely important that the decisions that need to be made filter up to the appropriate level. Whether a large crisis or a small one, the decisions must be made by the correct people, not delegated before getting to those people. In a major crisis, such as with the *Exxon Valdez* or Tylenol examples, the crisis decisions needed to be filtered all the way up to the top level of the companies. In the Exxon case, this seemed not to happen in a timely manner. While the CEO was made aware of the incident, it was widely interpreted that the decisions about cleaning up the spill and the response to the spill were made below his level. Even the CEO seemed to believe that the incident was something that was beneath his responsibility level at a company as large as Exxon. In the Tylenol example, on the other hand, the CEO became directly involved right from the beginning, taking control of the situation and making all of the important decisions. While he created a committee to devise the company's strategy, his constant involvement and key guidance to the committee were instrumental in ensuring the strategy's success.

> In crisis decisions, one of the most important things is to ensure that the decisions that need to be made filter up to the appropriate level.

Big Crisis, Small Crisis

Not all crises will be the same. Some crises are small ones that do not fundamentally affect the existence of the company. But others are major crises that, if not immediately addressed in the best possible manner, will spell certain doom for the company. One thing is in common among all crises, however: if the company is going to make it through the crisis successfully — whether that means losing the least amount of money, restoring consumer confidence, saving a deal gone sour, or any other measure of success or least amount of loss — actions need to be taken in a timely manner.

You will undoubtedly encounter crises in business that seem major, although in the long run they are relatively minor. You still need to treat these crises as extremely important immediately after they occur. The measure of success in any time of crisis is determined by the speed of your response as well as the decisions you make immediately following the onset of the crisis. A good example is that of a company whose CFO resigns from his position just before an SEC filing deadline. While this resignation is a potentially major problem for the company, a quick response to the crisis can prevent major damage. Likewise, if your company loses its largest client, you need to institute a process by which you will seek other clients relentlessly until you win back equivalent business.

> The measure of success in any time of crisis is determined by the speed of your response as well as the decisions you make immediately following the onset of the crisis.

Fast Crisis, Slow Crisis

Some crises are immediate, caused by one single event or decision that becomes an immediate threat to the company. An example of this was the *Exxon Valdez* crisis, which unfolded in a matter of hours from the initial crash of the ship onto the reef. A similar example is an airplane crash, where the response from the company whose plane has gone down is critical to the continued consumer confidence in that company. Not only would the response include a major public relations campaign, but also adequate actions taken to understand the nature of the incident and how a similar incident could be prevented in the future.

Other crises, however, unfold over the course of days, weeks, or even months. These will be the ones in which you may not even know you are facing a crisis because it materializes slowly and is not triggered by one single event. The Tylenol example serves as an example of a crisis that unfolded over several weeks, as the extent of the problem was explored and finally fully discovered. Recognizing these growing crises as they occur is one of the most important parts of understanding when and how to react.

Sometimes You Need to Overreact

One of the best pieces of advice I can give is that sometimes it pays to overreact to a crisis. A reserved response can possibly save time, money, and energy, but sometimes moderating your response can also lead to failure. When a crisis is of such proportion that it can completely drive the company into bankruptcy, underreacting may be a bad decision. During the Tylenol crisis, the company could have taken a number of less dramatic actions that would have cost a lot less, but would not have restored public confidence in their product at such a high level. This is not what happened in a timely manner with the *Exxon Valdez* crisis, something that made a large dent in the company's market share for years after the incident. Johnson & Johnson's bold decision to go above and beyond clearly was the right choice.

- All businesses face crisis decisions, and the company's response can determine success or failure.
- In any time of crisis, the most important step a business leader can take is to act quickly.
- When facing a crisis, failing to act is acting to fail.
- One of the most important things to ensure in any time of crisis is that the decision-making responsibility is filtered up to the appropriate level.
- All crises are different, but the common element in responding to them is speed and accuracy.
- Sometimes, it can pay to overreact in your response to a crisis.

CHAPTER 19

Hedging Your Bets

*Sometimes your best option is to
pursue more than one option*

In many decisions you do not have control over the outcome; you just decide and await the result. For example, you may make a job offer to a candidate, but still must wait for that candidate to accept the offer in order to reach your desired outcome. Or you could decide how to price a proposal, but you may or may not get selected. In cases where someone else determines the result of your decision, you may find it helpful to hedge your bet and keep a backup alternative active, too.

The director of human resources for a very large company was hiring a manager for one of the company's divisions. The director had finally settled on three good prospects after a round of interviews by company executives. Subsequently, the director called all three of the finalists to inform them of his decision. While he reached both of the candidates he was not going to hire and so informed them, he did not initially reach the candidate he was planning to hire for the position, so he left him a message. A few hours later, he received a return call from the chosen candidate, only to learn that the candidate had accepted a position with a competitor. The director of human resources was upset, but thought he had two other promising finalists for the position. He spent a few days trying to figure out which one of the two remaining candidates he thought would be the best fit, and came to a decision. Upon contacting that person, however, it turned out that she, too, had accepted a position at a different company. Not only that, when the di-

> Quite simply, hedging your bet is when you pursue more than one option at a time in an effort to maximize your gains and/or minimize your losses.

rector of human resources turned to the last candidate on his list of finalists, he found out this person had moved out of the area and was no longer interested in the position. Now the director of human resources had no candidates for the position and had to repeat the search process. Meanwhile, the position remained unfilled. He realized that his fault in this process was not in finding adequate candidates, but rather not hedging his bet in case his first-choice candidate did not accept the offer. A better way to proceed would have been to make the offer to the chosen person prior to informing the second- and third-choice candidates that they were not selected. He also should have asked about the timing of each candidate's decision time frame. Had he done that, he would have likely ended up filling the position with one of the top candidates in a timely manner.

Choosing one alternative instead of another is not always cut and dried. You may face a decision at your company where you have two or more options and you are likely to either lose something or gain something regardless of which option you choose. Or you may face a decision where you are unable to tell if you are going to come out ahead or behind. So what can you do under these circumstances? You can hedge your bet.

The term "hedging your bet" originates, obviously, from decisions that a person makes while gambling. Here is an example: A person betting on horses has the opportunity to take out a bet on the horse with the worst odds but the highest returns if that horse should win the race. One horse, Alexa, has odds of 22-1, so if the gambler places $100 down on Alexa and wins, the return will be $2,200. Another horse, Otis, the one who is strongly favored to win the race, has odds of only 2-1. This means that if the gambler places a bet of $100 on Otis and Otis wins, the return will be $200. The gambler decides to hedge his bet. He puts $100 on Alexa in hopes of winning big, but just in case, also puts $100 on Otis. If Otis wins, the gambler will lose the $100 he bet on Alexa but will win his money back on the bet on Otis. If Alexa wins the race, the gambler will lose the $100 bet on Otis, but will still win big.

Hedging your bet in business is when you pursue more than one option at a time, whether you pursue both options to the end or only for the early stage of

IN YOUR EXPERIENCE

Have you ever encountered a situation where you were uncertain about whether a choice you had to make would lead to success or failure? Were you able to pursue multiple options to reduce your risk?

the process. There are several different ways to hedge bets. The first is to keep your options open; even though you choose one option, keep some of the others as possibilities. When making investments, a business can hedge its bets by diversifying, even to the point of making competing investments. A third way companies hedge bets is to offset risks by buying commodity or currency futures to minimize cost fluctuations.

Keeping Your Alternatives Open

One way to hedge your bet is to keep more than one option open even after you have made a choice. One of the most common examples involves employee hiring decisions. Hiring decisions often involve pursuing multiple candidates at one time, from the lowest position in the company to the CEO and chair of the board positions. Once you reduce the number of candidates to a few who you think can do the job, then you can proceed to select your first choice and make that person an offer. It gets complicated, though, when the first person getting the offer wants some time to decide, perhaps while waiting for another preferred offer, and the backup candidates need to make their decision, resulting in conflicting timelines. I always try to ask each candidate the expected decision timing of other opportunities prior to selecting the final candidate and providing the timing for a decision. In some cases, the timing of a response to an offer may actually swing my decision on two candidates who are very closely rated.

Companies commonly invest in multiple options at one time in hopes of one of them panning out. For example, a company interested in acquiring another company in order to enter a new market may pursue multiple companies, all of which have some portion of the market share for a given product. While the company may not actually invest in the different companies, it will certainly do its research to make the best acquisition possible.

> In order to successfully apply the technique of hedging your bet, you need to do a cost-benefit analysis of all of the options.

Pursuing More Than One Option

Sometimes when choosing among multiple options it is best to select more than one. When I was contracting with an executive search firm to hire two senior consulting executives, I received proposals from three different firms. I asked each of them for a steep fee discount to hire two executives instead of one, but each held firm and charged the same fee for each candidate whether we hired one or two. So, I picked two of the firms instead of one. It cost the same and each brought a different pool of candidates, enabling me to hedge my bet. This was an easier decision than others where the cost is much higher to hedge the bet.

With emerging technology, it is sometimes impossible to predict which of two technologies could emerge as the standard, and it may make sense to hedge your bet by investing in both at the same time, knowing that only one of these bets will pay off. This was the case with the emerging standard for high-definition DVD. Toshiba developed and promoted its HD DVD technology, while Sony had a competing Blu-ray format. The battle was the first full-scale format war between two Japanese electronics companies since the 1980s, when Matsushita's VHS and Sony's Betamax fought to become the standard for videotape, with VHS prevailing.

The DVD situation resulted in a two-year pitched battle, in which both companies tried to woo Hollywood studios to release movies in their formats and computer and game console makers to use their disk drives. Some equipment suppliers decided to hedge their bets by offering both formats, sometimes in a single device. Some movie companies hedged their bets by offering both formats. And unfortunately many consumers hedged their bets by simply waiting until the standard was resolved before buying the equipment and DVDs.

Planting Strategic Seeds

A variation of pursuing two competing alternatives at the same time is a technique I call "planting strategic seeds." With this technique you make multiple strategic investments at the same time when you are unsure which ones will pay off, akin to planting seeds and waiting for the crop to thrive.

In 2001, with the management consulting business slowing and approaching a market decline, I evaluated numerous opportunities for expanding my firm into new service areas. Many of them seemed promising. Rather than placing a bet on one, I decided to hedge the bet and invested in five opportunities, since there was really no way of deciding which one would be the biggest winner. Of the five, one grew into a very big success; another was also successful, with a third doing all right. The other two did not succeed and were canceled. Planting the seeds allowed me to spread my risk.

Similarly, you can decide to plant seeds successively over time as a basic strategy. This is how Amazon unfolded its growth strategy. In 1998, it added music and video as a natural extension of books, which was very successful. In 1999, it created Amazon auctions to compete with eBay, but that failed. In 2001, it created Marketplace, a successful venue for third parties to sell used books and CDs. In 2006, Amazon entered the market for video download, and this is yet to be a success. In that same year, it also tried cloud computing with Ec2, enabling customers to rent space on Amazon's computers, and this is also yet to be successful. Then in 2007, Amazon released the Kindle, a lightweight e-reader, which appears on the way to be a tremendous success. Some of Amazon's seeds grew and others did not, but it decided not to place only one single bet.

Hedging Bets Financially

Many businesses and organizations make decisions to hedge bets financially, as illustrated in the way companies manage currency and commodity price risk. Global companies may maintain assets, particularly cash, in certain currencies, but purchase currency futures to hedge against fluctuations. Generally the objective is not to make money through hedging currency but to avoid losing money if currency rates change abruptly.

In a variation of this approach, Northwestern University (NWU) had a big payoff from its development of technology used in Pfizer's blockbuster pain drug Lyrica. Annual royalty payments were tremendous, and the forecast was that this would continue for many years. NWU, however, decided to hedge its bet in late 2007 and sold some of its royalty rights for $700 million in cash. While it continued to receive a portion of the royalties, it added $700 million to its endowment to support university research and scholarships. Most likely NWU would have made more money over the longer term by holding on to its entire royalty, but it decided to reduce risk and hedge its bet.

You Will Not Always Win

Be sure to realize, however, that hedging your bet does not always work. Sometimes you will still lose even though you have hedged your decision. Hedging is not a guarantee; it is simply a method for statistically reducing your chances of losing. Going back to the horse race example, there are more than two horses in the race, so just because the gambler places bets on two horses does not mean that either of those two horses is going to win the race. If a third horse wins, the gambler has now lost all $200 of his bet and received nothing in return.

United Airlines (UA) provides a case in point. In an attempt to hedge anticipated escalating fuel costs, UA contracted for future purchases of oil at current prices. Oil had spiked to $147 per barrel in July 2008, and Goldman Sachs predicted it would keep rising to $200. Of course the opposite happened; oil dropped to $41 per barrel and the hedge backfired, costing UA approximately $750 million.

As UA illustrates, sometimes there is risk in hedging your bets that may exceed the potential benefit. Other airlines, like Southwest, had successfully hedged oil prices as they were rising, gaining some significant competitive cost advantages. But this decision backfired on UA.

Determining When to Hedge Your Bet

In order to successfully apply the technique of hedging your bet, you need to do a cost-benefit analysis of your options. If you need to choose between two or more options, whether they are good or bad, try to understand the costs and/or benefits of each. Does it make sense to choose the option that you want the most or that you think would have the highest positive returns (or the lowest negative returns), and then spend a little extra (money, time, commitment, etc.) to choose a second option in the event that the first one does not work out? Here is a series of questions that should help you when you are considering a decision on which you may potentially benefit from hedging your bet:

- Is this a decision that affords you the opportunity to pursue multiple options simultaneously? How many options can you pursue at one time?

- Can you pursue more than one option completely, or will you be required to stop pursuing one at a specific time in the process? If so, how long will you be able to pursue more than one option? At what point will you need to stop pursuing multiple options and commit to the ones that will work?

- What are the additional costs in terms of time and money to pursue multiple options simultaneously? How much higher are they than choosing only one option? Are you willing to spend that much extra for the potential increase in the results?

- What are the risks involved in pursuing multiple options? Is there a chance that you may lose everything by not committing to one option from the outset? How much higher are the risks of pursuing more than one option and losing than pursuing only one option and losing?
- How do the costs relate to the benefits of pursuing additional options?

- In business, it can sometimes help to consider pursuing more than one alternative simultaneously.
- Hedging your bet allows you to maximize your chances of success while you minimize your risk.
- Be careful when hedging your bet because you can sometimes risk losing it all.
- One variation of this technique involves planting strategic seeds, which limits the risk involved by hedging.
- Apply the technique of hedging your bet only after a careful analysis of the costs and likely benefits of doing so.

CHAPTER 20

Seizing Opportunities That Cross Your Path

Applying the crossing-my-path technique to seize opportunities

Why do some businesses seem to be able to make decisions to seize opportunities while others overlook them? Sometimes it is just luck, but there is also a decision skill to discerning what opportunities to seize. It is not about opportunity knocking at your door; rarely if ever does that happen. But it is about opportunity crossing your path.

Here is how it works. There is something in the future — a strategic opportunity or operational move — that you might like to do if you have the opportunity. You identify it and are determined to watch out for opportunities that might help you realize that vision. In other words, you define a path that you might like to take if you have an opportunity. Over time you continue looking down these paths to see if an opportunity crosses it, a bit like serendipity. When one does, you can decide to seize it. However, if you have not defined these strategic paths, then you will not see the opportunity when it crosses that path.

Figure 20-1 illustrates the difference. The executive at the top is not looking for opportunities, so he does not see them as they pass him by. In contrast, the executive at the bottom of the figure is looking down a path for specific opportunities and sees two crossing the strategic path he defined.

> It is easier to take advantage of unexpected opportunities if you are prepared for them.

In 1973, Xerox, a company widely known for producing the leading photocopiers, invented what is arguably considered the first personal computer. Named the Alto, this computer used a mouse-driven inter-

178

Figure 20-1 Watching for Opportunities That Cross Your Path

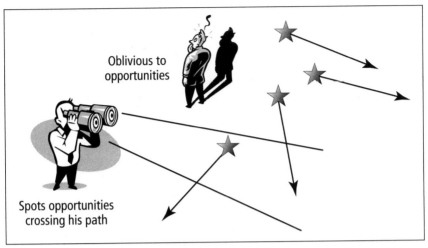

face and was the first computer designed to be used by one person at a time. While the executives of the company recognized the utility of the computer, even going so far as to pay for building 2,000 of the units for their own use and that of a select group of research institutions, they failed to make the decision to proceed with pushing the Alto as a commercial product for the company. In essence, the executives either did not recognize this opportunity when it crossed their path or failed to take advantage of this opportunity when they had the chance.

Within a decade, personal computers were beginning to be sold by a number of companies, most notably through the inventions of Steve Jobs and his company, Apple Computers. Jobs integrated the mouse-driven interface he had seen on the Alto on a visit to the Xerox facility where the computer was used. Bringing several of the engineers from Xerox over to his new company, Jobs jumped on the opportunity that had crossed his path while the executives at Xerox missed the opportunity.

> **IN YOUR EXPERIENCE**
>
> *Have you ever been presented with an opportunity that seemed to come out of nowhere but had the potential for bringing you or your business into new and potentially amazing places? Did you take advantage of it?*

By the time Xerox decided it wanted to enter the personal computer market, it was too late and the demand for their machines was so low they ended up leaving the market for good. The problem was not that Xerox did not have the technology or the product. The problem was that Xerox failed to set an established desire to take advantage of a strategic opportunity for expansion into a new market when the opportunity they sought crossed their path.

Always Be on the Lookout

Do you recognize unexpected opportunities when they arise? Xerox did not in this case. It is certainly easier to take advantage of these opportunities if you are prepared for them. To do so, when you are thinking about the future, take time to identify paths that you would like to explore if the opportunity presents itself. This is different from setting an objective and then planning for how to achieve it. The crossing-my-path approach lends itself to making an opportunistic decision when faced with this sudden opportunity. If you define and look down your strategic path, you will see opportunity crossing it.

Here is how I once used this technique when leading my management consulting firm, PRTM. The firm did extensive work in operations consulting in the 1980s, helping American companies to catch up with their Japanese counterparts that had made competitive advances with just-in-time manufacturing. I wanted to identify another opportunity for growing the business in a major new service area. After completing significant research and talking with clients, I identified a potential path for new services in product development, but did not know how to go about building a new practice around this business area.

One day, my firm received a request for a competitive proposal from a manufacturing company that wanted to improve its product development process. Typically, we would have decided to pass up this opportunity because it was highly competitive and we did not have much background. Instead, we decided to jump on it because it crossed our opportunity path. We worked night and day to learn as much as possible about improving product development in order to win that contract. We put an extraordinary amount of time into it because we recognized that this was an important opportunity. As a result of putting in this extra effort, we won the contract, beating out ten other major consulting firms that probably viewed it as just an average consulting project. PRTM went on to develop a methodology that became the industry standard for product development management. This business niche provided more than $1 billion in consulting as we introduced the methodology in more than 1,000 companies over 25 years. If we had not defined product development as a path that we wanted to go down if possible, we would not have seen this opportunity as crossing our strategic path.

I used the crossing-my-path technique with a European strategic opportunity. PRTM had an office in the United Kingdom but had yet to open one anywhere on the continent. Further European expansion was on our path, but we were not sure how to do it. About a year later, we learned about a consulting opportunity in France. The normal response would have been to ignore the opportunity because we had no office in France, but because it was on our strategic path, we decided to seize the opportunity. We learned more about the request, found a partner in France to work with, and won the project. The project ended up being the platform for PRTM to build its operations in France.

Planning Ahead Is Critical

When using this technique, it is important to identify ahead of time the path you want to take when the opportunity presents itself. You need to make yourself open to see the opportunity when it crosses your path and aggressively seize it when it presents itself. Do not fret or think it is impossible. Keep looking for the opportunity that might cross your path. Very likely it will. But be aware that you can easily miss it if you are not looking and open to new opportunities. You also need to be actively creating the possibility for more opportunities to arise.

How do you prepare to take advantage of opportunities that are in sync with your goals? First, you need to look far enough ahead. This technique takes time and patience, so the further ahead you look, the better. But be sure to set timelines. If you want to expand into a new market within the next five years, you need to strategize different opportunities now. If you want to expand your market share from one of your products, you should begin to look at ways to improve what you currently have and explore what existing clients need now. If you want to figure out how to open a new branch in a different location, you should begin to investigate various locations now that you think would produce the most business.

Where Are You Looking?

Your first decision is determining what major paths you want to look down. Focus on a few of them since you really cannot successfully undertake too many paths at any given time. Then, remain on the lookout for opportunities that cross that path. Most likely, the opportunity you are looking for will cross your path when you are busy or distracted; it just seems to work out that way. Maybe you will be so inundated with other projects that you will not recognize a new project as fitting the description of a path you have decided to look down. If you are constantly looking, though, you may find that you should drop other work to pursue this opportunity.

> It is very likely that the opportunity you are looking for will cross your path while you are busy or distracted.

I shared this technique with a CEO client, Jim, who applied it to finding a successor. He defined a path for finding someone who could be his successor. He was not ready to launch a search, but he had the succession plan on his path. About a year later, he met an up-and-coming young executive from a large company in a similar industry. Jim was intrigued by this man's potential and invested some time getting to know him better, inviting him to join a nonprofit board and to attend an executive symposium. Jim came to know him personally. Then Jim made his move, creating a new position for strategy in his company and recruiting him for that position. Three years later, Jim turned over the CEO position to his protégé successor.

You need to pursue with extreme aggressiveness this type of opportunity when it crosses your strategic path. It is not just another task you do to keep your business on track; it is *the* opportunity to do something that is very important to the success of your company. Give it the highest priority, and pursue it vigorously. Not all opportunities that cross your path actually lead to the results you want. You may not get the contract that you courted to help you expand your business, even after trying aggressively. In that case, keep looking down that path. Another opportunity will eventually cross it.

- One of the most successful ways to excel in business is to be constantly on the lookout for opportunities that will cross your strategic path.

- If you prepare ahead for the one or two opportunities you will vigilantly look for to cross your path and then aggressively pursue them when they do cross your path, you will be more likely to achieve your goals.

- Opportunities are more likely to cross your path while you are busy or distracted, so paying attention to the potential for these opportunities will help you find them and take advantage of them.

CHAPTER 21

Making Tough Decisions

*In tough decisions there are no
attractive alternatives*

I refer to "tough decisions" as those decisions you sometimes need to make where none of the alternatives are attractive. Tough decisions are different from a hard or difficult decision. Tough decisions are generally hard, too, but what distinguishes them is that there is no good alternative. You are forced to choose between bad alternatives. People tend to avoid, ignore, or delay a tough decision for this reason, which makes the situation worse.

Tough decisions are frequently a form of crisis decision, in that something has caused a problem to which you need to react. With a tough decision, the best decision is the least undesirable outcome; people are likely to be upset no matter what decision is made. In late 2008 and 2009 as the economy rapidly declined, many organizations unfortunately faced tough decisions.

In March 2009, National Semiconductor Corp., like many other companies, faced a steep decline in sales. Its sales fell more than one-third to $292 million from $453 million. "The worldwide recession has impacted National's business as demand has fallen considerably," chief executive Brian L. Halla said in a statement. National Semiconductor anticipated another 5% to 10% sequential decline in sales, which would put its fourth-quarter revenue between $263 million and $278 million. The executive team faced a tough decision: continue to have declining profits as sales dropped, or cut costs. Like other companies in similar situations, they reluctantly decided on an aggressive cost reduction program.

National Semiconductor Corp. decided to eliminate more than

> In tough decisions you need to select the least undesirable outcome.

one-quarter of its workforce, or 1,725 jobs. The company immediately began trimming 850 positions worldwide in its product, marketing, manufacturing, and support businesses. An additional 875 jobs would come from closing facilities in Suzhou, China, and Arlington, Texas, over the next few quarters. National Semiconductor had about 6,500 employees. None of the alternatives they considered was attractive. Nobody was happy with the decision, but it had to be made.

The executive team at Eastman Kodak faced a similar tough decision in early 2009. Sales fell 24% to $2.43 billion, as digital revenue fell 23% and traditional film-based revenue slumped 27%. The company incurred a loss of $137 million in the fourth quarter compared to a profit of $215 million in the same quarter of the prior year. They faced a similar tough decision to that of National Semiconductor and hundreds of other companies at the time. After agonizing over its decision, the executive team decided to eliminate 3,500 to 4,500 jobs, or 14% to 18% of its payroll.

Tough decisions are not limited to for-profit businesses. Nonprofit organizations also need to face some tough decisions from time to time. The trustees of Brandeis University were confronting a budget deficit of more than $10 million over five years, significant losses in its endowment, a drop in donations, and payment for extensive construction projects. These losses significantly impaired Brandeis's ability to fulfill its primary education mission because it would need to reduce faculty and curtail scholarship funding for students.

The school's trustees faced a tough decision, and after debate and realizing that they needed to make a tough choice, they voted on January 26, 2009, to close the school's 49-year-old Rose Art Museum and sell its art collection, which was appraised at about $350 million in 2007. With proceeds from this sale, Brandeis could replenish most of the loss in its endowment. Many protested that this was a bad decision, but whether it was the right decision or the wrong decision, it was certainly a tough decision to make.

Recognition and Acceptance

Tough decisions begin with the recognition and acceptance that you need to make a tough decision, which is where the first mistake is usually made. Tough decisions are uncomfortable, and ignoring them and hoping they will go away is easy, which is what the major auto companies did. They avoided the tough decisions about global over-capacity, quality, and market issues until it was too late. They avoided tough decisions on negotiating with the United Auto Workers union (UAW), instead choosing to push the burdens to the future. They used aggressive financing (the auto industry equivalent of subprime loans) to temporarily prop up sales in order to delay facing the tough decisions. Maybe they even fooled themselves into thinking that they would not have to face these tough decisions ever, but in the end they had even tougher decisions to make. The result of avoiding tough decisions is that they get worse.

The result of avoiding tough decisions is that they get worse.

Tough decisions get even tougher if you do not address them when they need to be made. Sometimes if you avoid tough decisions long enough, then you do not need to make them; someone else will, or it will be too late to do anything at all. It could be argued that this is what happened with the major auto manufacturers. They simply did not make the decisions until it was too late and they faced bankruptcy.

The bankruptcy reorganization of GM and Chrysler forced the tough decisions. With bankruptcy everyone – the unions, the debt holders, shareholders, management, and the United States government – were at risk of losing almost everything they had invested. They realized that almost everything could be lost, and only then could the tough decisions be made by everyone. Without bankruptcy, then each party thought it could remain whole, and the others should give in on the tough decisions.

In March 2005 when I took over responsibility for saving i2 Technologies, I faced some tough decisions. The company had lost money for years, was rapidly burning cash, had more than $200 million of debt coming due that it was unable to pay, and faced some legal problems. In the previous years, the company management was aware of its precarious situation but kept hoping it could grow out of the problem. They continually forecast increasing revenue to forestall tough decisions but always fell short. They recognized that they were in a difficult situation, but just could not accept it, so they kept hoping that business would get better. It is human nature to just hope that things will get better, which is why recognition and acceptance are easy to delay. The board of directors brought me in to make the tough decisions.

In contrast, the abrupt economic downturn of 2008 had the unique "advantage" of enabling most companies, their boards, their employees, and others involved to recognize that tough decisions needed to be made, and that making these decisions could not wait. Because most companies were hit hard by the economic collapse and the press was broadcasting nothing but bad economic news, recognition and acceptance were much easier — probably easier than at any other time I can remember.

This dilemma of tough decisions is an interesting one. Tough decisions are easier to make when there is broad acceptance of the situation, but by then the choices are more drastic, and the options available more limited. The tough decisions should be made earlier, even before there is broad acceptance, but then the backlash to the decision will be stronger.

Guidelines for Making Tough Decisions

1. *Don't procrastinate.* Tough decisions are distasteful, and it's really easy to keep putting them off, delaying the inevitable, or maybe even wishing things will change. Address the decision and get it behind you.

2. *Accept being unhappy making the decision.* In a way, making tough decisions is a little like going to a funeral. You need to accept it and do it.

3. *Make the decision quickly and carefully.* There will be a lot of anxiety awaiting the decision, so don't prolong the pain. Get it over with, but still make the decision carefully.

4. *Consider new priorities.* To make these decisions you frequently need to focus more on one priority; it could be a new one such as survival or returning to your basic priority or mission.

5. *Be prepared for a negative response.* With a tough decision, some people will be upset, others may be relieved, but nobody will really be happy. Be prepared.

6. *Don't try to make an optimum decision.* You won't have enough time to make the optimum decision, so be satisfied with the best decision.

7. *Accept uncertainty.* The outcomes of tough decisions are uncertain. Recognize the presence of uncertainty and figure out how to deal with it the best you can.

8. *Communicate.* Communicate honestly and as much as possible. Don't be afraid to say you don't know or you are trying your best.

When confronted with a tough decision, realize that it is just the situation that you are in, and you need to take the right corrective action. Do not dwell on how you got into this situation or who is to blame. Do not dwell on what you could have done or what you should have done. Do not become paralyzed by despair. The time for that has passed, at least for now. Maybe in the future you will have the opportunity to assess past decisions and to learn from them.

Accepting the need for a decision makes tough decisions stand out from other decisions. You really do not want to make tough decisions, but you have to. If you had your choice you would prefer not to have to make a decision.

When the board appointed me as CEO of i2 Technologies, it was with the express mandate to turn around the company as fast as possible. The company accepted and recognized that tough decisions had to be made.

Aggressive Timeline for Deciding

Set an aggressive timeline for making the tough decision. Tough decisions are frequently a crisis of sorts, but usually you will not need to respond immediately within hours or days. You will have weeks to make a decision, but do not stretch out the timeline because the decision is too painful.

> **IN YOUR EXPERIENCE**
>
> *Have you ever seen or read about a company that needed to make a tough decision, but the company just could not accept the facts?*

With most tough decisions you are dealing with a deteriorating situation where things are getting worse even while you are making the decisions. That was the case with National Semiconductor and Kodak, as well as thousands of other companies in 2009. They needed to make quick decisions once they confirmed how much sales had declined in the previous quarter. In the Brandeis example, the trustees had some more time, but the sooner they made the decision on the art museum, the less they needed to make other cuts.

Start with setting out a timeline for the decision or decisions. Mobilize resources necessary to make the decision, but also keep the group involved small, in order to minimize panic and confusion. In some cases, bringing in outside advisors or consultants is a good step in helping to facilitate and guide the decision process. This may avoid the decision becoming bogged down and will keep it on schedule.

At i2, I quickly established a rapid timeline. I announced that the cost cuts and layoffs would be done in 30 days, knowing that I planned to do them in three weeks. I also announced the intention to resolve the debt issue over the first six months.

Making the Tough Decision

As noted previously, the first step in making a tough decision is to actually decide that you need to make the tough decisions, which also involves defining the scope of the decision itself, as well as the potential alternatives to consider. This move then leads to the next step: making that actual decision.

The alternatives for tough decisions are usually ugly. The cases illustrated here all involved cost cuts. There is usually no good alternative, just some that may be less bad than others. Frequently, a list of options is devised that requires various actions to resolve the problems. National Semiconductor, for example, made layoffs in many areas of the company and closed two plants completely. Brandeis had to institute other cuts in salaries and develop a plan to bring in more students to cover costs in addition to its decision on the art museum.

> The alternatives for tough decisions are usually ugly.

A lot of factors come into play in making these tough decisions. Understand the longer impact of short-term decisions, but if it is a case of survival, there may not be a longer term if the company does not survive. Also, be fair in prioritizing the tough decisions. At i2 Technologies, I put together a list of potential cuts and then prioritized the list until we reached the targeted cut of eliminating more than $100 million in annual expenses. We made a commitment to lay off half of the 75 highest-paid executives and not just focus on lower-level layoffs. Employees — even those laid off — respected this decision.

One of the dangers of tough decisions is they are not always fair. Some people make more of a sacrifice than others. During the tough decisions on cost cuts made in early 2009, companies used a variety of ways to try to be fair: layoffs by seniority, voluntary buyout offers, across-the-board salary reduction, elimination of bonuses, reduction in benefits, and furloughs instead of layoffs, to name a few.

The alternatives for tough decisions also involve quite a bit of uncertainty. You do not know how long the situation will continue. You do not know how well the decisions you make will actually work. Yet you need to make your tough decision despite this uncertainty. Avoid making a series of tough decisions that merely drag out the process. While it is tempting to say, "Let's make some cuts now and avoid others until we need to make them," this approach may be more painful than making the tough decision just once and being done with it.

Other Types of Tough Decisions

I have focused so far on tough decisions for major business cost reductions, but you may encounter many other types of tough decisions:

- You may need to decide to cancel a project or even close a business in which you invested a lot of time, money, and energy, or let it continue to lose money.
- You may need to decide between firing an employee who is a good friend or letting him continue to perform below standard.
- You may need to decide between doing something that you think is right for a particular employee but which may set a dangerous precedent for the future.

- Tough decisions have unsatisfactory alternatives, but the decisions need to be made.
- Generally, few people are happy with the immediate results of a tough decision.
- Tough decisions have unique characteristics.
- The first step in making a tough decision is awareness and recognition that a tough decision needs to be made.
- Some guidelines to making tough decisions are as follows: do not procrastinate, accept being unhappy making the decision, make the decision quickly and carefully, consider new priorities, be prepared for a negative response, do not try to make an optimum decision, accept uncertainty, and communicate honestly and effectively.

CHAPTER 22

Performing a
Decision Autopsy

*Just because the decision is made does
not mean the process is finished*

A major investment company regularly hires dozens of new employees every year and is widely considered a great place for MBA graduates in New York City to cut their teeth in the financial world. Less than a year after one particularly large freshman class of new hires, the VP of human resources noticed that a very high percentage of them were either fired, left the company because they were underperforming, or were struggling to do their work. Concerned with the high attrition rate, the executive put together a committee to examine the hiring decision process to determine if there were flaws in it that contributed to what he perceived as a failure to hire the best new employees.

The committee reviewed the entire process of how new employees were hired, from the method of identifying potential applicants right through the time they were offered the position. What they found was striking. They found no consistency in the decision process, with a wide range of current employees being responsible for the hiring for different positions. There was no uniformity in any component of the hiring process. Some new employees were made offers after a grueling, four-part interview process and thorough reference check. Others were made offers after a simple 20-minute phone interview. After speaking with each of those responsible for the interviews, the committee determined that rarely were the same questions asked of different candidates for the various positions, and those chosen for an interview were selected based upon differing characteristics and qualifications — some for no other reason than they attended a good MBA program.

None of the interviewers used any type of questionnaire when performing the interviews, and the decisions on which candidate to hire were often made because the interviewer seemed to think one person was better than another. No specific assessment criteria were used to make these decisions, and to justify his or her decision, each interviewer mentioned a different reason or characteristic specific to the person hired. It became painfully clear to the committee reviewing the hiring process and to the executive who put together the committee that there was absolutely no uniformity in the process and that it was likely the cause of the longer-term problems the company was having with selecting and retaining the best candidates to serve in these entry-level roles.

What Is a Decision Autopsy?

An autopsy, also known as a postmortem examination, is a medical procedure conducted to examine a corpse in an effort to determine the cause and manner of death and to evaluate any disease or injury that may have been present. The term is used more broadly, as well, to describe an assessment of a process. In many cases, the purpose of an autopsy is to learn what went right and what went wrong in any given process in the hopes of improving the overall process and avoiding making mistakes in the future. A decision autopsy can be very useful to help you learn from your decision mistakes, so you can make better decisions the next time around. Decision making is a process and, like any other, one that requires continuous improvement. We can learn from our previous decisions — both good and bad.

> A decision autopsy can be very useful to help you learn from your decision mistakes so you can make better decisions the next time around.

We need to periodically review our decisions and determine if a particular decision was a good one, or if we could have made a better one at the time. The key is to identify what we did right and what we did wrong, and apply these lessons for decision making the next time.

The executive referenced in the beginning of the chapter who tasked the committee with examining the company's hiring process decided he was going to put a stop to loose and unstructured hiring. He looked at all of the problems identified by the committee and uncovered significant places to make improvements. First, he decided the company needed a hiring committee to focus specifically on these entry-level hiring decisions. The committee would be collectively responsible for selecting and interviewing each of the candidates. Each applicant would be reviewed along the same criteria, with education, experience, and references being assigned a value, with the top-scoring candidates offered interviews. A more structured and rigorous interview process would be instituted whereby each candidate would be asked the same questions. Responses to the questions would be evaluated along the same criteria for each candidate. After each round of interviews, the hiring committee would meet again and would discuss each of the candidates they interviewed, coming to a mutual decision about which candidates would be offered the positions. A year after the new process was instituted, the percentage of new hires who "washed out" dropped from 50% to 5% — a significant improvement. The executive and his review committee were widely credited with the improvement in the process, all of which was accomplished because he decided to perform a decision autopsy.

How Do You Perform a Decision Autopsy?

Following a purchase — of a new consulting service, for example — and being provided with the service by the company, you realize that you are either happy with your decision or you regret it. This is a good time to look back and learn from the decision process. How did you finally settle on a particular firm and a particular level of service? Did you meticulously research your options? Did you speak with others who have purchased similar services and ask for their advice? Or did you simply pick a consulting firm because you liked its website and merely called them up and asked them to tell you what they could provide, unsure of exactly what you were looking for, and hang up the phone having purchased one of their service levels? Whether you think you made a good decision or a bad one, take time to review the process you used.

> **IN YOUR EXPERIENCE**
>
> *Looking back at some of the decisions you have made, if you had to make them again, would you make them differently? What can you learn from your previous decisions?*

Use this checklist to perform your own decision autopsy:

- *Was this a good or bad decision?* Most likely you are more eager to learn from your bad decisions because you are more motivated to correct them.
- *What would have been a better decision?* With hindsight, you probably have an opinion of what you should have decided.
- *Why would this have been a better decision?* This question leads you to understand what you should have considered or tried to find out before making the decision.
- *Did you know there were other options available at the time of your decision?* Did you consider these sufficiently? Maybe you could have considered them but did not, or maybe they were unknown.
- *What should you have done differently?* The essence of the decision autopsy is identifying what you can do differently the next time around.
- *How can you use this experience to make a better decision next time?*

> You should not dwell on a good or bad decision, but you should learn lessons about how to make similar decisions better in the future.

You should not dwell on a bad decision — or gloat on a good decision, for that matter — but you should learn lessons about how to make similar decisions when you face them in the future. This process is particularly useful with repetitive decisions and those that include a longer decision process. Companies that make a large number of hiring decisions, as in the example at the beginning of this chapter, can learn to restructure the hiring process, significantly improving the quality of the employees at the company and, therefore, its profit capabilities.

Short-Term vs. Long-Term Results

One of the problems in judging decisions, however, is that short-term results tend to weigh much more heavily than long-term results. It is human nature to be short-term oriented, but a decision judged to be good in the short term may not be as good in the long term. For example, you may need to hire a new assistant because your previous assistant was promoted to a better job. You know such a promotion was the responsible thing to do for the growth of the company and for the personal growth of your former assistant, who had served you well for a number of years. You decide to go ahead and make the move. After all, how bad could it be to break in a new assistant? Six weeks after the change takes effect, you look at the situation and tell yourself you made a huge mistake. Your new assistant seems like a bumbling idiot, unable to perform the most perfunctory tasks. You just got off the phone with your old assistant, who is completely unhappy in his new role and is clamoring for you to take him back. Of course, you know you cannot oblige, but you wish you had made your decision more carefully.

As judged in this short period of time, you are certain your decision autopsy has proven you made a mistake somewhere along the way, and you want to know what the mistake was. Five months later — with the same new assistant who you have miraculously not fired — you reevaluate the situation. Your assistant has become an invaluable asset to you and your entire department. You recently had lunch with your old assistant, and his attitude has changed completely. Now he is not only fitting in better and excelling in his new role at the company, he absolutely loves the position.

> Do not neglect to consider the short-term and long-term consequences of your decisions in your decision autopsy.

He tells you it took him a while to become adjusted to the new situation, but once he did, he completely changed his outlook on the job. Now you decide to reevaluate the decision process one more time. Perhaps you made the best decision at the time, but originally did not realize it because the short-term ramifications of the decision seemed negative. Only once the longer-term ramifications became a reality did you realize your decision process was correct.

While the above example shows how short-term consequences can seem bad, only to be reconciled over the long term, realize that this can also happen the opposite way. Short-term consequences might seem excellent, yet you realize later you may have made a mistake. It is different to evaluate decisions in the short term alone. Quite often they have to be evaluated when you can understand both the short-term and long-term consequences together. (Alternatively, you can evaluate the decision in the short term, and then reevaluate your previous evaluation in the long term.)

Continuous Improvement

Managers who excel over time are committed to continuous improvement. They are constantly trying to improve their managerial skills. Continuous improvement applies to decision making as well; in fact, making better decisions may be one of the most important areas for continuous improvement.

You should perform decision autopsies not only following bad decisions — when you naturally ask yourself the question, "What did I do wrong?" — but also after making good decisions. In fact, as part of your annual self-assessment, you should look back on good decisions and do a postmortem. If you are trying to develop other people, you should require they also do an annual postmortem of their decisions.

To help you evaluate your decisions and learn how to make better ones, I have included a Decision Diagnostic worksheet in Figure 22-1. You can use this to evaluate your own decisions, or use it for a group to evaluate collective decisions. For the optimum learning opportunity, be sure to look at good decisions as well as bad ones.

- Once you have made a decision and implemented it, you can still learn from it.

- Performing a decision autopsy can help you improve your decision-making process for similar decisions in the future.

- Decision autopsies can be particularly beneficial for iterative or repeated decisions.

- Be sure to consider both short-term and long-term consequences of your decisions when you perform your decision autopsy.

Figure 22-1 Decision Diagnostic

Decision: _____

_____

Grade: ___

A	Perfect decision: great outcome, good process
A–	Almost perfect; could have improved a little
B+	Could have been a little better
B	Close to being a good decision; could have been better
B–	Not a good outcome; a better decision could be made
C+	Bad decision, but not sure why
C	Bad decision from poor decision process
F	What was I thinking? It was a disaster

Problems with the Decision:

☐ Didn't take enough time to make the decision
☐ Should have asked for advice
☐ Received bad advice
☐ Used my "gut feel" instead of a more rigorous process
☐ Didn't make any decision, and I should have

☐ Didn't consider all the alternatives
☐ Didn't use the right criteria for the decision
☐ Didn't understand the risk of the decision
☐ Could not get group consensus
☐ Group consensus led to mediocre decision

Better Decision:_____

_____

Lessons Learned:

1. _____
2. _____
3. _____
4. _____
5. _____

Section IV

Organizational Decisions

In businesses, particularly larger businesses, decisions are not just made by individuals; they are frequently made by a group, a team, or portions of the organization. While many of the decision pitfalls, techniques, and skills previously reviewed apply to groups as well as individuals, there is a fundamental added dimension when people in an organization or group work together to make decisions. This added dimension can make it more difficult to reach a decision. I have learned during many years of helping companies make decisions that organizations which work hard on improving the way group decisions are made reach far superior decisions, hands down.

Indeed, groups or teams make some of the most important decisions. Groups include standing committees such as an executive committee or a recruiting committee, as well as boards of directors or trustees. Teams are generally temporary and focused on projects, but could be in place for several years. Team dynamics are complex and subtle. Personalities differ, and people approach the same decision very differently. Teams that work well together make great decisions and then follow these decisions with a shared commitment for implementation. Successful teams agree on the decision process up front and understand the give-and-take required. Teams that do not work well together become easily frustrated and take longer to reach a decision, and more often than not their decisions are mediocre.

In large companies, decisions are made by organizations, not individuals. Fundamentally, organizational structure defines the authority for decisions, but often this definition is incomplete or confused, resulting in friction and missed decisions. Organizational decisions are also influenced by other factors, such as the political, bureaucratic, and cultural aspects of an organization. Company culture in particular has an increasingly evident role in influencing decisions.

To truly understand how groups make decisions, you first need to understand how others may approach a decision differently than you do, which I delve into in this section's first chapter. Everyone tackles decisions uniquely, and research has found that personality types are a primary factor in determining the way people formulate decisions. When working with groups or teams to arrive at a decision, you must first appreciate how others make their decisions, and personality types are the best place to start. This chapter uses the proven Myers-Briggs personality type indicators to explore decision making.

Team or group dynamics add another dimension to decision making. Sometimes team decisions can be substantially more successful than individual decisions; other times they can be mediocre or misdirected. In my extensive experience with team decision making, I have found that misunderstood practices and ignorance detract from effective decisions. Chapter 24 takes a comprehensive look at the advantages and disadvantages of team decisions and clarifies the guidelines and best practices that make these decisions effective and more successful.

Research demonstrates that the culture of a business shapes the decisions within that business — both good and bad. Strong or unique cultures, in particular, influence the tone and direction for business decisions. Chapter 25 uses strong culture examples to illustrate how decisions are shaped by varied cultures, providing insights on how to understand the important role that culture plays.

Making sure that important decisions are made is an essential leadership characteristic. If you look at successful senior executives, particularly CEOs, they do not so much make all of the decisions as they make sure that the right people make the right decisions at the right time. Chapter 26 provides an overview on how to ensure that organizations make decisions.

In 1971, Graham Allison published an insightful book titled *The Essence of Decision*, which examined the different decision processes behind the Cuban missile crisis. He interpreted the decisions of the crisis through three different models: rational decisions, organizational decisions, and bureaucratic/political decisions. This book became a standard for understanding the different ways that organizations, not just governments, make decisions, and for many years I gave a copy of this book to my consultants to help them understand the way our clients made decisions. The final chapter in this section examines the differences in these three models and how they exist simultaneously in an organization.

CHAPTER 23

Understanding Personality Types and Decisions

People approach decisions differently depending on their personalities

Have you ever wondered why you and your business associates make decisions in such different ways? Not everyone approaches decisions the same way. While variables — such as prior experience, decision priority, and time available — play a role, I have found that the primary reason for these differences relates to each individual's personality. It is not that one person approaches a decision correctly and the other does not. Sometimes two people arrive at the same decision through almost opposite mental processes. How does that happen? The reason is that our decision processes reflect our personalities. Different computers, for example, have different operating systems. Similarly, individuals have different personalities, leading to different processes for making decisions.

As I wrote in my first book about decision making, *Decide Better! For a Better Life,* the theory of cognitive differences based on personality type, originally posited by C. G. Jung in 1923, was expanded into a widely used diagnostic framework by Katherine Briggs and her daughter, Isabel Myers. The framework, which has become known as the Myers-Briggs Type Indicator (MBTI), is extremely useful for determining personality-based differences in how people process information and make decisions. The MBTI defines four dimensions of personality characteristics, with two opposite personality types for each characteristic. Here is a fun example.

Eight people were appointed to a committee to consider various candidates for an executive position to head up a new division in a major financial company. The position was an important one, and the search committee was composed of experts in a wide range of financial and operational matters, each with individualized experience and knowledge to add to the decision. After interviewing a large number of people for the position, carefully reviewing their resumes and experience, the committee began to discuss how to proceed. Edward (E) thought the committee should talk through all of the candidates until they came to a consensus. Isabelle (I), however, disagreed and said that she wanted to have some time on her own to think about the candidates, rather than jump to a conclusion. Sam (S) responded that he thought it was important to get all possible information about each of the candidates ahead of time, including checking all of their references, reviewing their previous experiences in detail, and finding out as much as they could about each one. Nelly (N) disagreed, believing that the group members should use their intuition about which candidate they believed would fit in best and would achieve the most for the new division. Intuitive judgment, she believed, trumps any detailed examination of the facts surrounding a particular candidate.

Terrence (T), on the other hand, believed the committee needed to focus on those things that mattered most in the decision, namely how well the candidates' experiences prepared them for this position and how well the candidates could achieve the goals set out for them. At this point, Fay (F) jumped in and said she thought each person on the committee should discuss how they felt about each candidate, not restricting the conversation to those two or three items focused on by Terrence. Jake (J) became agitated with the lack of progress of the committee and proposed holding a vote right away on which candidate would be offered the position. The information was there, and he believed it was time to make the decision. Pamela (P) interrupted Jake and argued that she thought they needed to keep weighing their alternatives, and they were not even close to being able to make a decision. She thought they needed to consider whether

IN YOUR EXPERIENCE

Have you ever noticed that some of your colleagues focus on different things than you do when making a decision? Which one of you is right? Maybe you both are.

they had acted rashly in eliminating three of the lower candidates for the position already, and she believed they needed to keep all of their alternatives open at this point. The meeting continued for a while and eventually ended in gridlock, with the members agreeing to meet again a few days later to once again seek a decision. Before discharging them for the day, however, the CEO of the company directed each member of the committee to examine their own personalities and how they shape their decision-making attitudes, as well as how the personalities of their colleagues on the committee shape their ability to make decisions. Coming back a few days later, the committee finally made a decision on how to proceed.

How Personality Type Shapes Decision Making

In this example, we see an extreme illustration of different approaches to how a common decision is made. There is no right or wrong approach, just varied ways of reaching a decision. These differences are commonly encountered when you work with others to make a decision, but rather than become frustrated, you should learn about people's differences based on their personality characteristics.

Using MBTI, the personality spectrum in decision making is summarized in Figure 23-1. Every person falls into one of the two opposing categories for each of the four dimensions of this spectrum. This provides as many as 16 different combinations in the ways someone could approach a decision, causing a frustratingly wide variety of approaches when people work together on a decision.

Introverts vs. Extroverts

The first characteristic separates Extroverts (E) from Introverts (I). Extroverts prefer to reach decisions interactively — that is, by talking them through with others. They believe in consensus through discussion, assuming all involved will express their opinions. When people do not express an opinion, the Extrovert interprets their silence as consent, even though that may not be the case. Introverts (I) do not make their decisions through interaction with others, but rather through private reflection. Here is an example in the business world of how an Extrovert and an Introvert differ. One of the two members of a hiring committee, an Extrovert, may say to the second member that she thinks it would be the best for the company to hire candidate A rather than candidate B. This statement was merely her way of thinking out

Figure 23-1 MBTI Personality Spectrum of Decision Making

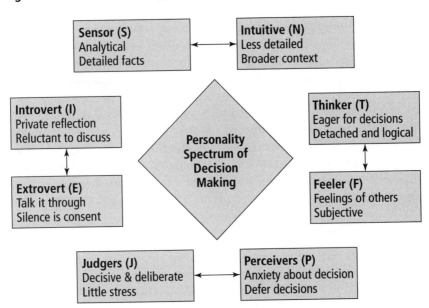

loud about that option in order to solicit the other's opinion. But the Introvert committee member interprets this as his partner's unilateral decision to hire candidate A and becomes upset because "she was not even willing to discuss it. I thought we should have considered candidate B instead of candidate A, but it made no difference what my opinion was." Introverts have such a strong preference for making decisions in private that they may even prefer a written proposal to a verbal argument. As you may be able to tell, this personality difference can be a major obstacle in an Extrovert and an Introvert making a joint decision that satisfies them both.

Sensors vs. Intuitives

The second Myers-Briggs characteristic relates to the information that different people need to consider in order to make a decision. Sensors (S) prefer to make decisions by looking at detailed facts and are very reluctant to reach a conclusion until they have all of the facts they think they need. Sensors, in other words, are analytical and wary of analytical error. In contrast, Intuitives (N) typically want to consider alternatives at a less detailed level so they can make decisions within the context of the broader picture. Here is an example: Coworkers S and N are responsible for coming up with location options for the company's annual conference the following year. S begins by gathering details on various destinations, including hotels, costs, weather, and possible activities. N becomes resentful of too much detail being kicked in his face and pushes back. "We are getting way ahead of ourselves," says N. "We may want to do it in a location that is close to the office, or that can serve as a vacation for our overworked employees. We have not even discussed the options we will want to consider before making the decision, and you are plunging into all kinds of details." To this S responds, "How can we decide where to have the conference without knowing any facts? If we do not have any information, we are just speculating." An S and an N must both be very tolerant in order to make a decision together.

Thinkers vs. Feelers

The third major division in the Myers-Briggs Type Indicator is between Thinkers (T) and Feelers (F). Thinkers do not mind making the difficult decisions themselves, and cannot understand why anyone gets upset about topics that are not relevant to the decision. They tackle decisions in a detached fashion and tend to be objective and logical, rarely getting emotionally involved. They tend to assume that every problem has a correct answer, and their task is to figure out that answer. In contrast, Feelers believe that a good decision must take into account the feelings of others. They are driven by interpersonal involvement and tend to approach decisions subjectively, trying to incorporate all of the expressed points of view into a decision that everyone will find acceptable.

Even though they may go about it very differently, Thinkers and Feelers do not always end up in disagreement. Consider two managers in a company who were charged with deciding whether one of their subordinates should be promoted into a management position. Feeler may state this particular employee should be promoted because he works very hard and deserves the promotion. Thinker disagrees because he believes the employee should not be promoted simply because he works hard. Thinker does not disagree about the promotion, however, because he believes the employee would be the best person for the job. They disagree on

> Knowing your decision-making personality will help you to understand why you make decisions the way you do and will help you to work with others who make decisions differently.

how to make the decision, but they agree on the outcome. Although many of the MBTI personality categories are not related to gender, the Thinker/Feeler personality characteristic tends to be. Thinkers tend to be male, and Feelers tend to be female, which is not to say females do not think and males do not feel.

Judgers vs. Perceivers

The final personality characteristic influences how easy or difficult people find decision making to be. Judgers (J) are decisive and deliberate, and they reach decisions without much stress. They like everything organized and controlled, and they readily make the decisions necessary to achieve and maintain control. At their extreme, Judgers sometimes make uninformed and even indefensible decisions, just to have them off their agendas. Furthermore, they may find it very difficult to change a decision once they have made it, even an obviously bad one. Perceivers (P), on the other hand, do not want to be forced to make a decision. They like to keep their options open. Making decisions causes them anxiety. They prefer to take a wait-and-see attitude, deferring decisions until they have gathered more information. At their extreme, Perceivers are virtually incapable of making decisions, and make every decision more complicated than necessary. When a J and a P face a joint decision, it is often an exercise in mutual exasperation.

Applying Personality Types

At my consulting firm, PRTM, we used this personality type indicator both internally and externally. I had all of the firm's directors and many others take the type indicator classification test in order to determine their personality types. I put the results on a chart posted behind my desk and would refer to it often when working with directors, so I could better understand how they would approach a situation.

> The more you take your personality into account, the better you will be at making good decisions.

We also used MBTI with client project teams. We had all project team members classified, and then they discussed their styles at an early team meeting. This technique was very successful in helping the project team work through decisions together, because they could appreciate the differences in others.

The better we understand our personalities, and the more we take them into account, the better we will be at making good decisions. I am an ENTJ, for example, based upon the Myers-Briggs Type Indicator. Knowing this about myself has helped me understand why I make certain business decisions the way I do. It has also helped me to constantly improve my decision making. To help you achieve the same, think about yourself and the people with whom you make decisions in terms of these personality dimensions. If you do, you may be able to frame your choices in a way that is more agreeable to coworkers. At the very least, you will be a more tolerant and tolerable decision-making partner.

- Different people make decisions in different ways, but that does not mean one is correct and the other is incorrect.

- Understanding how your personality affects your decision making helps you make better decisions by yourself and with others.

- Knowing how your personality affects your decisions helps you figure out the strengths and weaknesses of your decision-making process.

CHAPTER 24

Making Successful Team and Group Decisions

*How to make the best team
and group decisions*

In businesses as well as other organizations, groups frequently make important decisions. The dynamic of the team or group adds another dimension to decision making. Team decisions can potentially be much more successful than individual decisions, yet they can also be mediocre or misdirected.

Decisions made by teams or groups are often better than those made by individuals, simply because the combined experience and brainpower of a team can trump that of one person. The additional viewpoints and collective experience help to clarify objectives, define better alternatives, assess potential risk, and evaluate alternatives. This is almost always the case when a decision is complex and requires broad experience.

In consulting to project teams I often used an exercise called "Lost at Sea" to show how teams make better decisions. In this exercise, each person is asked to decide and rank the importance of particular objects to take if forced to survive a sinking ship. Then they form teams, and the teams determine the rankings. Every time, the team ranking is better, according to U.S. Coast Guard guidelines. (For a more detailed description of this exercise, see *Decide Better! For a Better Life.*)

> **IN YOUR EXPERIENCE**
>
> *Have you ever wondered why some teams and groups make good decisions, while others don't?*

Group and team decisions can also be frustrating and slow, and lead to mediocre results. In my extensive experience with team decision making, I have found many people misunderstand practices and are ignorant about the way team and group decisions should be made. In this chapter, I share some of the most important guidelines for different group decisions and look at how successful teams go forward implementing consensus decisions.

Project Teams

A team is basically a decision-making unit. Businesses rely on project teams to make decisions on new initiatives and improvements. A typical large company could have hundreds of project teams at any point in time. The way these teams function determines how efficient they are and how well they accomplish their objectives. This chapter considers how the teams themselves function; section V looks more broadly at project decision processes.

Project Team Organization

Successful project team decisions start with properly organizing the team. Prior to the late 1980s, functional project teams were the most popular team model. In this model, different functions of a business delegated representatives to a project team. These team members represented their functions, but usually did not have the real authority to make decisions. Instead, decisions were usually made by the functional organization. Project team members were really messengers who went back and forth. When this model worked well, it was simply slow. When it worked poorly, project delays and inefficiencies were enormous.

In the late 1980s, along with Mike Anthony, I studied different project team models to determine which were better, particularly in making project decisions. We looked at projects with different teams for each phase, program coordination models, matrix organization-based models, and autonomous teams. In the end we concluded that what we called the "core team model" was the far superior project team model.

Figure 24-1 shows the traditional functional team project organization model. Project team members were assigned to represent their functional organizations, and their primary reporting responsibility was back to their functional organization. Any decisions had to be brought up a level or two to the functional manager or director and

Figure 24-1 The Functional Team Project Organization Model

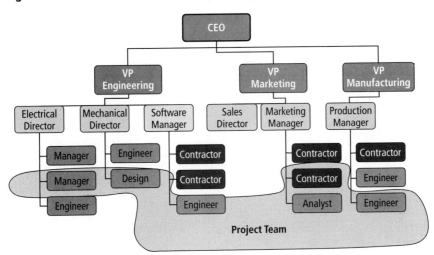

then passed back down to the project team. With this model, projects tended to move from function to function and back again. Decisions were frequently inefficient and frustrating, and much project time was wasted trying to make and reconcile decisions across functions.

The core team project organization model illustrated in Figure 24-2 is very different. A core team generally consists of up to 10 individuals with different skills and a core team leader. It does not use a classic hierarchical approach; hence it is illustrated by a circle. All project responsibilities and work are divided among the team members, with these responsibilities usually related to each member's skills. Recognizing the need to move away from vertical hierarchies, strict functional representation, and pay-grade-level politics, the core team structure is represented by a continuous circle. All team members are equal, and no function has more authority than another.

> Everyone on the team has the same objective, and they work together as a group.

The circle also emphasizes that everyone on the team has the same objective, and they work as a group. The full project team can be much larger than the core, and core team members frequently work with, supervise, or lead others outside of the core as part of the complete project. The team members are the core of the complete project team, and everything funnels through them. The core team has the primary responsibility for making project decisions. We will look at core team project organization in chapter 29.

Figure 24-2 The Core Team Project Organizational Model

I have seen many different models of project team leadership, and the following are the most prevalent ones:

- *Teams with strong project leaders,* who are fully in charge of the project, tell others what to do, and make all the decisions. In this model, the project team really functions as the staff of the project leader and is not really a team, even though it may call itself one. The decision process for this model is really the functional leader model.

- *Teams with confusion over project leadership,* where all team members collaborate, but nobody is in charge. Teams without a leader tend to flounder. Some of the small tasks, such as scheduling meetings, setting an agenda, and guiding discussion, tend to slow progress. Sometimes a very small team — three or so — can function without a formal leader if each member takes the initiative to lead from time to time.

- *Teams where each member is a leader of the area that he or she represents.* This approach is more of a delegate model than a project team.

- *Teams with collaborative leaders,* who keep the team on track and make decisions when needed, but encourage the team to function as one group. This is the best model for a core project team.

The core team leader is the hub of the core team. In my experience, the role of the core team leader varies in a subtle, but significant, way from that of a traditional project manager. The core team leader is more of a team captain than a part-time boss. The emphasis is on leadership, not control. A good core team leader motivates, inspires, and supports team members, and resolves issues and decisions when necessary. The core team leader is usually responsible for managing the project budget and schedule.

Guidelines for Successful Project Team Decisions

I have worked with project teams extensively over the last 25 years and have developed the following proven guidelines on how the most successful project teams work, especially in making decisions.

1. *Clearly empower teams with the decisions they should make.* The biggest confusion that project teams wrestle with is just what decisions they are supposed to make. A team must be clearly empowered to make specific decisions. Empowerment comes from the executive or executive team that initiated the team in the first place. Empowerment is discussed more in the project management section.

2. *Staff teams with the breadth of experience necessary.* In order to make successful decisions, project teams need to have all, or at least most, of the experience to make those decisions. This level of experience enables fruitful discussion and informed decisions. If the team is stacked with members having the same skills, discussion and solutions shift in one direction, which might not be the best direction.

3. *Make team meetings effective.* Teams meet regularly to progress toward the decisions they are empowered to make. Many times I have seen that the difference between successful and unsuccessful teams is the effectiveness of their meetings. An effective meeting is held on schedule, is attended by everyone, has a set agenda, lets everyone express opinions, and records action items and follow-up.

4. *Recognize individual experience and skills.* A team with balanced membership has a diversity of skills and experience. Successful teams take the time to understand each other's experience and turn to it during discussion. In some cases, members without experience on a particular decision defer to a member who has that experience.

5. *Train and facilitate teams.* Most teams are brought together for the first time when they are chartered to make a decision. Do not take it for granted that they will automatically begin to work together effectively. Companies with the most successful teams put each team through training, especially on how to make team decisions, before they begin to work together. Some companies also provide facilitation for the first few team meetings to establish the right pace and ways of working together.

6. *Commit to a common goal.* Successful teams work toward a common goal, not individual goals. They agree up front to this goal, subordinate individual goals to the team goal, and make decisions consistent with this overall goal.

7. *Have fun.* The most successful teams bond together and have some fun. This not only makes work easier, but also helps team members work together more effectively. Some bonding experiences include having team dinners, going out for drinks together, and establishing a team identity (team shirts and coffee mugs may seem trivial, but do work).

Boards of Directors or Trustees

Businesses are guided by a board of directors, and nonprofit organizations are guided by a board of trustees. I have had the opportunity to serve on many boards and consulted for countless others. The differences in their ability to make good decisions have been wide. Some are incredibly effective while others are amazingly dysfunctional.

Governance Responsibility

Boards are appointed with the governance responsibility to represent shareholders and, in the case of nonprofit trustee boards, to represent various stakeholders. The specific responsibilities of board members are set by the organization's bylaws, but generally include:

1. Provide continuity for the organization by setting up and maintaining the corporation or legal entity, and represent the organization's point of view.

2. Select and appoint a chief executive to whom responsibility for the administration of the organization is delegated, including regular performance review and evaluation. When necessary, the board is responsible for recruiting and appointing a new chief executive.

3. Govern the organization by broad policies and objectives, formulated by the chief executive and employees, including assigning priorities and ensuring the organization's capacity to carry out its mission.

4. Acquire sufficient resources for the organization's operations.

5. Account to the public for the products and services of the organization and expenditures of its funds, including providing fiscal accountability, approving the budget, and formulating policies.

Boards usually deal with relatively easy decisions such as approving the following items: bonuses, policy changes, the appointment of new officers, the auditors of the company, and the financial statements of the company. Most of the detailed work on these decisions is done in subcommittees that usually spend the time needed to make good routine decisions. Boards also make approval decisions on some major items, such as annual plans, but boards do not prepare the plan. The problems with boards come with nonroutine, difficult decisions.

Difficult Decisions

The difficult decisions boards face include the appointment of a new CEO, acquisitions or the sale of the company, major expansion investments, or new financings such as debt or equity. With these types of decisions, boards can become divided — even at the times when it's important for them to be unanimous. Chapter 7 presented the example of the indecisive board of directors that could not agree on a new CEO candidate. This is not atypical. Most boards are made up of experienced executives who have different backgrounds, so they look at situations, including the requirements for a new CEO, very differently.

> The problems with boards come with the nonroutine, difficult decisions.

Similarly a board may be faced with an offer to sell the company and have different views on the company's value, the most important terms of the sale, or how to negotiate. Discussion may take time, and usually out of respect for each other, all board members listen to each other's opinions. In the end unanimous agreement may still be hard to achieve. But these major decisions are the board's most important responsibilities.

Guidelines for Successful Board Decisions

In my experience, boards of directors or boards of trustees make more successful decisions if they follow these guidelines:

1. *Have the necessary experience for the decision and apply it appropriately.* Most boards strive to have broad experience among their directors just for these difficult decisions. If the board is missing specific expertise for the decision, it should employ experienced advisors. When making a difficult decision, you should be able to rely on other board members with the appropriate experience. For example, when dealing with a complex legal matter, I defer to a board member who has legal experience or one who has already been through a similar situation.

2. *Discuss objectives of a decision up front, and agree on the process and schedule.* As we saw in the earlier example, if there is con-

fusion over the objectives, such as the most important criteria for a new CEO, well-intentioned board members often come to several different recommendations.

3. *Be prepared for all meetings.* Critical decisions must be informed decisions. For complex board decisions, this requires, first, that the appropriate briefing materials are prepared. This may require presentations by management, investment bankers (in financial decisions), attorneys (in legal decisions), recruiters (in hiring decisions), compensation specialists (in compensation decisions), or consultants (in strategic decisions). Next, the board members must spend enough time to prepare for the meeting. This can be a challenge since most board members have full-time jobs and need to free up enough time for these major decisions. While most board members put in the needed time to be prepared, I have seen some board meetings where board members are totally unprepared.

4. *Have respectful discussion at all times.* A board needs to have an open and lively discussion to reach the best decision, but it also needs to be respectful. Where passionate differences of opinions exist on an issue, discussion can get heated. When this happens, board members tend to get more vocal and entrenched in their opinions. This situation can be exacerbated when a board deals with difficult issues, because meetings frequently need to be called quickly and usually go late into the evening to fit everyone's schedule — which adds stress for all parties involved.

5. *Keep the board focused on the decision.* In open discussion on major decisions, it is very easy for the conversation to drift off into different directions. The chairman of the board is responsible to keep the board focused on the decision, while at the same time allowing open expression of opinions.

6. *Determine the right voting process.* On most major decisions by a board of directors, a majority vote is sufficient, but there can be wrinkles. For a major issue, all board members need to be present at the board session to vote, because an absent director could change the vote. There may also be votes where one or more of the board members abstains either because of a poten-

tial conflict or for other reasons. Finally, on some major issues, it is best if the board is unanimous, and working toward that point is important. For example, the board should be unanimous in major personnel votes, particularly for CEO positions. Otherwise, friction could arise later if the CEO finds out that some of the directors voted against the executive.

Executive Committees

Many businesses use an executive committee (EC) made up of the senior VPs and CEO to make major business decisions, instead of having the CEO make decisions individually or each VP making decisions without the input of others. A typical EC meets regularly, such as every month or every few weeks.

Advantages of Decisions by Executive Committee

The EC format has many advantages. First, important decisions arrived at through the executive committee provide a more balanced perspective on the pros and cons. A typical EC includes a range of expertise in finance, marketing, sales, service, manufacturing, and human resources, which supports today's cross-functional business structure. Second, ECs avoid conflict over who has the authority to make decisions that affect many others. Finally, ECs can achieve unified agreement to implement decisions.

Guidelines for Successful Executive Committee Decisions

Some executive committees are successful in making very good decisions on a regular basis, while others tend to be argumentative and dysfunctional. Here are the guidelines I recommend to my clients for their executive committee decisions.

1. *Define rules of engagement.* These rules include how the EC works together, distributes materials in advance of the meeting, and listens and talks with one another. The rules also cover how decisions are made. Sometimes a unanimous decision is needed, other times EC members actually vote (although there are disadvantages to this), and on occasion the CEO makes the decision after listening to everyone's input and recommendations. The rules of engagement should be determined at the outset, not made up as they go along.

2. *Use the two-step decision process.* In chapter 9, I discussed the two-step decision process, which can be very effective for executive committee decisions. The key is to schedule decisions enough in advance to use it.

3. *Identify which decisions come to the EC.* Some decisions should be made by the individual VPs or their staff. Others are best made by the CEO. It is most effective to clearly define and schedule what decisions come before the EC. A good example of an appropriate EC role is the appointment of all new VPs, as this better ensures consistency throughout the organization.

4. *Require attendance, especially at critical meetings.* Depending on frequency and schedule, it may be difficult for all EC members to attend every meeting. I have found it is important to have them all there for critical decisions and use conference calls and mutual availability (i.e., late night) to facilitate inclusion. I recommend not allowing substitutes for meetings because they really do not have the authority for decisions, although sometimes I use substitutes as a training opportunity for those who are close to promotion.

5. *Agree to support all decisions.* One of the requirements I have is that whatever the decision, everyone has to support going forward with it. Buy-in and presenting a united front are the prices to being on the EC, which is discussed further in this chapter.

6. *Consider outside training and facilitation.* I have found that committees, especially critical ones such as an executive committee, benefit a lot from training. Hiring an outside expert to help define the way the executive committee functions and to provide training and facilitate a few meetings can be invaluable.

Other Decision-Making Groups

A wide variety of standing committees can be used to guide a business for areas such as sales, operations planning, and recruiting. These committees usually oversee standard operating decisions and make decisions on exceptions. For the most part, the decisions of these committees follow defined guidelines, but occasionally they need to make more difficult decisions, which is when problems often arise. As these occur, recognize them as more difficult decisions, allocate the time to make them, and work as a group to achieve the best decision.

A "task force" is a term sometimes used for a group formed to carry out a specific task or complete an objective. Although the term is borrowed from the military, where it defines a team on a mission, in business usage today a task force generally is a team used to investigate a problem and recommend a solution. It may or may not make the final decision. In general, a task force can follow the same decision guidelines that project teams use.

Strategic planning committees are similar in that they are usually chartered to make recommendations on strategy rather than make final strategic decisions. In this case, the group evaluates all of the alternatives to arrive at a recommended strategy. In this sense the committee goes through all of the decision process except that it does not provide the final decision. The failing I see in strategic planning groups is that they do not always perform the rigorous process needed to make the best recommendation. Instead many of them just share their creative ideas on a strategy.

Consensus Decisions

Consensus decisions can be powerful or they can be mediocre. Results really depend on two sets of motives: those for making a consensus decision in the first place and the individual motives of the participants. If the goal is to bring diverse knowledge, skills, and insights to bear, and if the participants all have the same goal — to arrive at the best possible decision — then consensus can produce excellent decisions.

But when consensus decision making is an attempt to satisfy everyone involved — or, more accurately, to placate everyone involved — then the process dissolves into a competition, often resulting in a worse decision than the best-informed person would have made alone.

I have seen firsthand how consensus decision making can lead to a terrible result. One company I worked with employed consensus decision making to determine the specifications of a new product for development. The engineering VP wanted to incorporate a hot new technology to make the product "edgy." The marketing VP wanted to include a long list of features from a major competitor's product. The CFO wanted some changes for the sake of cost reduction. Around and around they went.

In the end, they all got a little of what they wanted, but the result was a hopelessly compromised product. It was late to market because of the bug-infested new technology. Its performance was slow because the product was stuffed with so many features. The quality was second rate because of the penny-pinching.

We constantly see the downside of consensus decision making in the political realm. Every year, the U.S. Congress passes a series of spending bills that collectively become the federal budget. Too often, however, members of Congress support or decline to support a spending bill based on what is in it for them and their districts or states. They cram each bill full of spending for special interests, bloating the costs. If these provisions are stripped from it, members of Congress will oppose the bills. No wonder so many bills are little more than political bone-dispensing machines.

The problem is not that consensus decision making is bad. In fact, it can often prove to be very useful. The problem is that it is frequently misapplied. The goal is not to make everyone happy, but to arrive at the best decision based on the experience and talents of those involved. Over my years of consulting, I have found the following principles helpful in making better consensus decisions.

> Consensus decision making can prove to be very useful, but is also frequently misapplied.

1. *Understand what "consensus" means.* To reach a consensus decision means to reach a general agreement that a majority of the decision makers believe is the best to achieve the objective. A consensus agreement does not mean a uniformity of opinion or a solution that pleases everyone. The goal is to arrive at the best decision, not one that is acceptable because it satisfies everyone's personal agenda.

2. *Keep the decision group small.* Consensus decisions are practical only in a group of approximately four to eight. A smaller group than this may be easier to manage, but it may be missing expertise on some aspect of the problem to be solved. A decision complex enough to warrant a consensus process warrants a complete and well-rounded decision team. Loaded with too many participants, the group tends to become a debating society rather than a decision team.

3. *Pick the right people.* Skill, experience, and judgment are obviously important to the decision group, but so is compatibility.

A disruptive personality or several strongly clashing personalities can poison the process.

4. *Establish guidelines on the scope and process of the decision.* Groups that make effective consensus decisions usually establish operating guidelines up front. Agreeing on a few basic rules of the road can prevent accidents and traffic snarls. (The two-step decision process described in chapter 9 is highly recommended.)

5. *Realize that some opinions outweigh others.* Everyone's opinion should not be equally valued on every issue. Opinions of those who are more experienced or skilled in some issues should carry more weight. The process is not an exercise in democracy.

6. *Be prepared.* Each member of the decision-making group must get up to speed on the issues prior to the final decision meeting. If some members of the team do their homework, while others do not, conflict is inevitable. People with knowledgeable and carefully considered positions do not often take kindly to off-the-cuff opinions from ill-prepared participants.

7. *Apply consensus decision making to the right types of decisions.* Consensus decision making is more appropriate for strategic (what to do) than tactical (how to do it) decisions. It is particularly suited to "go/no go" decisions — for example, where a project team formally proposes a new product to a company's management and asks for permission to commence the design process. Group brainstorming should not be confused with consensus decision making. They are entirely different in both purpose and process.

> The dynamics of arriving at a consensus decision enable everyone contributing to the decision to own it.

The dynamics of arriving at a consensus decision do more than shape better decisions. They enable everyone contributing to the decision to own it — to form a commitment to the decision and its implementation. Consensus decision making is a very adult process. Unlike the political process, it is not about who gets what. It is about the decision group doing its collective best for the common good. Everyone, in the end, can live with the right decision because each person knows it has been reached after thorough consideration of alternatives, benefits, and risks.

Going Forward United

One of the most significant benefits of a group decision comes when the group implements the decision. If they are united in their commitment for implementation, it will alleviate a lot of potential problems.

Once a group reaches a decision, then everyone in the group must commit to following it. I have witnessed how a lack of this commitment too often undermines group decision making, particularly in business situations. For example, a CEO and his management team met regularly to discuss their opinions and reach necessary business decisions, allowing everyone the opportunity to present and discuss his or her views. There were always differing viewpoints from representatives of various departments. The perspective of the vice president of marketing was not the same as that of the vice president of manufacturing, and they were both different from the perspective of the vice president of finance. Sharing opinions was an important element of the decision-making process in this company because many decisions were difficult and required a broad understanding.

However, the process broke down after the decision-making meeting ended. Some of the participants would openly complain about the decision in hallways and at lunch with others, particularly those who reported directly to them. This only served to undermine the decisions the company made as a team, and it often prevented the decision from being successfully implemented.

A group decision-making process does not end when the decision is reached. It continues with unanimity of support behind the decision while it is being implemented. The price you pay for having a voice in a group decision-making process is a commitment to support the decision reached by the group. If you want to be involved in the process, you are responsible for the decision — like it or not. If you have reservations about the decision as it is being made, then you need to raise these issues during the discussion, not after it is over.

> The price you pay for having a voice in a group decision-making process is a commitment to support the decision reached by the group.

In this example, the lack of support for decisions eventually undermined the company's CEO, who was replaced. The new CEO set down his rules very clearly for his management team. "I want to hear your opinions on all major decisions, and I would like to get a reasonable consensus whenever possible. If not, then I will make the final decision. But once we make the decision, we all support it. I do not want any of you complaining about the decision, telling others you do not support it, or being critical of it. We need to be unified in implementing the decisions we make — even, and especially, the difficult ones. Now if you cannot play by these rules, let me know now and I will replace you." This clarification worked. Interestingly enough, other managers and employees felt like the new CEO made better decisions than the former one. In reality, however, he just made sure everyone understood the process and was committed to it before he began.

- Team and group decisions can be much better than decisions by individuals, but team and group decisions can also be mediocre decisions — or even bad decisions.

- Teams and groups should follow proven guidelines to be more successful.

- Consensus decisions can be powerful if they follow proven guidelines for reaching that consensus.

- One of the benefits of a team or group decision is united support when implementing the decision — a shared ownership of the decision.

CHAPTER 25

Shaping Decisions with Business Culture

*Strong corporate cultures influence
and bias decisions — good and bad —
throughout an entire organization*

An important factor that is often overlooked is how a company's culture shapes its business decisions. To some extent, the strength or weakness of the culture determines how much it shapes decisions. In strong business cultures, decisions are definitely shaped — good and bad — by the culture. A weak business culture may still influence decisions, but not to the same degree. By shaping decisions, I mean exhibiting a bias or tendency toward a particular decision alternative. In fact, in some cultures certain decisions become almost automatic.

Examples of Culture-Shaping Decisions

The best way to understand how a business culture shapes decisions is to look at some examples. I have chosen four examples: two showing how culture negatively affects decisions and two showing how culture positively shapes decisions.

Growth-at-Any-Cost Culture (Washington Mutual)[15]

Loan approval officers at Washington Mutual (WaMu) repeatedly approved bad mortgages for applicants who did not meet income levels or had unverified inflated earnings. These were not isolated cases; these approvals permeated the entire company from top to bottom with few exceptions. These decisions were not just tolerated, they were encouraged through incentives and performance reviews, starting with executive bonuses that were based on the volume of mortgages processed, not the quality of those loans.

WaMu initiated new mortgage products, such as option adjustable rate mortgages (ARMs), which encouraged — some say tricked — homeowners into loans for which the payments would increase after a couple of years to a rate the purchasers could not afford. The company frequently bundled and resold its mortgages in order to provide additional capital to make more mortgages and reduce its risk from the bad loans it made. The company has also been charged with providing incentives to brokers to pass along mortgages, even poor ones, and work with appraisers to be "flexible" on appraisal values.

> These systemic bad decisions were not a conspiracy; rather they demonstrated the way a strong business culture can influence and bias the way decisions are made.

These systemic bad decisions were not a conspiracy; rather they demonstrate how a strong business culture can influence and bias the way decisions are made throughout a company. In some cases, company culture can make decision bias almost automatic — with good and bad results.

WaMu's culture was aptly illustrated by the theme of its television commercial: "The Power of Yes." WaMu was obsessively committed to writing as many mortgages as possible. The more mortgages it wrote, the faster the company grew, the bigger the management bonuses were, and the faster the stock price rose. Employees were constantly encouraged and even pressured to write as many mortgages as possible, regardless of the quality.

To fuel the growth of mortgages even more, the company expanded the number of branch offices by 70% to 2,200. Rapid growth like this certainly has an impact on quality, but even more important was the overriding culture of accepting mortgages.

The WaMu culture permeated the decisions that lenders made on accepting mortgages. This culture is best expressed by an employee who said, "We were giving loans to people who never should have had loans. We were told from up above that that's not our concern. Our concern was just to write the loans." Mortgage loans were approved for millions of people who did not qualify. In many cases, the underwriters never verified the income claimed by those applying. Sometimes underwriters even approved mortgages without verification even though they doubted the facts on the application.

To further expand its business, WaMu decided to emphasize variable rate mortgages. Option ARMs became attractive because they carried higher fees than other loans and further increased WaMu's revenue. Its adjustable rate mortgage business increased dramatically from about 25% of its mortgages in 2003 to 70% by 2006. Within WaMu's culture, those who wrote the most mortgage loans were heroes. One broker wrote $1 billion worth of mortgages in 2005 and was called "the king of the option ARM."

To a large extent, WaMu's business culture was shaped by the terms of executive compensation. WaMu's CEO's compensation increased to $24 million in 2006, because his incentive was based on total mortgages approved without penalty to loan losses. This unbalanced compensation plan apparently caused him to push employees to write as many loans as possible without much concern as to the viability of those loans. In fact, the WaMu executives even excluded mortgage losses from their bonus calculations.

WaMu grew rapidly based on its loan aggressiveness regardless of quality, and this practice became ingrained in the culture from top to bottom. Incentive compensation was based on it. Recognition and status within the company were based on it. Promotion and performance reviews were based on it. The other lesson here is that rapid growth enables a culture to be created more quickly than it could with slower, more deliberate growth. If WaMu had not grown so fast, more than likely its culture could not have been transformed so quickly.

Cost Management Culture (Wal-Mart)[16]

Wal-Mart's business culture is as instinctively and reflexively frugal as Sam Walton was himself. Cost management became the very fabric of the way managers in the company made decisions. Every time they spent a dollar, they would think about how many dollars of merchandise they needed to sell to make that dollar back.

Cost management was reflected in the decisions on how the company spent, or refused to spend, money. For example, it required vendors to provide a toll-free telephone number or accept collect calls from Wal-Mart buyers. It measured its overhead fanatically and managed costs by the numbers. A store manager with a payroll of 8.1% instead of the 8% standard might be forced to transfer an assistant manager to another store to come back to the target cost.

When Wal-Mart makes store management decisions, the emphasis is on saving money. The stores are big, and not a lot is spent on making them attractive. The parking lots are big, making it difficult to get into the store. Wal-Mart puts skylights in many stores to reduce the cost of electric lighting. There is rarely help in the store available to answer your questions. It takes a lot of time to check out. But Wal-Mart's revenue per employee is higher than any other retailer.

Wal-Mart is renowned for its decisions on suppliers, forcing suppliers to sell at the lowest possible price, even with small margins. Wal-Mart also innovated many cost reductions. For example, in the early 1990s Wal-Mart decided to eliminate deodorant boxes and sell deodorants without their protective boxes. This saved about a nickel for every box no longer used and also consolidated shelf space.

Wal-Mart has always stayed true to its original core value — always low prices through its cost-conscious culture, which shapes its decisions. In this example, cost reduction and cost management decisions are almost reflexive. These decisions are put into the forefront of all decisions, giving them a higher priority than other decisions. The company culture also places a bias toward cost savings in all decisions.

Obsessive Sales Culture (Software Company)

The example of a software company that I used earlier provides another cultural perspective. The company emphasized sales, and while sales are important, extreme emphasis can distort a culture. This rapidly growing large software company established a strong sales culture, which was reflected in many ways.

Salespeople were glorified in the company. Good salespeople were rewarded financially, sometimes paid more than $1 million including commissions. They received many perks, such as generous expense accounts, reward trips to great locations, and recognition at company events. In general, salespeople ruled the company. The CEO came from a sales background and spent most of his time selling. Everyone in the company learned to respond to what the salespeople wanted.

The company invested more in sales, at the expense of other functions that were frequently understaffed. Competition among salespeople to outdo each other was fierce. This pushed the company to larger and larger sales. There was also a lot of pressure to close sales by the end of the quarter since a software company's sales can be shipped immediately for revenue recognition, and the company needed increasing revenue to justify its high stock market valuation.

This sales-dominated culture eventually had severe consequences. The enthusiasm for larger and larger sales led the company to sign contracts that it could not deliver on. In some cases, salespeople were able to make sales for products that did not even exist at the time (typically called "vaporware" instead of software). In these cases, salespeople, as well as the managers and executives, were influenced into making decisions shaped by the dominant sales culture. Others in the company, especially in the accounting and finance areas, were also swayed by the sales culture in revenue recognition decisions.

Eventually these sales-dominant decisions became increasingly aggressive and questionable. The company collapsed under the weight of these decisions and needed to restate almost $1 billion of revenue. The stock price collapsed and lawsuits followed, as did an SEC investigation. The board fired the CEO and VP of sales, both of whom eventually paid millions in fines to the SEC.

> Salespeople, as well as the managers and executives, were influenced into making decisions shaped by the dominant sales culture.

While dramatic, this example illustrates how the entire culture of a company can be dominated by one aspect at the expense of a more balanced culture. The underlying cause of these problems was not just a few people who acted improperly, or any conspiracy; it was a business culture that got out of control, eventually to the point of shaping bad decisions.

High-Performance Culture (PRTM)

This next example comes from the management consulting firm, Pittiglio Rabin Todd & McGrath (PRTM), that I founded and managed for 28 years. Right from the start the founders (myself and three others) focused on building a high-performance consulting firm. I am not sure that we did this intentionally; rather we just assumed that was the right thing to do. The philosophies we established along the way ended up becoming embedded in the strong PRTM culture. Eventually PRTM was recognized in the consulting industry as the highest-performing consulting firm with the highest profitability. PRTM exemplified how three aspects of culture — client results, productivity, and cost management — shape decisions.

We started out emphasizing client results, which was factored into almost everything we did. We used the saying "results not reports" in describing the firm. We only proposed on projects that delivered results for our clients, turning down work that ended in just a study (sometimes when we needed the work, this decision was painful). We promised results to our clients and were willing to be measured by them. In our recruiting, we only hired people we thought wanted to do results consulting, turning away some very bright people who went on to work at other firms. The emphasis on results eventually became part of our culture and shaped proposal, project management, and recruiting decisions. We did not need to discuss alternatives; the decisions emphasizing results shaped them.

The second significant element of the culture that shaped decisions was PRTM's emphasis on productivity. In consulting firms, productivity comes from high utilization of the consulting staff. At PRTM, we fanatically emphasized high utilization and regularly achieved 90%+ utilization when other firms were averaging 60% to 70%. The emphasis on utilization shaped many decisions, including how we proposed and managed projects, how we worked with clients, how we distributed bonuses, how we planned and measured performance, and how we scheduled staff on projects. After a while, decisions that emphasized utilization were ingrained in the culture.

The third element of the culture that shaped decisions was an emphasis on controlling costs. PRTM had the lowest overhead in the consulting industry. When it came to costs, our culture was stingy, which came from the early emphasis by one of our founders on cost management. Any expense, no matter how small, had to be approved in advance, and he did not approve anything. For example, people did not attend conferences that required travel. We placed offices outside of cities, where the rent was low, and the offices were not fancy. We applied this low-cost approach to client expenses as well, passing the benefit on to clients. This attitude was so ingrained in the culture that nobody spent money on anything. As an example, when a company asked us to visit and tell them what we could do, they had to agree to pay our travel expenses or we would not go.

It took a decade or more to build this culture, but it made many decisions efficient. Decisions were made a certain way just because we did it that way. It is also important to realize that these culture-based characteristics reinforced each other. You cannot build a culture with contradictory characteristics.

How Business Cultures Shape Decisions

These examples illustrate clearly how decisions can be shaped by a business culture. Let's look a little more at what I mean by "shaping decisions." A culture can shape decisions in several ways:

1. *A culture gives a priority to certain types of decisions.* Businesses have many opportunities that require decisions, and the priority of these decisions can be determined by the business culture. Wal-Mart's focus on cost-reduction decisions is a good example.

2. *A culture can determine the way decisions are made.* In the WaMu-example, decisions on mortgages were sloppy and aggressive, and there was not much concern for the details on a mortgage application or much concern about the validity of the data.

3. *A culture influences the alternatives considered.* When decision alternatives are considered, a business culture may exclude options that might otherwise be considered. The cost management examples in Wal-Mart and PRTM exclude high-priced locations for new stores or offices.

4. *A culture biases certain alternatives in a decision.* When decision alternatives are considered, certain criteria used to evaluate those alternatives are weighted in importance, either subconsciously or consciously. A business culture influences that weighting or bias. This was seen in the PRTM example on the bias in recruiting decisions to hire consultants who wanted to do implementation consulting and in the WaMu example on the bias to approve a mortgage no matter what.

5. *A culture can go as far as compromising business ethics.* In the cases of the software company and WaMu, decisions were influenced by the culture to the point where they crossed the boundary of ethical business decisions. Sometimes cases where a company crosses the ethical line are labeled as a conspiracy to do what is later seen as evil. However when seen through the lens of the business culture, it can be seen as more of an exuberance that went too far.

The broader issue of how businesses build cultures and why some companies have strong cultures is beyond the scope of this book, but I can offer a few observations. A business culture is formed as the company grows. I used to say a business culture is formed over time, but the software company and WaMu examples show that growth, not time, forms a culture. These examples also point out companies that grow rapidly risk creating a culture based on that growth — good or bad. I will not go as far as to say all companies that grow fast have bad cultures, for some companies with positive cultures grew fast.

Business cultures become strongly entrenched and are not easily changed. After PRTM, I led the turnaround at i2 and tried to introduce some of the PRTM culture, but attempts to change the culture in a short period of time were not very successful.

Incentive compensation practices, reward and recognition practices, and values are the biggest influences on a business's culture. WaMu's incentive compensation clearly biased decisions toward aggressively accepting mortgages at any cost. If executives were rewarded on the quality of mortgage loans and penalized for bad loans, I do not think WaMu's problems would have happened. At PRTM, all consultants were given incentive compensation for high utilization, reinforcing the culture of high productivity.

The reward and recognition practices at WaMu and the software company were instrumental in forming their cultures. Throughout the company, people were recognized for extreme sales and penalized for not achieving sales goals. Finally, values form a culture. Sam Walton's value of cost management clearly formed Wal-Mart's culture. At PRTM, the value placed on results for clients became well ingrained in the culture.

- Business culture can shape decisions – good or bad.
- Strong business cultures are more likely to shape decisions than average cultures.
- As was seen in the examples, a culture's impact on decisions can be profound – maybe even fatal.
- Rapidly growing businesses tend to also grow their cultures rapidly, but sometimes the culture is obsessed with growth.
- Other examples of a culture affecting decisions include a cost management culture, obsessive sales culture, and high-performance culture.

CHAPTER 26

Ensuring Organizations Make Decisions

*Organizations need to make
sure decisions get made*

An essential characteristic of successful organizations is making sure that all the right decisions are made. Successful senior executives, particularly CEOs, do not so much make all of the decisions as they ensure that other people make those decisions that are necessary. As the primary leader, the CEO must know that the most important issues are addressed and decisions are made at the right time and by the right people.

> Successful companies are decisive; they know what decisions need to be made when, and they make them.

Decision making can be defined and encouraged in an organization in different ways. We look at the following aspects of decision making in this chapter:

- Formal management processes define who needs to make what decisions, when they need to be made, and in some cases how they are made.

- Many decisions in a process are later embedded in automated systems that actually make routine decisions and flag exceptions for intervention.

- Leaders in an organization, especially the CEO, can foster decisiveness throughout the company in many informal and subtle ways.

- If there is confusion about who makes a particular decision, it needs to be clarified; in other words, who is the "decider"?

- Sometimes people need to be pushed to make decisions for their own benefit.

Successful companies exhibit decisiveness. While decisions are not always perfect, leadership knows when decisions need to be made, and makes them. This is done regularly through decision reviews and appropriate decision processes. Lately, companies that aspire to better decisions hire consultants for decision mapping to identify decision gaps and areas where decision making can be improved.

Decisions in Management Processes

Over the last decade, most companies have implemented new management processes and improved outdated ones. This includes a wide range of processes, such as sales pipeline management, order fulfillment, production scheduling, material acquisition, performance evaluation, product development, and recruiting. The fundamental objective of these management processes is to make better business decisions by (1) establishing consistency in decisions, (2) ensuring that decisions are not overlooked, (3) prompting decisions when they need to be made, and (4) putting decisions in front of the right people.

> The fundamental objective of management processes is to make better decisions.

A performance-appraisal process and schedule are designed to force managers to make decisions on salary increases for their employees. Without such a system in place, a supervisor could put off the review because so many other priorities seem to come first. Sanctioning this process and a schedule for reviews ensures that employees get the appropriate review and know when to expect it. The review process is a forcing mechanism because it mandates supervisors to provide a review of their employees' performance in writing and make a recommendation for salary increases and progression within the company. Regularly scheduled performance reviews make for happy and higher-performing employees.

In a similar way, the annual planning process forces decisions. For most companies, however, the focus of annual planning is on budgeting, not strategy, which is where companies are most vulnerable to overlooking or deferring strategic decisions. The most important element of annual planning should be strategic decisions. I am a big advocate of Peter Drucker's thinking, "Strategic planning does not deal with future decisions. It deals with the futurity of present decisions." Good annual planning processes include strategic decisions.

Management processes are critical to decisions, and better management processes drive better business decisions. Companies committed to excellence in their decisions continually make management process improvements. In section V, I look in detail at one such management process: the product development process. I compare the quality of decisions in an informal, inconsistent process to those made in an upgraded, high-performance process to show you that the decision benefits of the improved management process are enormous. I have found this to be the case in almost all management process improvement. Just remember to keep a focus on how decisions are made within a process, not just the processing of transactions.

Decision Making Embedded in Systems

Over time, some of the routine decisions in a management process get embedded in an automated system. For example, a material-requirements planning (MRP) system, using somewhat sophisticated mathematical algorithms, automatically decides what quantity of materials and parts need to be ordered and when. The system also alerts a purchasing manager, for instance, when a more difficult component reordering decision needs to be made. Prior to the advent of such systems, material planners had to make hundreds of material purchase decisions every day, frequently falling behind and making errors.

Successful companies continue to use automated systems for increasingly complex decisions. Optimizing supply-chain management decisions provides an example. When I was at i2 Technologies, we implemented complex, powerful systems that could process enormous amounts of data, which could not be done manually, to make optimization decisions, such as the best shipping routes or rapid changes in the mix of retail inventory based on daily consumer buying patterns.

Newly emerging decision analytics systems provide advanced analysis to help make decisions based on critical information that may not have previously been visible in the right form for a decision. A good example of this is Eidetics, which uses decision analytics to assess strategic alternatives for new pharmaceutical products.[17]

Routine systems, such as the MRP system, automate thousands of routine decisions, making them faster, cheaper, and more consistent than personnel could achieve. One word of caution, however: sometimes these systems fail and make bad decisions because the data they rely on have errors or because they encounter an unanticipated situation or new facts. More advanced systems usually present decision recommendations for managers to use in making decisions. The final decision maker needs to understand and agree with the logic behind the calculations, or a bad decision could result.

Fostering Decisiveness in Others

Decisiveness is not a universal trait in people or businesses. Not all businesses act decisively and opportunistically, but they can improve. Decisiveness can be enhanced in an organization in several ways. One way is through leaders who set examples, not only demonstrating decisiveness, but also using it as a teaching opportunity to explain why and how the decision was made. Leaders who provoke others to make decisions also can aid a company's decisive processes.

> Good managers should work to provoke decisions in those who work for them, their coworkers, and even their supervisors.

Management processes, as we saw earlier, encourage or even require managers to make timely decisions. A performance appraisal process, for example, could require all managers to submit performance evaluations for all their employees, along with a ranking of the top 10%, by a certain date. The process at least forces decisions, if not decisiveness.

Several ways are available to provoke decisions in those who work for you, those with whom you work, and sometimes those *for* whom you work. To encourage someone else to make a decision, sometimes you may simply challenge individuals: "Decide what you think we should do about this problem, and let me know by the end of next week what you decide."

Pushing coworkers and people who work for you to make decisions is an important leadership trait — perhaps even more so than making good decisions yourself. The lesson is that it is often necessary to push others to make decisions that they either are hesitant to make or do not know they need to make. This situation is quite common in the business world, where the consequences of our decisions are enormous, and the day moves so quickly that some decisions we face fall by the wayside.

In the best companies, decisiveness becomes culturally ingrained among everyone from the CEO on down throughout the organization. Some of the best companies also invest in decision skill training to help improve decisiveness throughout the company.

Clearly Identify Decision Makers

All too often, decisions can be delayed or ignored because of confusion over who should make them and when they should be made. For example, a major electronics company identified an exciting new market opportunity and launched a team to develop a product to take advantage of this opportunity. Soon after the project started, however, it began to drift. Several important design alternatives were identified, but precious months slipped by with no decision as to which design the company should use to proceed. Later, another delay of several months occurred due to the lack of a decision regarding initial functionality of the first product release. In the end, the actual decisions were unimportant because the delay in making them proved to be fatal to the project's chances of success. A competitor beat the company to the market opportunity, so the company never released its product. If someone had just pushed the company to make these decisions, the company could have increased its profits significantly. Instead, someone who worked for their competitor was successful in provoking the decisions that ultimately led to the competitor reaping the profits.

> **IN YOUR EXPERIENCE**
>
> *Have you ever seen confusion over who is supposed to make a decision?*

Many companies have solved this problem by using management processes to trigger important decisions such as these. Over the past decade, for example, most companies have implemented a phase-based decision-making process to force "go" or "no go" decisions at clearly defined phases of product development. The process identifies who is responsible for making these decisions and when they make them. Simply correcting this decision-making deficiency can take a third of the time out of a company's development cycle. It also creates a new respect for senior management: "They sure know how to make the difficult decisions!"

Another concept is one I call the "decider" (after President George W. Bush, who pointed out that he was the "decider" on the war in Iraq).

When there is confusion over who is supposed to make a decision, designate a decider. A group could agree that one of the members is the decider for a particular decision, or an executive could appoint someone to fulfill the role. This alleviates all confusion as to responsibility. Sometimes as CEO, I would pick someone on my staff and say, "You are the decider. Let me know what you decide." It was a great way to cultivate decision-making skills in others.

Pushing Others for Their Own Benefit

Sometimes people do not even get around to making a decision that is in their own best interest. During such instances, you just need to push them to make it. For example, a major manufacturing company offered a very attractive 401(k) plan for its employees — full matching payments into the benefits system up to $25,000 per year, something few other companies offered. For years, only a very small percentage of the employees took part in the plan, and executives were hoping to increase participation as a method for employee retention and recruitment. After studying the reasons for non-participation in the plan, it was clear that employees were interested in participating; they simply did not take the step to actively file the forms required to initiate their participation.

Considering many different options for increasing the percentage of employees who took advantage of this benefit, the executives decided that they would provoke their employees into making this decision by simply pushing them to participate. Rather than requiring them to file a form to trigger their involvement — including taking 2.5% of each paycheck and depositing it into the account — they began automatically enrolling employees in the program, letting them opt out if they really did not want to participate. Amazingly, almost all employees continued their participation, and virtually all of them expressed how excited they were with the amount of money they were now saving. Simply provoking employees to make this decision, which they otherwise put off as not being important or pressing, led to many more of them making the better decision.

Decision Mapping

One proactive way that businesses are improving business decisions is called decision mapping. Decision mapping is essentially a diagnostic to examine an organization's decision effectiveness. It maps decisions made (and those overlooked), who makes them, and how they are made. It looks at decisions made in management processes and information systems. It examines nonroutine decisions such as strategic decisions, planning decisions, and project decisions. Finally, the decision-mapping process entails interviews with managers and executives to understand where there are decision problems and how decisions can be improved.

The result of a decision mapping exercise is a decision improvement plan including training, process and system improvement plans, and clarification of decision authority through policies and practices. In some cases, the decision culture is also evaluated. Decision mapping can help companies improve the quality of their decisions, avoid missed decisions, and reduce bad decisions.

- The ability to provoke decisions in others is an important characteristic of successful business executives.

- You should be able to provoke decisions in those who work for you, your coworkers, and even those you work for.

- Many companies provoke their employees to make decisions by instituting decision triggering mechanisms, including pushing them, encouraging them, and forcing them to make decisions.

- Successful companies are decisive; they may not always make perfect decisions, but they know when decisions need to be made, and they make them.

CHAPTER 27

Recognizing Political and Bureaucratic Decisions

"The essence of ultimate decision remains impenetrable to the observer — often, indeed, to the decider himself. . . . There will always be the dark and tangled stretches in the decision-making process — mysterious even to those who may be most intimately involved."

— President John F. Kennedy[18]

In 1971, Graham Allison published an insightful book, *The Essence of Decision,* which examined the different decision processes behind the Cuban missile crisis. His goal in writing the book was to understand why the Soviet Union and the United States made the decisions they did throughout the crisis. More specifically, he wanted to understand why the Soviet Union decided to place offensive missiles in Cuba, why the United States responded to the missile deployment with a blockade, and why the Soviet Union decided to withdraw the missiles.

In his thesis, he notes that most analysts explain decisions made by governments by considering that each government acts as a unitary, rational actor. As he notes, "Predictions about what a nation [or company] will do or would have done are generated by calculating the rational thing to do in a certain situation, given specified objectives."[19] In other words, governments theoretically act rationally by weighing the circumstances of their current situation and making a decision that maximizes their objectives. Allison did not believe this was always the case, however. He went on to state, "Although the Rational Actor Model has proved useful for many purposes, there is powerful evidence that it must be supplemented by frames of reference that focus on the governmental machine — the organizations and political actors involved in the policy process."[20]

Understanding that decisions are not always rational, Allison explained the decisions of the Cuban missile crisis as having been interpreted through three different models: the rational actor model, the organizational behavior model, and the governmental politics model. This chapter examines the differences in these three models and how they exist in an organization at the same time. The most important lesson you can learn from this chapter is that you cannot assume that businesses — and decision makers within all levels of business — are always going to make decisions in a rational manner.

The Setup

A mid-sized company was in the process of a deal to be acquired and merged into another, larger company. The executives of the mid-sized company and its board members weighed in on the acquisition very early in the process. Steven, the CEO and chairman of the board, attempted to navigate the entire process, negotiating the needs, wishes, and advice of each senior member of the company. It seemed that everyone from the largest shareholders to the COO and CFO had their own ideas about whether the acquisition would be in the best interests of the company.

Upon carefully reviewing the details and recommendations of the various individuals who had major input into the acquisition, the CEO was faced with a decision: whether to recommend some sort of acquisition for the company, or whether to recommend the company hold off on any negotiations and continue operating on its own. While performing this review, Steven realized clearly that there was no uniformity in the advice he was given. His job as CEO was to do what was best for the company, but not all of the advice was necessarily equivalent, nor was it all based upon what could be considered best for the company. But he still had to make a decision, including how to navigate all the advice he was given. While the decision was not his alone, his opinion and recommendation on whether to pursue being acquired and what course to pursue in this regard would certainly be given the most consideration when it came time for the decision.

Rational Actor Decisions

Under the rational actor model, governments — and, in our case, businesses — are considered to act like unitary, rational actors. These units, rather than making a decision based upon the individual actors involved in actually making the decision, are theoretically aligned and make one single unified decision based on the company's own self-interest. Under this model, the company looks at a decision, examines the various options, and evaluates the pros and cons of each of the options. It weighs the factors that can be used to make the decision. Then it comes to a rational decision based upon what is best for the company in terms of its short- and long-term interests. In Allison's words, "Rationality refers to consistent, value-maximizing choice within specified constraints."[21]

> Under the rational actor mode, businesses are considered to act like unitary, rational actors.

If this theory were to be taken as given, Allison believed that the Soviet Union placed short-range nuclear weapons in Cuba because the United States called them out on not having as many nuclear weapons as they had claimed. Upon learning of the placement of the missiles, the United States made the decision to blockade Cuba after evaluating a full range of options, ultimately selecting the blockade because it pushed the actual decision about confrontation onto the Soviet Union. The Soviet Union then evaluated its own options in response and, based upon a cost-benefit analysis, realized that its best option was to remove the weapons from Cuba. Both sides made their decision based upon a completely rational evaluation of their respective situations, including the ramifications of selecting a specific option.

In respect to the situation Steven faced regarding the company being acquired, were the decision to be made in a rational actor model, there would be no question about what course to take. The company, acting as a single unitary actor, would make a deal to be acquired at or above a specific financial level, whether that be in terms of cash or stock for current shareholders. Acquisition simply made complete sense in terms of better performance and return to the shareholder.

Organizational/Bureaucratic Decisions

According to the organizational/bureaucratic decision-making model, governments and businesses do not act as one single actor, but rather break down their decisions by department. In this model, relevant components of a decision are assigned to the specific department that handles that specific part of the decision. In government, this approach specifically is important when it comes to a major crisis. When a government faces a crisis, under this model the leaders who are responsible for determining what course of action to take do not look at the problem as one complete problem. Rather, they assign portions of the problem to varying departments within their bureaucracy. Allison describes this well:

> For some purposes, governmental behavior can usefully be summarized as action chosen by a unitary, rational decision maker: centrally controlled, completely informed, and value maximizing. But a government is not an individual. It is not just the president and his entourage, nor even just the presidency and Congress. It is a vast conglomerate of loosely allied organizations, each with a substantial life of its own. Government leaders sit formally on top of this conglomerate. But governments perceive problems through organization sensors. Governments define alternatives and estimate consequences as their component organizations process information; governments act as these organizations enact routines. Governmental behavior can therefore be understood, according to a second conceptual model, less as deliberate choices and more as outputs of large organizations functioning according to standard patterns of behavior.[22]

Following Allison's examination of the Cuban missile crisis, the organizational/bureaucratic model can explain the decisions made by each side in the crisis. According to this model, the United States was able to learn of the existence of the short-range missiles placed in Cuba because of the fact that each department within the Soviet military carried out procedures that were the same as those carried out by the military for facilities within the Soviet Union proper. Not taking proper steps to customize their nuclear facilities to the Cuban situation enabled the United States to spot the missiles. In response to these missiles, the United States decided to pursue a blockade because it had only considered to select either that option or air strikes. The air strikes were not selected because they were not determined to be accurate enough to destroy all of the missiles without extensive collateral damage. The navy was much more well-equipped to undertake a blockade; therefore, it was selected for the solution. Being provided with the requirement to make the next move, the Soviet Union simply did not have an accurate response available to any of its components, therefore requiring it to remove its missiles.

In a business, this process operates in much the same manner. Looking back at the business example, Steven, the CEO, had solicited opinions as to what key company individuals and board members thought about the ability to be acquired and under what terms and arrangements such an acquisition should be pursued. The inability of the company to act as a single, unitary actor as in Allison's rational actor model was clear to Steven almost immediately. One example of how that came into play was related specifically to the finance department. Steven had requested a detailed report and recommendation from the CFO about the possibilities for acquisition. The CFO presented him a report that strongly recommended against any acquisition of the company, which was a little confusing to the CEO because the potential financial gains in the report were tremendous, and the recommendation to not proceed with the acquisition did not seem to be in line with the data presented in the report.

> According to the organizational model, businesses do not operate as one single actor, but rather break down their decisions by department.

Upon a more thorough discussion with the CFO, the CEO clearly understood other factors were in play here. The entire finance department had severe reservations about the acquisition, not on its own merits, but because the department knew it was highly likely that it would be merged into the finance department of whichever company undertook the acquisition. This merger would mean a loss of control for the department, and a finance department recommendation to proceed with the acquisition would be a recommendation to dismantle itself and render its entire purpose moot.

Governmental/Political Decisions

Organizational models and rational actor models are not the only ways to view how major businesses and governments make decisions. Allison proposed a third model: the government/political model. This model is largely based upon the theory that statesmen and stateswomen make decisions based upon the negotiations conducted among top leaders. While some of the leaders within a government may share some of their goals, they often differ in how to pursue those goals, often for personal reasons. According to this model, the makeup of the top leader's entourage has a large effect upon what decision is ultimately made. The interests, beliefs, and interpretations of the members of the leader's key staff not only shape how the decision is made but also how it is implemented and whether it is followed correctly.

As Allison notes,

> The leaders who sit atop organizations are no monolith. Rather, each individual in this group is, in his or her own right, a player in a central, competitive game. The name of the game is politics: bargaining along regular circuits among players positioned hierarchically within the government. Government behavior can thus be understood according to a third conceptual model, not as organizational outputs but as results of bargaining games. Outcomes are formed, and deformed, by the interaction of competing preferences. In contrast with [the rational actor model, this model] sees no unitary actor but rather many actors as players: players who focus not on a single strategic issue, but on many diverse intranational problems as well; players who act in terms of no consistent set of strategic objectives but rather according to various conceptions of national, organizational, and personal goals; players who make government decisions not by a single, rational choice but by the pulling and hauling that is politics.[23]

This model also can be used to explain what decisions both sides made in the Cuban missile crisis. According to Allison, Khrushchev's power was particularly threatened because the United States pointed out the dearth of intercontinental ballistic missiles and because of the Berlin airlift success. In addition, military leaders were displeased that Khrushchev had reduced the size of the military, and the economy was faltering. He needed to act quickly to regain his power, and placing these missiles in Cuba was a quick and inexpensive method for achieving that. In responding, congressional Republicans were preparing to use the issue of Cuba as a major policy difference in the 1962 elections. Kennedy therefore decided on a national security response rather than an ambassadorial one. Debates continued between the members of the executive committee (EXCOMM) the president created for the crisis, with each member voicing individual opinions about which option to select. These were often based upon their own background, experiences, and interests. For example, the air force kept pushing the strategic air-strike option. Ultimately the blockade option was selected because of the specific combination of opinions. Khrushchev attempted to recover the situation by looking for an agreement to remove American missiles from Turkey, but ultimately decided to remove the missiles from Cuba after a public promise by Kennedy not to invade Cuba and a private guarantee to remove the missiles from Turkey months later.

Returning to the business example, as the CEO examined the process of working toward a potential acquisition, it became clear to him that much of the advice he received was political. Some of the members of the board supported an acquisition based upon the details of the package, but also based upon other considerations. Each of the board members personally held different stock positions in the company. Some bought their stock many years ago and had the opportunity for a large gain. Others had only recently purchased stock and would only have a small gain. A few purchased stock at the peak of the market for a price greater than the selling price, so they would see a loss. Each of the directors also had different liquidity interests in selling the stock.

> While some decision advisors may share the same end goals, they may vary widely in the methods to take to achieve those goals.

The COO was looking out for the good of his employees as well, knowing full well that many people would be laid off were the acquisition to go through without certain guarantees for key personnel. The CFO was concerned he would lose his job and someone else would be given the credit for the acquisition. He knew the CFO of the new company would be likely to assume the top finance position. Each of the key political players within the company had the CEO's ear. The top executives and the members of the board essentially represented a similar function to President Kennedy's EXCOMM; they were the CEO/chairman of the board's top advisors.

- Decisions are not always made using the same model, and quite often you can examine a particular decision using multiple models.

- Not all decisions in business can be described as having been made using the rational model.

- According to the organizational decision model, businesses do not make decisions as one single actor, but rather break down their decisions by department.

- Under the government/political model, businesses make decisions based upon the negotiations conducted among top leaders.

- While some decision advisors may share the same end goals, they may vary widely in the methods to take to achieve those goals.

SECTION V

Project Decisions

Projects are essential to all businesses and organizations. They are used to create and launch new services and products, build and expand facilities, formulate process improvements, create new advertising or marketing campaigns, make investments, and explore changes in strategic direction, to mention a few examples.

While projects are very important to the success of an organization, I have found that projects often take longer, cost more, and fail to deliver the best results — and this failure is more often than not due to flawed project decisions. Project decisions are unique. Rather than single decisions, projects are actually a series of different — but related — decisions that occur throughout the project. Better project decisions lead to better project results, yet despite the importance of project

---

Project Decisions Are Different from Operational Decisions

- Projects involve two layers of decisions: high-level decisions to authorize the project, and project management decisions.

- Projects are not repetitive; project decisions tend to be made uniquely for every project.

- With projects, less opportunity exists for improvement by learning from mistakes. Projects evolve as the work progresses toward completion, and as the project evolves, the types of decisions change.

---

decisions, most organizations fail to apply the right combination of processes, techniques, and skills to make project decisions properly. There seems to be an assumption that everyone involved somehow knows how to make appropriate project decisions. This is rarely the case, so focusing on how to improve these decisions is critical.

This section explores the unique characteristics of project decisions, defining typical failures of project-related decisions and the impact they have. Section V defines the four aspects of project decisions and the correct way to make these decisions.

Research and development (R&D) and product development are among the most important types of projects in business. Each year corporations and organizations throughout the world invest $200 billion in R&D. Outstanding R&D projects make companies successful, while project failures can have detrimental impacts. In the late 1980s, R&D was transformed by new approaches to project management, most of which focused on improving the way project decisions were made. The impact was dramatic. By the end of the 1990s, benefits from these improvements in project decisions were benchmarked in excess of $75 billion per year. In other words, companies saved or made more than $75 billion every single year by focusing on how to make better project decisions.

The best known of these new decision methodologies was called PACE (Product And Cycle-time Excellence), which I created at my management consulting firm, Pittiglio Rabin Todd & McGrath. More than 1,000 of the largest companies in the world have successfully implemented the PACE decision process to transform their project decisions. In this section, I introduce project decision techniques through a PACE case study, illustrating the before and after of project decision making at a typical company. After the stage is set for how improved project decisions transformed R&D, I explore the four aspects of project decisions in subsequent chapters.

- *Who* — First, I will look at who makes project decisions, which is frequently where the confusion begins. Chapter 29 defines the differing responsibilities for strategic project decisions and project management decisions. Strategic project decisions are used to (1) initiate a project; (2) continue, cancel, or refocus the project at each phase; (3) approve the plan for the next phase; (4) fund and provide resources for the next phase; and (5) empower the tactical project decisions. I then examine decision authority for project management decisions, paying particular attention to the decision confusion between project teams and functional organizations.

- *When* — Chapter 30 defines when decisions are made during projects. This chapter introduces the importance of a phase-based decision process, where phases progressively define the major work on a project and different decisions are made at the end of each phase. Chapter 30 illustrates phase definitions across a variety of projects, and provide an example of when decisions are made.

- *What* — Next it is important to understand what decisions are made at the end of each phase. The fundamental decision is to decide among three options: continue the project, cancel it, or redirect it. But the key to making these decisions, as explained in chapter 31, is defining the right questions to ask at the end of each phase.

- *How* — Section V concludes with a look at how decisions are made at each phase. Chapter 32 explains specific best practices for making great project decisions.

CHAPTER 28

Setting Amazing PACE®

"PACE was the most important management improvement ever in the history of DuPont."
— Charles Holiday, chairman and CEO,
E. I. DuPont, September 22, 1999

A company that designed and manufactured communications equipment, which I will call Dynamic Global Communications (DGC), was excited about its latest new product development project, *Maverick*. Everyone thought *Maverick* would be a big success. Development was launched initially with a $10 million estimated investment, and the CEO told the board that it would be ready for market launch in 18 months. While it was one of 25 product development projects within DGC, *Maverick* had the most visibility, funding, and attention.

Two and a half years and $25 million later, *Maverick* was almost a year from being ready and DGC's competitors had by then introduced several similar products, already reducing DGC's potential market share. And this was not the only disappointment at DGC in its research and development (R&D) projects. When I came in with my consulting firm to assess the problem for the board of directors, the diagnosis pointed directly to flaws in project decisions for new products.

To start with, nobody at DGC knew who was responsible for approving a new product development project. We interviewed 40 managers and executives, and most had a similar response: "I have absolutely no idea who makes that decision." Others identified specific executives, but none of the same names were mentioned twice. In tracing the history of recent projects, most just seem to have started in some mysterious way, and eventually people began working on them and called them projects.

This lack of knowing who made decisions to initiate projects certainly points to a fundamental decision gap, let alone indicating a serious void when making more advanced decisions on priorities among alternative product opportunities. The CEO responded to the question on responsibility for this decision as follows: "That is a good question. It probably should be me, but I don't recall formally making these decisions. Perhaps this is a big part of our problem." It was, but it was not the only problem.

The decision on what resources were allocated to specific projects seemed to be made by the developers themselves or by managers fighting over scarce resources. "We make the decision by working on the projects we are interested in doing," was stated more than once. Everyone recognized this problem and complained about it, but nobody was able to fix it. "Nobody can make decisions around here," became a regular complaint. In some cases, the opposite was true; sometimes multiple managers thought they had the same decision authority and argued about who had the right to make decisions, particularly specific product design decisions. There were frequent disagreements on the decision authority of the project teams versus department managers. Resolving these disputes required executive arbitration, necessitating meetings of multiple VPs to fight for their group's point of view.

All of this led to an odd decision structure — what I refer to as an *inverted decision pyramid*. Top executives, who were supposed to set the strategic direction for the company, were involved late in the development process, arbitrating disputes on detailed project decisions. Yet they were not involved enough at the beginning of the development process where the strategic decisions were made.

We also found there were no formal approval points or hurdles throughout the project to make a decision to continue or cancel the project. Once a project was started, it continued indefinitely until it was deemed to be completed, or until people lost interest and it simply died from lack of attention. As one executive described it, "Because of this, our product development pipeline is bloated in the middle like a big bubble where everything sits, and new products do not so much get launched as they escape."

Yet another decision problem related to when decisions were made. When an early project review was held, one of the executives would say, "I need to see a physical prototype before we approve doing this project." Then another would say, "How can we approve this without a complete market study?" A third would state emphatically, "We need to have the complete software architecture done before we proceed to develop it." By the time all of their requests were satisfied, half of the cost of the project was already invested. Then they would find that it did not make sense to develop it at all — which they could have figured out without all this additional work, and canceled the project a year earlier, saving $5 million.

Finally, DGC did not know how to make project decisions. Too many meetings were wasted discussing projects without making any decisions. There was no structure or purpose for many meetings.

Overall, DGC paid a considerable price for its project decision problems. The company wasted millions of dollars annually on projects that could have been canceled or refocused much earlier. Even more important, it took the company much longer to complete new products than necessary. The opportunity cost in terms of lost revenues was estimated to be more than $100 million annually.

Although striking, the project decision problems at DGC were far from unique at the time, and unfortunately these problems still remain at many companies today. We corrected these problems at DGC using PACE — a decision process that was subsequently implemented at more than 1,000 other large global corporations. But first, a little background.

PACE®

Back in 1987, I was studying the management of research and development (R&D) and product development in the high-technology industry, as part of my responsibility to lead the strategy for my consulting firm, Pittiglio Rabin Todd & McGrath (PRTM), and to identify opportunities for major management breakthroughs for our clients. It became apparent to me that significant opportunities existed for managing R&D more effectively and efficiently. Most new product projects were late and over budget, and a company never had enough resources to do everything it wanted. Moreover, the benefit of improving time-to-market in technology-based industries with short product life cycles was enormous because it meant increased revenue from new products.

Working with several initial clients, we developed the management process and practices called PACE (Product And Cycle-time Excellence). PACE initially included three primary new management practices:

1. A phase-review process for project approval decisions
2. Cross-functional project teams for making decisions within the project
3. A structured development process to consistently guide projects

PACE introduced extraordinary management changes, most significantly by dramatically altering the way project decisions were made. At its foundation, PACE was a revolutionary new way to make project decisions. Let's use the DGC case to illustrate how PACE works. The process and benefits were similar in hundreds of other companies.

Phase Review Process at DGC

The first change we undertook at DGC was to implement a *phase review process*. This new management decision process required project approval decisions at each phase of a project, based on specific criteria for completion of the previous phase and preparedness for the next phase. The authority for making these "go/no go" decisions was clarified with the establishment of a new cross-functional executive group, typically referred to as the product approval committee (PAC) or something similar.

Each phase review decision was made promptly at the end of the phase, as opposed to being made periodically or when the executive team got around to it. This schedule helped to establish a cadence for each project and set deadlines for the phase approval decisions. This change alone began to accelerate new product development.

> The phase review process established a cadence for each project and set deadlines for phase approval decisions.

Phase review decision deadlines, set by standard, significantly compressed development cycles and helped reduce development costs. These deadlines also put the appropriate amount of pressure on the project team developing the product. Work had to be completed within a specified, but reasonable, period of time. Previously, project teams had a tendency to complete most of the work in the last two weeks leading up to the deadline — no matter how much time was allowed.

With the new phase review process, DGC began to make decisions progressively by phase. Here is an example.

- *Phase 0 (Feasibility)* — The question answered was, "Does this product look like it could be financially viable?" Concerns and issues were examined a little more closely, but the question was answered based on common sense and experience.

- *Phase 1 (Planning)* — "Do we expect that this product will be financially viable?" Now the question was answered based on the results of a rough design and high-level planning. High-level financial estimates were used to answer the question, but these were all based on rough projections.

- *Phase 2 (Design)* — At this point, the product was designed and ready for development. Product cost estimates could be made much more accurately and enough marketing work had been completed for reasonable revenue estimates. So the question at this phase was, "Is the ROI on this product sufficient?"

- *Phase 3 (Development)* — At this point, the product was actually developed from the design and ready for launch. Now the question was more of a validation: "Is the projected ROI still acceptable?"

- *Phase 4 (Launch)* — Prior to officially launching the new product, DGC held a final phase review to make sure the product was sufficiently completed, tested, and ready to be sold. Here the question was, "Is the product ready?"

By making progressive decisions, DGC cut its losses earlier with less wasted investment, canceling or redirecting projects with the minimum investment lost to that point. Prior to the implementation of a phase review process, DGC wasted 22% of its R&D budget on products that were not released. With the new decision process, this figure was reduced to 5%. Since it invested a little over $100 million a year on R&D, improved project decisions saved them approximately $17 million per year, which it reinvested in developing more products, effectively increasing its R&D productivity by 17%.

Project Management Decisions

We placed the authority to make all project management and development decisions with the cross-functional project team, which we called a "core team." This team typically consisted of four to eight dedicated managers or developers who represented the critical range of expertise needed to develop the product. At DGC, the typical core team consisted of a manager from these areas: electrical engineering, mechanical engineering, software, marketing, finance, manufacturing, and quality. One of these was designated as the *core team leader,* who had overall responsibility for the team.

The core team's authority to make these decisions came from the PAC when it approved the next phase of the project. The team was authorized to make all the decisions needed to develop the product as presented to the PAC, according to the approved plan and schedule, and within the resources approved for that phase. In other words, the decision authority of the team was empowered by the PAC within specific, agreed-upon constraints.

While on the surface this step seems obvious, it was a significant shift from what was previously done at DGC and virtually all other companies at that time. In most cases, project team members were simply designated representatives of the various functions within the company. The decision authority remained with

> The decision authority for the team was empowered by the PAC within specific, agreed-upon constraints.

the functional managers who made the decisions from their functional standpoint across all projects. This approach to decisions had two problems. First, the functional managers were not close enough to the details of most projects to make informed decisions, which resulted in too many poor decisions. Second, they usually made decisions based on their own functional bias. Electrical design decisions were based on the bias of the electrical design manager. Mechanical design decisions were made based on the best interests of the mechanical design department. This held true for every department. The resulting products were hopelessly compromised and quite often disappointing in the marketplace.

In many cases, these individual functional designs conflicted. To resolve these conflicts, decisions were escalated to the company's VPs, who then were put into the uncomfortable position of battling to defend their functions. For the most part, the VPs were even further away from the details of the new product and even less likely to see what was best. In many cases, the CEO needed to arbitrate a decision. As a result, too many detailed design decisions were being made by executive management, who were not as qualified as the department engineers. This was a poor use of executive time, not to mention the fact that it ended with poor decision making.

PACE® at DuPont[24]

In the late 1980s and into the 1990s, DuPont implemented PACE throughout most of its divisions. At DuPont, PACE was a highly structured process for making decisions on what products to develop and where to allocate resources. While varying some by division, this process involved several aspects.

The process unified management decisions through a formal program approval committee (PAC) in each division, which was composed of the business leadership responsible for managing product development activities. The PAC held decision-making meetings at key milestones (phases). These decisions required either a decision to continue through the next phase (Go) or a cancelation (No Go) decision. In some cases the PAC could also offer a redirect to change the project direction. The structure of this decision authority was a major change for DuPont, which previously relied on individual project sponsors to push a project through to completion.

Because the PAC had clear authority to allocate resources at these phase reviews, the decisions it made were fully implemented throughout the company. Resources were available as promised, and potential roadblocks were removed before they became serious. With this new process, DuPont divisions tackled fewer projects than before because they were more focused. But because the resources were available, they were able to cut development times in half.

The project teams at DuPont were relatively small multifunctional teams (typically four to nine members), called "core teams." The teams were typically formed in the beginning of a project and stayed together for the entire project. Most important, the PAC empowered these core teams with the decision authority for the next phase of the project. In other words, their decision authority for the project was generally greater than that of functional groups within the company, making decision authority clear. DuPont also defined a standard process for the ways these core teams worked together and trained them extensively on how to make project decisions. All of this paid off as the teams functioned at a high performance level.

The benefits of the PACE decision process at DuPont over a wide range of products was considerable. Product development cycle times were generally improved by 30% to 50%, enabling DuPont to increase revenue by bringing more new products to market faster. In one DuPont business, for example, revenues from new products soared from

5% to more than 75% of total business revenue. Overall, the revenue increase for DuPont attributed to the PACE decision process was very significant.

By making clear decisions earlier in the product development cycle, DuPont focused its R&D budget on products that were viable, rather than wasting funds on projects that would never be completed. This change allowed the company to invest more in products that came to market, significantly increasing R&D productivity.

Years later, on September 22, 1999, at a CEO luncheon, I had the opportunity to speak again with Charles Holiday, the chairman and CEO of DuPont. He recognized me as the creator of PACE and shared with me that "PACE was the most important management improvement ever in the history of DuPont."

PACE® Benefits

Overall, the PACE process was implemented in more than 1,000 major corporations to improve their R&D project decisions. In addition to DuPont, some of the biggest and best companies in the world used PACE: most divisions of IBM, Xerox in conjunction with its transition to digital copiers, Merck, NCR, Autodesk, Dow, and BBN.

The results at the companies that implemented the PACE decision processes were impressive:

- Almost all companies reduced new product development time by 50%.
- By bringing products to market faster, most companies achieved significantly increased revenue from new products.
- Project costs were typically reduced by more than 25%.
- The amount of the R&D budget wasted on projects that were never completed dropped significantly. Typically, companies lost more than 15% of their R&D budgets on projects that were never completed; with PACE this was typically reduced to 3% to 4%.
- On a qualitative basis, project decisions were made with much more confidence and significantly less turmoil.
- Many companies reported that they developed much better products.

Unfortunately, some companies that improved project decisions with PACE have slipped back to some bad habits, losing the crispness of project decisions. They and other companies can benefit from reviewing the project decision basics discussed in this section.

PACE®

- Project authorization decisions by an executive product approval committee (PAC)
- Phase-based decision process
- Go/No Go decisions at the end of each phase
- Progressive decisions at each phase
- Empowerment of a core project team to make project management decisions within a phase

CHAPTER 29

Clarifying *Who* Makes Project Decisions

Defining who makes project decisions includes determining the authority for authorizing new projects and selecting the decision authorities of project teams

The problems of project decisions often begin with confusion over who makes the decisions. As you can see in the three examples that follow, without a clear definition of decision responsibilities, poor project decisions are likely to occur.

The administration of a college planned to build two new dormitories to expand residential housing capacity to keep up with its growth in enrollment. The VP of students decided on the specifications for residential facilities that he believed would provide the best learning environment, as well as safe and comfortable living conditions. He studied recent construction at other colleges and came up with what he called "the best of the best, something we can be very proud of." The VP of operations, who was responsible for construction, worked with the architects to design the building to those specifications. They made many decisions on the design to be sure that it was attractive from the outside and fit "the feel of the campus." Then they put the design out to bid and decided on a contractor, and while not the lowest bidder, the company was proven, reliable, and easy to work with. The VP of finance decided how to fund the project.

As a formality and as required by the college bylaws, the project came to the college's board of trustees for approval. Each of the three VPs made their presentations: the building would be great for the students, looked beautiful, and was financeable with debt. Everyone thought it was a no-brainer until one of the trustees asked some questions. "How much was it going to cost, and how many students would it house?" The answer was a full cost of about $18 million and it would house 200 students. The trustee pointed out that equaled $90,000 per bed. Then he asked how much it would cost annually for the interest on the debt, depreciation, maintenance, and other costs. The VP of finance estimated about 10% of the building cost, or about $9,000 per year per student. "How much do we charge for housing?" After a few minutes the VP of finance estimated about $6,000 per student for room and board after deducting the other costs for food and so forth. "Are we OK with subsidizing student housing $3,000 per student every year from tuition?" the trustee asked.

After some discussion, the board decided it would not approve subsidizing housing, and it directed the VPs to redesign the building, keeping costs closer to $60,000 per bed. This decision kept students paying the full cost for their housing without requiring any subsidizing by the college. This example illustrates a typical problem of project decisions. Because there is no permanent project organization, project decisions tend to get made functionally and sequentially. Everyone makes decisions they prefer based on their experience, focus, and interests. They are not being evil or deceptive; they are just using their own experience base to make project decisions that should be made cross-functionally, with broader expertise. It also illustrates another problem with project decisions: it is often unclear who has the final approval authority. In this case, did the board of trustees really make that decision, or was it reviewed with them as a formality?

> Because there is no permanent project organization, project decisions tend to get made functionally and sequentially.

Similar problems occur time and again in product development projects. Here is an example at TG Electronics. The VP of marketing identifies a market opportunity and decides that a new product could be very successful, so his team develops the requirements for the product and then passes it to the engineering VP to design. He makes design decisions for a terrific product, using advanced technology. The VP of manufacturing makes decisions on how to build the product and how much it will cost. Finally, the VP of finance decides on the price for the product so it will provide sufficient profit margins, and the VP of sales decides on a sales forecast that he is willing to commit the sales force to sell. When you put together all of these individually good decisions, you end up with a losing product: one that is too expensive for customers, costs too much to produce, and fails to meet sales requirements.

Similar to the DGC example discussed earlier, when I interviewed the executives and key managers at TG Electronics about project decision making, another problem became apparent: nobody knew who in the company had the authority to initiate new product development projects, and nobody knew who approved development. Some looked back at how projects got started and could not figure out who approved the initiation. When we got into the discussion, others expressed frustration about low-priority projects that were started because they were some manager's pet project, while other, more critical projects never got the necessary resources. The only correlation was that managers with resources (people and budget) were able to decide what projects their people worked on.

The impact of this confusion was severe. New products did not support the company's strategy, and it lost ground to competitors, despite outspending them in research and development. Investments in product development were very inefficient due to this lack of process control for making good project decisions.

Without a clear project decision process, effective leadership is difficult, if not impossible, as demonstrated in a story told to me by the CEO of a consumer products company. The CEO was frustrated with his inability to implement his company's innovation strategy through R&D projects. He awoke one morning full of enthusiasm and a renewed desire to lead innovation in his company. He knew that innovation leadership must be more than arbitrating disputes between functional managers. That morning he spent time in the lab with the engineers and designers. They enjoyed his attention and the pizza he bought for lunch, but the CEO did not feel he had made much headway in resolving problems. Next he went to marketing to look at market research and was inundated with so much data that he took some home to review. As a result of these meetings, he decided to call for project reviews of all projects.

> Without a clear project decision process, effective leadership is difficult, if not impossible.

All 14 project teams scrambled to pull together status reports and presented them a week later. Each presentation was different, making it difficult to analyze the material, but each had one common element. Every project team asked for more resources. In the end, the frustrated

CEO realized he really did not know how to lead innovation in his company.

Issues with *Who* Makes Project Decisions

These examples are not unique; they illustrate characteristics that many companies experience with unclear project authorization decisions. While there are a range of issues related to unclear project decision authority, there are three primary problems:

- *Decision-making authority as part of the traditional functional organization structure does not work effectively for project authorization.* This is usually why the sum of what appeared to be functionally good individual decisions in the college and product development examples cited earlier resulted in combined bad decisions. Due to the predominance of the primary functional organization, project decisions are distorted because most assume that decision making works within the functional organization, even when it does not.

- *Unless there is clear responsibility for who initiates projects, then the wrong projects will inevitably be initiated, while the more important opportunities may be overlooked.* Strategically critical projects can be overlooked or not funded while pet projects with a lower strategic priority are funded. In some cases, functional managers with the resources really make the strategic decisions regarding company investments, instead of the executive team responsible for implementing the company's overall strategy.

- *Unless clearly defined, project management decision authority can be confused.* Members of the project team and functional managers may argue about who has decision authority or who is to blame for a bad decision. Executive management can sometimes get involved in making decisions that should be made by the project team when functional managers bring them to executives for resolution. On the other extreme, the project team may overstep its authority, making decisions that exceed project authority or compromise company policies.

Levels of Decisions

A useful approach is to separate project decisions into two levels. At the highest level is the authority to make decisions to initiate, fund, approve, and cancel projects. I refer to this as "project authorization decision authority." A company's strategy is executed by initiating and funding projects. For large projects, authorization decisions are usually made by the CEO, executive team, a portion of the executive team designated with this responsibility, or the board of directors of an organization. For smaller projects, typically the senior executive who has the responsibility and resources for the project makes the call. Because of the strategic importance of large projects in some companies, it is the board of directors' responsibility to make sure these decision authorities are clear.

Figure 29-1 illustrates the levels of project decision authority. In this example, an executive team called a PAC, as discussed in the previous PACE examples, has the project decision authority. The PAC makes its project decisions at the conclusion of each phase, using a phase review process, which we look at in the next chapter.

The next level of project management decisions are those decisions related to management of the project itself. In this figure, this is referred to as a core team. These include decisions made by the project team as part of its work on the project. In construction projects, project management decisions would include design and architectural decisions, contractor selection decisions, and budget and spending decisions. In product development decisions, these include product specification, design, development, and launch. In process improvement projects, these decisions include identification of process issues and improvements to the process. In a marketing project, they include the focus and content of advertising and promotion programs. While the team has the primary authority for these decisions, some of the decisions would be subject to approval by the executive or management team with the overall project authorization responsibility. Generally, this approval is most effectively given in clearly defined phases, as described in subsequent chapters.

Project management decision authority also includes the decisions related to project management, including project planning, meetings, project staffing, and spending within the approved budget. Issues about how the project team makes these decisions — specifically who in the project team makes these decisions — are detailed below.

Figure 29-1 Project Decision Levels

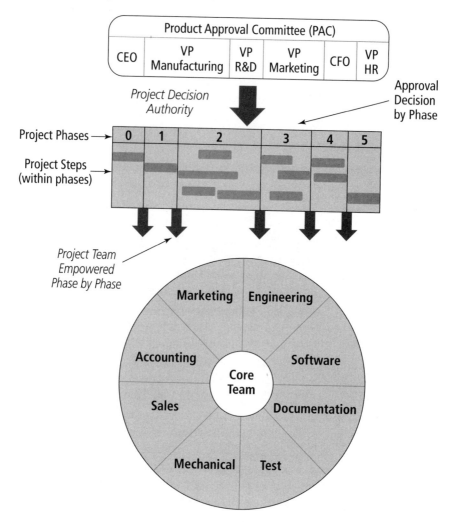

The link between these two levels is the empowerment given to the project team by the authorizing decision authority. This empowerment of decision authority supersedes the authority of the functional organization for this particular project. In other words, this new organization for this particular project supersedes the traditional organization of the company. Without this empowerment, the project team would be subjected to being pulled in multiple directions by the traditional functional organization.

Project Authorization Decisions

Who has the authority within an organization to initiate and fund new projects? That is the fundamental project authorization question. It can be the leader of the organization — the CEO, president, or general manager. It could be a group of top-level managers. It could even be a functional VP in some cases. For large projects that require cross-functional resources, such as product development, I recommend an executive team. Typically, this small team would consist of the CEO/COO/GM, VP of marketing, CFO, and VP of operations.

BBN Communications, for example, formed a product review board (PRB) consisting of the president and the VPs of manufacturing, development, and marketing. The PRB reviewed development projects at the conclusion of each phase and determined whether the project should continue (Go/No Go). The PRB reviewed projects thoroughly at each phase review, and then made its decisions in closed session, canceling some projects and redirecting others. The executives gained much greater confidence in their project decisions through the thoroughness of this process.[25]

In the college example discussed at the beginning of this chapter, the college formed a construction approval committee (CAC) for all construction projects over $1 million. The president of the college chaired the committee, and the three VPs, as well as the provost, made up the committee. Based on the success of this decision process, the college later made other major project decisions, such as IT improvements, through this committee. Academic decisions remained with the college's academic community.

The executive team with the project authorization decision authority, or the executive in the case of a single decision maker, is usually given specific authority to:

- Initiate major new projects of a specific type, such as product development in the case of BBN Communications and DGC, and construction projects in the college example
- Cancel projects if they fail to achieve the expectations of each phase
- Redirect projects with new objectives or a new scope, if necessary
- Ensure that approved projects fit the organization's strategy

- Approve the budget for the project and allocate necessary resources
- Approve the project plan for the next phase
- Make decisions to reprioritize one project over another
- Empower the project team to make decisions between phases

When you look at the significance of these project authorities, it becomes clear that these decisions are best made by a cross-functional executive team at the highest level of the organization. The first step we took at DGC was to clearly define who had the authority to make decisions on whether to initiate a new product development project. While the ultimate responsibility rested with the CEO, there were many benefits to having the senior executive team collectively make these decisions. So we formed what the company called a product approval committee (PAC) that consisted of the CEO, CFO, VP of engineering, VP of marketing and sales, and VP of manufacturing. The PAC was specifically authorized to approve and prioritize new product development investments. While this now seems obvious, the formal clarification of this decision authority significantly transformed the organization and was the starting point for an entirely new management decision process.

Tips for Defining Authority for Project Initiation

- Understand the types and nature of projects within the company and define the authority to initiate and oversee them.
- Projects that require resources across functions are best approved by a cross-functional executive team.
- Smaller or routine projects may be exceptions to the formal project decision process.
- Where projects are repetitive, it usually makes sense to define a standard decision process for everyone to follow.
- When an executive group is making project initiation decisions, it should define the way members interact, run their meetings, and reach a decision.

Because the PAC is a decision-making group, it should remain small. Four to five executives is an appropriate size, but some organizations may prefer a larger team. Other senior managers may be invited to attend the decision session but do not participate in the final decision. This became the new approach at DGC, and we defined how the PAC should reach a decision and took them through a day of training in decision-making techniques. We then facilitated their first three phase review decision sessions, helping them to get into the mode of working together to make decisions. The change in this company was remarkable. One manager commented that he "never realized that the senior executives could actually make decisions." The problem previously was not that they could not make these decisions; it was that they did not know that they needed to, and as we will see, they did not know what decisions to make and when to make them.

At DGC, as was the case in almost all other companies that implemented this phase-based decision model, the executive team canceled or redirected most of the first few new product opportunities they reviewed. The CEO commented after the first three project decisions, "Today we saved almost $15 million! Previously we would have let these projects continue, and then they would die after a few years when we spent millions of dollars on them."

Empowerment

Empowerment is a powerful way to delegate decision authority, especially for project decisions, but empowerment is sometimes misapplied. One consultant stated that true empowerment is when the project team can do whatever it wants, spend what it needs, and complete the project whenever it will. This is *not* the interpretation of empowerment used in this book.

In project decisions, the group or person with project approval authority (such as the PRB or PAC in the previous examples) grants the project team specific decision authorities at each phase of the project, giving the team authority to make the decisions that take it to the end of the phase, but not beyond. Typically, these empowered decision authorities include:

> Empowerment is a powerful way to delegate decision authority.

- Deciding how to use the approved resources (usually the purview of the project team) to accomplish what was planned

- Making the project decisions necessary to achieve the objectives of the next phase, within the objectives previously proposed and approved

- Investing the project budget approved to accomplish the project objectives

Note that the empowerment is granted within the context of the approved objectives. For example, the dormitory construction team is empowered to design a new building within the financial constraints of $60,000 per bed, the project schedule to complete construction is as proposed, and the design budget is not to exceed the amount approved.

Project Management Decisions

In the college dormitory project example, the board of trustees was able to see the problems that occur when project decisions are made sequentially by a functional organization. Another way this can be manifested is through conflict between the project team and functional organizations. Without clear decision authority, conflicts that arise regarding project decisions can delay projects and take them off course.

TG Electronics, not surprisingly, also had problems with confusion over project management decisions. One project exemplified these problems. The project team leader and the engineering manager argued over product specifications, each insisting it was his decision. The manufacturing manager and the project team disagreed over components specified in the product. The marketing manager and the project team disputed product pricing. Each of these arguments escalated to the VPs for arbitration. The result of this was a weird decision structure. The strategically critical decisions on which projects to invest in were made by lower levels of the organization based on the personal preferences of the managers who had the resources, while the specific detail design decisions were made by the senior executives only because they were forced to arbitrate the conflicts between the project team and the functional organization.

Once the team is empowered to make project management decisions, the focus then turns to how the team itself makes decisions. There are several ways to define decision authority within the team. One decision model is to have the project manager make the final decisions — the *authoritarian model*. Another model is to disperse decisions among team members, with each member making specific decisions — the *populous model*. The third is to form a small team that has the authority to make project decisions collectively — the *core team model*. For most large projects, this last model works the best. I discussed project teams more closely in chapter 24.

TG Electronics corrected its problems by implementing a core team model. Figure 29-2 illustrates the way project teams worked previously. The original team "organization structure" looked like a spaghetti chart, with everyone directly and indirectly on the team communicating with all others and making decisions independently and, in some cases, differently and inconsistently. When they actually mapped the way that project decisions were made, as illustrated in the simplified version in this chart, it was surprising that any decisions were made.

Figure 29-3 illustrates the new core team structure that TG Electronics implemented. The core team consisted of the project manager, a marketing manager, a financial analyst, an engineering manager, and a quality analyst. Collectively they made project decisions, meeting weekly to manage the project. Each of the core team members in turn had the responsibility to oversee the work of various people in the company who worked on the project. As illustrated in Figure 29-3, the team

Figure 29-2 Previous Project Team Organization

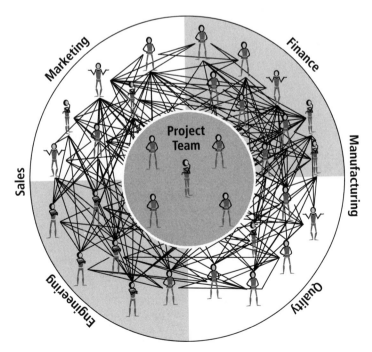

members had different ways to integrate the full team working on the project: a traditional functional organization, several external people directly assigned to the project, or a sub-team assigned to the project. The work of the full team involved in the project was pulled together and integrated by the core team through its project decision authority. The improvement in execution by the core teams at TG Electronics was so great that it achieved a reduction in project completion time of more than 30% and budget reductions approaching 20%.

Figure 29-3 Core Team Organization

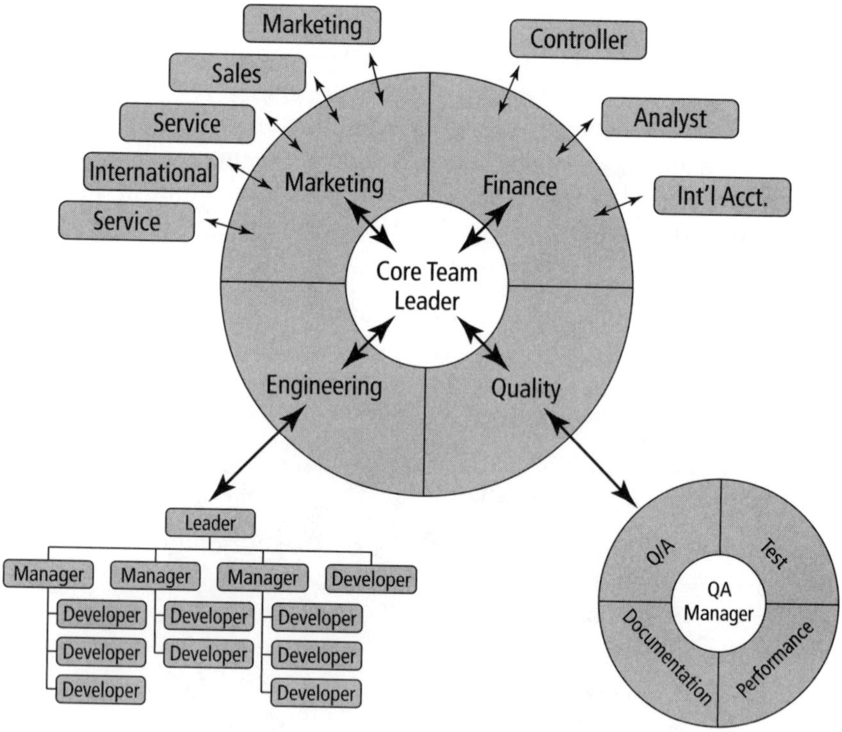

Organizational Decision Authority vs. Project Decision Authority

Changing the responsibilities for project decisions can essentially be a massive reorganization of responsibilities and authority. Many large companies have organization charts that go down to seven or more levels. Organizational decision authority moves down and back up these organizational levels very slowly.

With the project decision process of authority described here, organizations are essentially compressed to two levels: one for project approval and one for project management. The initial model for this organization structure was venture capital funding, where funding decisions are made at one level and the company develops its products with that money. While in many large companies this involves a massive reorganization of authority and responsibility, the key to implementing it is to do it subtly.

If we had advised a large multinational company to reorganize its seven-level organization into two levels for project decisions, one to authorize and approve the project and the other to make all of the specific project decisions, they would have laughed hysterically at the impossibility of implementing such a dramatic change. By focusing on making this change outside of reorganizing the traditional organization of the company and only utilizing it for project decision making, companies could find the ability and the will to implement the new approach. Empowerment by the higher level is what defines the decision authority of the project level.

- Without clearly defining who makes project decisions, you should expect many problems.
- There are two levels of project decisions: project authorization and project management.
- These two levels are linked through the empowerment of the top level to the next level.
- Small core teams are generally the most effective model for project management.

CHAPTER 30

Defining *When* Project Decisions Should Be Made

Project decisions should be made phase-by-phase as the project progresses

Another cause of poor project decisions comes from when they are made. One mistake is making the authorization decision for the entire project at the project's inception. The other mistake is not knowing when to make what decision, incurring too much advance work before making basic decisions. The two following examples illustrate these decision-timing problems.

In addition to confusion over who made project decisions, Dynamic Global Communications (DGC) also had a problem understanding when to make project approval decisions. As we saw in the *Maverick* project, even though it was expected to cost $10 million and be ready for market in 18 months, work continued long after that time frame. In the end, it took two years longer than projected and cost $30 million to complete. Moreover, by the time the project was completed, it was no longer competitive. How could this happen?

Without a formal decision process that required approvals at critical points in the project, the assumption was, as one engineering manager explained, "Once started, projects are approved for whatever it cost and however long it took." On *Maverick*, like other similar projects, cost overruns and delays occurred for many reasons. One delay occurred because critical resources were unavailable when needed (software resources were unavailable because of turnover, and testing resources were unavailable because of conflicts with testing other products) and because the software development work grew more complex than originally planned. Project costs increased substantially because the software development requirements were underestimated, and, since the project took longer, new improvements in technology necessitated hardware redesign. Once a project takes longer than expected, costs inevitably escalate.

DGC also had the opposite problem when it came to when to make project approval decisions. Typically, groups of executives and managers gathered to discuss the merits of a new product and inevitably set higher and higher requirements for supporting a new product. An example of this was its *Neptune* project. The team presented the project opportunity, and one executive said he needed to see a prototype first, so they built a prototype. Then another said he needed to see a detailed market and competitive study, so they spent six months doing a detailed study. After that, another executive said she needed to see the complete software architecture, which took another six months to complete. After a year and a half and wasting $5 million, everyone realized this product did not fit the company's strategy. Unfortunately, by point TG Electronics was well into development work. Had the company looked at strategic fit initially, this decision could have been made in a month at a nominal cost.

Issues with *When* Project Decisions Are Made

When project approval decisions are not made at the right time, the cost of wasted projects is much higher. For example, DGC estimated it wasted 22% of its total R&D budget on projects that were never completed or brought to market, much more than the 2% to 5% wasted by other companies that had much better project decision-making processes. For DGC, this savings was approximately $17 million annually.

In addition to the basic problem of failure to make any decisions, two major issues occur with project decision timing:

- *Launch and forget* — Many companies simply make a decision to launch a project and then let it go until completion or until it loses momentum. Executives lose the opportunity to keep projects on course, and all too frequently projects drift out of control.

- *Putting the cart before the horse* — In many cases, too many decisions are made at the beginning of the process, causing too much project work to be done before the project is evaluated and a Go/No Go decision is made. This results in much more squandered project investment than is necessary.

Phase-Based Project Decisions

Project decisions are best made phase-by-phase as the project progresses, with early-phase decisions used to help weed out poor projects early in the process before investment increases. A good phase-based decision process enables canceling or refocusing a project at the earliest possible point, saving money and time that would have been misused, and helping to prioritize the right projects.

Figure 30-1   Project Decisions Phase-by-Phase

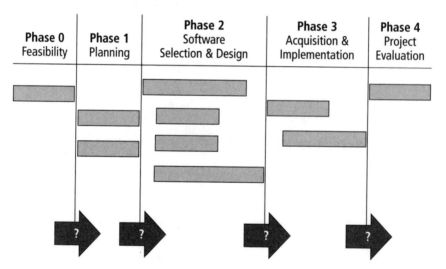

The information technology group in a large insurance company had just implemented a phase-based decision process for all major IT projects. The company spent about $30 million annually on new software systems, including implementation costs. Its new project decision process is illustrated in Figure 30-1. Project approval was required at the completion of each phase, prior to the start of the next phase.

- *Phase 0 (Feasibility)* — In this phase, the feasibility of a new system is evaluated, so the focus is on whether it would be a good investment. A typical feasibility phase involved only a few people working part time on the project for two to three months, so the investment was minimal. Only a rough project budget is used to estimate the cost since the objective of this phase is quick screening. Typically, half of the projects were approved in this phase, and the other half were deferred or rejected. Approved projects progressed to the next phase.

- *Phase 1 (Planning)* — In this phase, the company formed the core project team that created a more detailed project plan. At this point, the project plan included estimated software acquisition costs, the implementation schedule, implementation resource requirements, and a more accurate assessment of benefits. At the end of the phase, the project came back to the IT project approval committee (IT/PAC) for approval of the next phase. Generally 75% to 80% of the projects were approved at this phase, and the rest were deferred or rejected.

- *Phase 2 (Software Selection and Design)* — Most IT systems for this insurance company used acquired software, so the primary work of this phase involves solicitation of proposals from software vendors and evaluation of those proposals. The output of this phase is a recommendation for software acquisition. The project team recommendation goes to the IT/PAC for approval at the end of the phase. Approval at this point means the commitment for investing most of the project costs since the software license and the implementation costs are typically 80% of the project costs.

- *Phase 3 (Acquisition and Implementation)* — The new software is acquired and implemented in this phase. At the end of this phase, the team goes back to the IT/PAC for approval that the project is complete. While this may seem like a formality, it was not, because there were always a number of new features that users wanted, so disagreement occurred over when the project was actually complete and when maintenance began.

- *Phase 4 (Project Evaluation)* — This was a new phase added to the original phase-based decision process to evaluate the success of the project. The project team, along with key users, performs a postmortem evaluation in this phase to judge the success of the project and lessons learned for potential implementation in subsequent projects. This phase review was done six months after project completion.

Let's look at how this phase-based decision process worked for a recent IT project at this insurance company. The project was a new business intelligence (BI) system, which included several capabilities:

- *Revenue and Expense Planning* — Revenue forecasting would enable forecasting new and renewal premiums and exposure, as well as policy cancelations and lapses. Expense forecasting included commission calculations, total policy acquisition costs, and expense ratios.

- *Claims Planning* — Claims planning would enable planning for gross and net claims estimates, cost recovery, claims handling expense, reserves estimates, loss-ratio calculations, and evaluation of prior year claims.

- *Project Planning* — Project planning would provide analytical assistance in identifying new product or service opportunities.

- *Business Segment Reporting, Analysis, Dashboards, and Scorecards* — This feature would provide executives and managers with performance information on business segments and products, including revenue, claims, and segment profitability.

This new project was approved at the end of Phase 0 and moved into Phase 1 since it projected favorable benefits relative to the anticipated software costs. But when it came to the Phase 1 review decision, there were some significant concerns. First, it would be expensive to integrate the BI system into other applications in order to extract the data in real time, as required by the BI system. Second, the BI system necessitated several management process and organizational changes in order to be effective, and these would be difficult to implement. Third, there was mixed support for the new system. Some managers were threatened by it since it would report their performance "around them" instead of going through them — a cultural change for the company. Finally, the benefits, while potentially high, were very soft in that they were conditional on the new system identifying business strategy changes.

At this point the IT/PAC canceled the project because of the additional complications relative to the potential benefits. The CFO praised the phase-based decision process, noting, "Prior to this new decision process, we would have initiated this project based on preliminary evaluation, but it would have failed. We would have spent more than $4.5 million on software we probably would never use and, even more importantly, it would have disrupted the company while we were trying to implement it."

The *when* in project decisions is determined by the definition of the decision phases for the project. While some projects are unique and phases need to be defined individually at the initiation of the project, most projects fall into categories where common phase templates can be applied. The next section looks at some of these phases.

Decision Phases in Different Types of Projects

The most important reason for defining a phase-based decision process is making easy decisions early in the project before committing the majority of the project expenses. Here are some examples of decision phases by type of project:

Advertising Program

Advertising programs generally have two major expenses: the cost of advertising production and the cost of placement in publications or on the air. For this reason, the early phases are most important. But there are also two major decision points in the process. In some cases, even though an advertisement might be produced, it may be a waste of money to pay for placement. (See chapter 4 on throwing good money after bad.) Here are the typical phase decision points for an advertising program:

- *Phase 0 (Evaluation)* — The purpose of this initial phase is to evaluate the rough financial feasibility of an advertising program, before completing design work and planning the media placements. Financial estimates are generally based on experience instead of price quotes. If the benefits are not worth the estimated cost of the program, it should be canceled or redirected at the conclusion of this phase.

- *Phase 1 (Campaign Planning)* — The advertising campaign is planned in more detail in this phase, including themes, approach, potential media, and more accurate cost estimates. At this point, preliminary budgets and quotes are used to estimate the investment, and forecasted increases in sales are used to estimate the benefit. Sometimes several alternative programs or program sizes are considered in this phase. The approval at the end of this phase includes the approval for the ad production budget.

- *Phase 2 (Production)* — The advertising is produced during this phase, and typically the proposed advertisements are shown for approval at the conclusion of this phase. In some cases, especially where there are significant production costs, the approving authority may ask for a mock-up or preview of the ad prior to completion in order to redirect it if necessary. This would be referred to as a Phase 2A approval point with the final approval being the Phase 2B approval. The advertising placement budget would also be presented at the conclusion of this phase. The decision at the end of this phase includes the go-ahead to place or run the advertisement.

- *Phase 3 (Ad Placement)* — The advertising program is run during this phase, and generally there is little to approve at the completion, but some companies do an evaluation of the advertising program at the completion of this phase. In this case, they look at the final costs of the program and measure the results. Best-in-class companies establish metrics for measuring success in Phase 1 and evaluate them at the conclusion of this phase.

Companies that follow these decision phases realize much more benefit from their advertising budgets because they make clearer decisions early on. Those involved know what is being approved at each phase. They also are able to redirect the program at key points in the process. Companies that do not follow these phases tend to spend more money on ineffective campaigns that could have been refocused or canceled.

Process Improvement Project

Process improvement projects involve making changes to the way an organization manages a particular aspect of its business, such as supply chain, customer billing, manufacturing, or order processing. While there are many types of process improvement projects and the required phase-based decision process may vary accordingly, the following phase-based decisions are typical:

- *Phase 0 (Scope and Objectives)* — In this initial phase, the project is initiated through a decision based on the intended outcome and the processes involved. The primary objectives of this phase are to define the scope of the project, the approximate expected benefits and cost, and the general priority of the project. In many cases, this is primarily a screening phase.

- *Phase 1 (Assessment and Process Improvement Plan)* — Based on the approved scope, the project team completes an assessment or diagnostic of the opportunities to improve the process. Typically, this is the most important phase since it identifies what needs to be done to improve the process and the cost to make those improvements. A project plan is completed from this assessment. In some cases, several alternative plans at different levels of investment may be presented for approval. Approval at the end of this phase is the approval to make the process changes.

- *Phase 2 (Implementation)* — In this phase, the process changes are made by defining and implementing new practices. Some companies may separate this work into two distinct phases — one for defining the new practices (Phase 2A) and another for implementing them (Phase 2B). This approach is generally recommended for large process improvement projects. Completion of this phase is generally the completion of the project. Similar to IT projects, approval of this phase may include approval that the project is indeed complete.

- *Phase 3 (Project Evaluation)* — In this final phase, the project team, along with key users, performs a postmortem evaluation to judge the success of the project and lessons learned that could be implemented in subsequent projects. Success is generally measured by benefits established in Phase 1 of the project. This evaluation phase review is done in the future, when benefits are expected, but avoid waiting too long, though, because this step could be overlooked if too much time intervenes.

Process improvement projects lend themselves to a common, highly structured process. Following this method for process improvement projects ensures the best process is implemented, that decision makers have similar expectations, and that best practices are learned and communicated across other projects.

Acquisition and Merger Project

Acquisitions and mergers are generally very large projects with significant investment and strategic impact. While acquisition plans vary widely, a general phase-based process can be applied. Use the following decision process for a deliberate acquisition, as opposed to one that is opportunistic:

- *Phase 0 (Strategic Assessment)* — This phase initiates the evaluation of the strategic need or advantage for an acquisition. The evaluation might be brief or involve a significant amount of strategic work. Sometimes this phase is best done by an outside consultant or investment advisor. Approval at the completion of this phase is simply an approval to make the investment in the next phase, not to make an acquisition. Frequently, it also includes agreement on the criteria for a target acquisition. If no agreement is made or if the strategic need cannot be defined, then the next steps for an acquisition are put on hold and revisited at a future time.

- *Phase 1 (Acquisition Planning)* — This next phase of an acquisition process involves some work but is not generally expensive relative to the final costs. It includes the evaluation and prioritization of potential acquisition targets. The acquisition team generally applies alternative evaluation techniques. At the end of this phase, the team presents the business case for making an acquisition and recommends a target company or companies. Approval of this phase is the go-ahead to incur significant legal, investment banking, and related fees. It is frequently difficult to put a cap on these fees once Phase 2 starts, so the approach is a somewhat more open-ended budget and flexible time approval than other types of projects. It also includes tentative, but not final, approval of how much the company might want to invest in an acquisition and how to finance it.

- *Phase 2 (Negotiation and Agreement)* — This phase is very different from those of other projects. The company may determine an acquisition candidate, either directly or most likely through its investment banker. This phase entails multiple approval points, requiring a continuous series of phase review decisions. The first would be approval of the terms of a preliminary offer, or letter of intent, to acquire the company.

This will go through many iterations as the offer changes, each requiring approval. To expedite matters, the approving authority, which is generally the company's board of directors, may empower a subcommittee to meet as needed to approve minor variations of the offer until reaching a definitive agreement for the acquisition. At the completion of this phase, the acquisition is formally approved by the board of directors. This can involve the commitment of millions, hundreds of millions, or even billions of dollars. If no agreement is reached, then the process ends or another acquisition candidate is identified, and Phase 2 begins all over again.

- *Phase 3 (Acquisition Closing)* — The actual closing of the acquisition takes place sometime after the formal agreement completed in Phase 2. The closing could include approval by the shareholders of one or more companies, completion of financing, approval by government authorities, and satisfying other contingencies.

- *Phase 4 (Acquisition Integration)* — After the agreement closes, the acquisition integration begins. Depending on the acquisition, this most likely will be another project entirely, and follow new phases, starting with a phase for the acquisition plan.

Acquisitions tend to be unique from other projects and vary from acquisition to acquisition. They are also projects that are not done repetitively, as were the previous projects discussed. Yet an acquisition's costs and high stakes necessitate clear process oversight to avoid squandering funds.

New Office or Factory Location Project

New facilities projects for moving offices or adding a new building have similar characteristics. The primary cost and commitment ensues when the lease is signed, but until that point, critical phase decisions need to be made. The following is a typical phase-based decision approach:

- *Phase 0 (Decision to Look for New Location)* — This phase initiates approval of a project to investigate location alternatives. Approval at the end of this phase includes the scope of the project and a rough estimate of the expected costs and timing, but is not a commitment to acquire or lease a new facility. Most important, this phase identifies the objectives, which will be used later to evaluate the alternatives. These objectives can be refined in Phase 1 as the project team learns more about the location decision.

- *Phase 1 (Detailed Planning and Alternatives)* — This phase includes the identification of alternatives and more detailed planning and typically involves refining the objectives. At its conclusion, approval includes those alternatives for consideration along with the possibility of other alternatives. The example in the alternative evaluation section of this book ties in with these steps.

- *Phase 2 (Selection)* — In this phase, the project team recommends one of the alternatives, which green lights this alternative for pursuit. Typically the project team would present its analysis and reasons for the recommendation. Approval at the conclusion of this phase is also a go-ahead to negotiate terms of a purchase or lease.

- *Phase 3 (Negotiation)* — In this phase, the lease or purchase is signed as long as the terms are within the parameters agreed upon in Phase 2. If the terms are not within these parameters, then approval is required of the new terms. Approval of the lease or purchase is the result of this phase approval.

- *Phase 4 (Moving or Start-up Plan)* — After the lease is signed, then the moving or start-up plan needs to be undertaken. Approval of this phase is generally a Phase 0 approval of a new project for moving or start-up.

Facility purchase or lease decisions are best made phase-by-phase. While the final approval is the formal commitment, the intermediate decisions on objectives, alternatives, and criteria for evaluation are important discriminators for the final decision.

General Guidelines for Defining Phases

While the phases of different projects tend to vary based on the nature of the project, these examples show the similarities in the way phases are defined. It is important to define the phases so that early decisions can enable the cancelation or redirection of projects with the least amount of up-front investment. It is also important that the phase approval decisions set the boundaries and expectations for decision empowerment. Finally, there are major decisions during a project, and these are best made at formal phase review decision points, not made informally throughout the project.

- Project decisions should be made at the end of each phase.
- They should be made progressively, requiring less work in the early phases.
- Making decisions at the wrong time or simply making them without regard to the best time to make them is a haphazard process that ultimately leads to bad decisions.

CHAPTER 31

Specifying *What* Project Decisions Should Be Made

An effective project decision process requires a common expectation of what decisions are made at each phase

Now that we have looked at who makes project decisions and when they make them, we can now turn our attention to what decisions are made. The previous chapter gave an indication of these decisions, and this chapter entails a more complete explanation, starting with a few examples.

An electronics company, International Microelectronics (IM), read about the importance of phase-based project decisions and attempted to implement the company's own version of it, but misunderstood the nature of approval decisions and defined "approval" as completion of specific milestones. Each phase was defined as the completion of certain deliverables, such as product function specifications, product design, and marketing plans. The phase reviews deteriorated into work approval sessions: Was the work completed? If so, then the project automatically continued to the next phase. Even if the project no longer made sense, the next phase was approved because the work was completed. No decisions were made about whether the project continued to be worth the investment or had a sufficient priority for receiving resources.

> The best way to determine what is needed to enter the next phase is to define the criteria as the answer to specific questions, not deliverables.

For IM, this new process turned out to be almost as bad as no process at all. Work continued on projects that no longer had appropriate business impact for pursuit. As a result, the company wasted almost half of its budget on projects that failed or were only marginally successful. It fell behind its competition. Managers and employees lost faith in company leadership and joked about how dumb it was to continue some of these projects just because someone was able to get them started. Employees began to leave IM to work for other companies with better leadership. Eventually, the board of directors replaced some of the key executives — all because the company misunderstood what project decisions needed to be made throughout critical projects.

Another client, a successful consumer electronics company, considered a project to diversify into a very different market. Although it was pointed out that the company did not have access to distribution channels for this product, the company went ahead with the project and completed the product. It spent $7 million developing and testing the new product and then launched it. The company withdrew the product from the market a mere six months later after selling only 10 units at $450 each. Why? The company, as warned, was unable to access necessary distribution channels.

When I met with the former CEO shortly after he was fired, he said that he should have canceled the project as soon as he realized that channels of distribution would be a big problem, and he knew this as soon as the project started. It would have saved a big mistake, $7 million, and his job.

Issues with *What* Project Decisions Should Be Made

While some companies, like those in these examples, get the *who* and *when* of project decisions right, they fail to properly identify the right decisions to make. Here are some of the issues they have:

- *They confuse the completion of work with the approval to continue to the next phase of the project.* A phase review is the approval to continue to the next phase of a project, not just validation that work during the previous phase was completed. The work in the phase is done to answer the questions needed for approval; simply completing the work does not mean the answers are acceptable. It would be like grading a student paper with an

A because the work was completed, even though the answers were wrong.

- *Approval of a phase is considered as approval of "exit criteria."* This is similar to the point above, but a variation that emphasizes "exit criteria" instead of "entry criteria." Approval should not be that the phase is completed; it should be that the project deserves to go into the next phase.

- *Important questions are overlooked or missed.* The questions asked at the completion of each phase are critical. If an important question is overlooked, then the company will eventually find that missing questions can be very costly.

- *The quantity and size of presentations and documents are given too much importance.* The objective is to answer the questions as accurately as possible, not pore through long presentations. One of the most effective phase review decisions I ever participated in used a simple two-page summary clearly answering all of the questions for that phase.

- *The questions asked at the end of the phase are not progressive, even though the project is progressive.* An effective phase review process asks questions progressively as the project advances and, as necessary, enables early project cancelation, thus minimizing labor costs and other pursuit expenses.

As these issues show, the best way to determine what is needed to enter the next phase is to define the criteria as the answer to specific progressive questions, not the completion of deliverables.

Progressive Decisions

Projects progress as the work is completed, and as they progress the project team gains more certainty about previous assumptions and estimates. The simple key to understanding what project decisions are made throughout a project is based on this progressive nature of projects. The purpose of making progressive decisions is to cancel or redirect a project that is no longer feasible before expending even more resources on it.

> The simple key to understanding what project decisions are made throughout a project is based on the progressive nature of projects.

For example, in Phase 0 of a project, decisions can be based on assumptions. The assumptions can be discussed and debated, but the Phase 0 decision is nonetheless based on these assumptions. If the project does not make sense based on the assumptions, then it is canceled or redirected. Granted, the assumptions may not be validated at this point in the process. Validating these assumptions is one of the purposes of the next phase. But if the project does not look feasible or attractive even with ambitious assumptions, then why waste the time and money on proving assumptions?

Phase 1 decisions are usually based on plans and estimates. While estimates are better than assumptions, they are still only estimates, not facts. In this phase, estimates replace the assumptions, and in some cases a project may be canceled because the new estimates now show that the project does not make sense, either because the assumptions from Phase 0 were wrong, new information has arisen, or situations have changed.

Phase 2 decisions are based on a more accurate combination of actual facts, refined estimates, and forecasts. Overall, the quality of information for the Phase 2 decision is much more reliable, but in most projects the majority of the costs and work have been incurred.

Decisions by Phase

As previously discussed, project decisions should not be made on achievement of milestones or completion of deliverables. They are best made by asking specific questions and then making a decision based on the answers to these questions. In any project decision process, these questions are most helpful if well defined ahead of time so the project team and the project approval group understand what questions are asked when.

> The purpose of making progressive decisions is to cancel or redirect a project with the least amount of wasted work.

The questions for each phase were ingrained into the culture for a particular client of mine. At one Phase 0 review meeting, a new executive participating in her first meeting interrupted and said, "Shouldn't we be asking this question?" In unison the entire project team and executive approval committee responded, "That's a Phase 1 question!"

Although decisions and the questions that prompt them differ by the type of project, there is some commonality. The following list outlines questions applicable to each phase.

Phase 0 Questions

For most projects, Phase 0 is a screening and evaluation phase to determine if the project makes sense and has an appropriate priority level. Here are the types of questions that should be answered to make those decisions:

- Does this project fit strategically?
- Does it appear like it will have a sufficient return on our investment, based on the assumptions we are making?
- Are the assumptions reasonable, even if yet to be proven?
- Do we have the resources to complete Phase 1 of this project, and the remainder of the project after that if it passes Phase 1 approval?
- What are the risks of this project? Are they acceptable?
- Do we have the technology and other skills to be successful?
- Does this project have a priority over other projects that may require the same resources? Where does it fall in terms of priority with regard to these other projects?

Phase 1 Questions

Phase 1 is usually a planning phase. Estimates of the work required to complete the project are based on a project plan with a reliable degree of accuracy. The ability of the project to achieve the initial objectives is clarified, and project objectives may be refined. If the project is for the development of a new product, the functionality of the product and its competitive comparisons are clearer.

- Does the project continue to make strategic sense?
- Does it still achieve its original objectives, or are the redefined objectives sufficient?
- Is the return on expected investment still viable based on revised estimates?
- Do we have the skills to complete this project?
- Do we have the resources to assign to complete Phase 2 of the project as now planned?
- Are the risks still acceptable?
- If this is a product development project, are the market analysis, competitive comparisons, and financial projections acceptable?
- Can we complete this project to our quality standards?

Phase 2 Questions

In most projects, the majority of the work is done in Phase 2, so the nature of the decisions and questions at the end of this phase change from deciding if it makes sense to invest in the project to checking that it accomplished its goals.

- Did the project complete what it planned to in Phase 2?
- Has the project achieved its intended objectives at this point in the project?
- Does it still make sense to complete the project based on more accurate actual data, revised estimates, and forecasts?
- Are there any significant barriers to success from this point on in the project?
- Are the risks still manageable?
- Has there been a change in the strategic fit, priority, or competitive positioning for completing this project?

Final Phase Questions

Some projects have more phases than others, so consider this as the final phase after the project is completed. The nature of these questions entails a postmortem of the project to see what can be learned and what may still need to be done. This phase is usually finalized after the project has been sufficiently completed to begin to judge its success.

- Did the project achieve its stated objectives?
- What else needs to be done to maximize success?
- What did we learn from the project, and what should be done differently next time?

- Too often the wrong project approval decisions are made at the wrong time in a project.
- Project approval decisions should be made progressively as the project itself progresses.
- Project decisions are best made based on the responses to specific questions for each phase.
- The questions to be answered at the end of each phase should be determined at the start of the project, if not defined by a standard process.

CHAPTER 32

Understanding *How* Project Decisions Are Made

Best practices for how project decisions are made can lead to more effective decisions

Even with a good definition of who makes project decisions, when they make them, and what decisions they make, there is still a final element needed to achieve effective project decisions: how the decisions are made. This chapter examines best practices for how project decisions should be made.

A major consumer products company followed a textbook phase-based decision process, but failed to implement it correctly. The company just told everyone to start making project decisions phase-by-phase. It seemed so simple. But it did not work. It only caused confusion. Without a common process, everyone involved had their own ideas as to how the process should work. The initial meetings turned into chaos, with most of the time spent arguing over how the meeting should run.

> Applying best practices is the best way to ensure how projects decisions are made.

Phase review meetings were difficult to schedule, and many were canceled just prior to the meeting for various reasons. Executive attendance at the meetings was inconsistent, and when substitutes attended, they did not have the authority to make the decision, so the meetings were continued at a later point. Some project teams came into the meetings unprepared; others distributed books of information to the execu-

292

tives only hours before the meeting. Each meeting followed different agendas, and each team presented differently.

Meetings ran over schedule, and most concluded without reaching a decision, requiring additional meetings. Even with a "new project decision process," decisions were not made. After nine months, the new process just died away, and most people were relieved, but the company still did not have a project decision process.

The company ignored working on the *how* and failed to implement the new decision process properly. The remainder of this chapter reviews some of the best practices to implement successfully an effective project decision process. The chapter looks at best practices for defining the approval process, scheduling phase decision meetings, running the meetings, and project team decisions.

Issues on *How* Project Decisions Are Made

As seen through these examples, even a phase-based decision process can fail if not implemented correctly. Here are some of the issues companies experience:

1. *Phase review decision processes are most effective if clearly defined as a standard.* Otherwise, if each process follows a different process or variation, the lack of consistency will lead to inconsistent results. Decision approvals will be confused, expectations frustrated, and the opportunity for continuous improvement diminished.

2. *Without attention and commitment to maintaining scheduled phase review meetings, projects easily slip or slow down.* Phase review process decision meetings set the cadence for the project. Delaying or compromising these meetings can slow down or diminish project effectiveness.

3. *Phase review meetings themselves must be run crisply to be effective.* Ineffective meetings can discourage the project teams and result in poor project decisions. I recommend that meeting guidelines be clearly defined and that the executive approval team practices prior to its first decision.

4. *Finally, project teams must function effectively for the project to be successful.* This cannot always be assumed, so a formal process for the way teams are expected to work together and a guideline for team meetings and decisions can be invaluable.

The way to address these *how* issues is by understanding the best practices used by successful companies.

Best Practices for Defining the Approval Process

Best practices for how project decisions are made start with defining the process itself. Companies that are best in making project decisions have a formally defined process that becomes ingrained in the company's policies and culture. Here are some best practices:

- The phase review decision process is formally defined so that those involved know how it works and have the same expectations.
- In the best companies, this process is ingrained in the company culture as "the way things work."
- Executives make it clear that the primary purpose of the meeting is to answer the questions posed at the end of each phase, and not the amount of information presented. The easier the questions can be answered, the better.
- The process is clearly defined and updated from time to time based on continuous improvements.

Best Practices for Scheduling the Phase Decision Meeting

The next set of best practices has to do with how the phase review meetings are scheduled. Companies that make the most effective phase-based decisions follow some specific best practices:

- The phase reviews are held as scheduled at the completion of the phase and not rescheduled or postponed. The executive team realizes there is a cost associated with delaying the meetings, as it also delays the project and wastes resources working on it.
- There should be a simple way for the project team to request short delays of a few weeks, if truly needed for project reasons.
- The best companies conduct these meetings in person, especially for the largest and strategically most important projects. If done remotely, these companies institute guidelines for conference call attendance (such as prohibiting on-the-fly cell phone participation).

- The best companies also have rules for executives who need to have a substitute attend the meeting. If a substitute is needed, that substitute has full decision authority and does not need to check with his or her boss prior to making a decision. He or she is also expected to be fully prepared for the decision meeting.

Best Practices for Running the Meeting

The phase review meetings and how well they are run have an impact on the success of project decisions. Here are some of the best practices followed by the most successful companies:

- Each phase review is done through a formal presentation by the project team to the executive approval group, such as a project approval committee. This provides a sufficiently serious forum for the decision, increasing respect for the importance of the decision. It also creates the decision as an event rather than just a meeting.

- The project team is expected to present the appropriate materials necessary to answer the questions defined for that phase and to provide the necessary plans and resource requests for the approval.

- The executive approval team is expected to be prepared for the meeting by reviewing these materials in advance and asking the appropriate questions to reach a decision. This not only makes the phase review meeting more effective, but it also creates a mutual respect with the project team.

- The executive team practices prior to the first phase review meeting. Understanding how the meeting will likely be conducted before jumping into making important decisions helps keep the first phase review meeting from encountering common difficulties. Usually, a mock case review is used for this practice session.

- The executives empowered to make the authorization decision meet in closed session to make the decision after the presentations and discussion. This gives the executives the ability to talk candidly in confidence about the project (without the pressure of individuals present who have a stake in the project) to arrive at the best possible decisions.

Best Practices for Project Team Decisions

Finally, how project teams function and make decisions has a bearing on the success of the project and the effectiveness of the teams. Here are some of the best practices for project teams:

- Project teams meet at regularly scheduled times — weekly for large projects.

- Project teams meet in person when possible so they can develop better working relationships.

- Moving forward entails that those involved in the project decisions are appropriately empowered. An important factor of this empowerment is to understand project boundaries or tolerances; how much leeway is the team given? In a strong empowerment process, the team has some degree of freedom within its empowerment. For example, the team empowered to design the college building may have tolerances to complete the design phase within a month of the original objective, with an expense budget not to exceed 5% of that authorized, and the building design should accommodate the planned number of students within the overall cost range. If during that phase, the team realizes that any of these tolerances could be exceeded, then their empowerment ceases and they need to go back to the approval committee for project reapproval or cancelation.

- Even after determining the *who*, *what*, and *when* of project decisions, the *how* is important to implementing the process effectively.

- *How* is best expressed through best practices.

- Best practices include defining the approval process, scheduling phase decision meetings, running the meetings, and project team decisions.

Notes

1. David Leonard, "How Lehman Brothers Got Its Real Estate Fix," *New York Times*, 3 May 2009.

2. Janet Morrissey, "Credit Default Swaps: The Next Crisis?" *Time*, 17 March 2008.

3. William D. Cohan, "Rating McGraw-Hill," *Fortune*, 4 May 2009, 104.

4. Beth Healy, "Fund Firm Behavior Faces State Scrutiny," *Boston Globe*, 6 May 2009.

5. Tim Arango, "The Struggles of a Game Maker Bog Down Viacom," *New York Times*, 2 November 2008.

6. Ronald D. Utt, "The Subprime Mortgage Market Collapse," Heritage Foundation, 22 April 2008, No. 2127.

7. Andrew Ross Sorkin, "A Bridge Loan? U.S. Should Guide G.M. in a Chapter 11," *New York Times*, 18 November 2008.

8. Katie Benner, "The Public Pension Bomb," *Fortune*, 25 May 2009, 74.

9. Peter S. Goodman and Gretchen Morgenson, "Saying Yes to Anyone, WaMu Builds an Empire on Shaky Loans," *New York Times*, 28 December 2008.

10. William D. Cohan, "Goldman Questions Bear's Marks," http://money.cnn.com/2009/03/02/magazines/fortune/cohan_houseofcards5.fortune/index.htm, online, 3 March 2009.

11. Jessica Vascellaro, "Radio Tunes Out Google in Rare Miss for Web Titan," *Wall Street Journal*, 12 May 2009.

12. Report of the Presidential Commission on the Space Shuttle Challenger Accident, "The Rogers Commission Report," June 1986, 82.

13. Richard Siklos, "Bob Iger Rocks Disney," *Fortune*, 19 January 2009.

14. Peter Gumbel, "Saving Britain's Broken Bank," *Fortune*, 11 May 2009, 77.

15. Background for WaMu from Goodman and Morgenson, "Saying Yes to Anyone."

16. Some of the background on Wal-Mart from Charles Fishman, *The Wal-Mart Effect* (New York: Penguin Books, 2006).

17. Courtesy of James C. Kirk, vice president, Eidetics — A Division of Quintiles Consulting.

18. Graham T. Allison and Philip Zelikow, *The Essence of Decision: Explaining the Cuban Missile Crisis*, 2nd ed. (New York: Longman, 1999).

19. Ibid., 5.

20. Ibid.

21. Ibid., 18.

22. Ibid., 143.

23. Ibid., 255.

24. Information on DuPont came from the following sources: Dean Gilmore, "Keeping PACE with the Market," *World Class Design to Manufacture* 1, no. 1 (1994): 12-16;

   Roman Boutellier, Oliver Gassmann, and Maximillian von Zedtwitz, *Managing Global Innovation: Uncovering the Secrets of Future Competitiveness*, 3rd ed. (Berlin: Springer 2008);

   Robin A. Karol, Ross C. Loeser, and Richard H. Tait, "Better New Business Development at DuPont," *Research Technology Management* (January–February 2002);

   Richard H. Tait, "The Sponsorship Process to Strengthen Innovation," *R&D Innovator* 5, no. 11 (November 1996): article 247.

25. Rick Whiting, "Managing Product Development from the Top," *Electronic Business*, 17 June 1991, 42.

Index

Numbers in *italics* indicate figures.

About the Author

Michael E. McGrath is the creator of the popular *Decide Better!* decision-making series and the bestselling author of *Product Strategy for High-Technology Companies*. His recent book *Decide Better! For a Better Life*, published in 2008, has been nominated and selected as a finalist for numerous book awards.

In addition to being a successful author, Michael is an expert on decision making. He is a successful turnaround CEO, renowned management consultant, experienced board member, and powerful speaker who has taught decision-making skills for 25 years. Michael also has a top reputation and track record for being able to make tough, strategic decisions in the corporate world and is highly sought after for his insight and opinions. Michael is frequently featured on ABC, CBS, FOX, and CNN as an expert in business and decision making.

Michael was a cofounder and managing director at Pittiglio Rabin Todd & McGrath (PRTM), a leader in helping global technology-based companies make better decisions by developing management processes and methodologies. In over two decades of management consulting, he has worked with more than 1,000 companies in the United States, Europe, and Asia. Michael initiated PACE (Product And Cycletime Excellence), PRTM's product-development consulting practice that applied an innovative decision process reducing time-to-market in a variety of global companies.

In addition to advising others on decisions, Michael has demonstrated exceptional decision-making skills as CEO of the turn-around of i2 Technologies and as president and managing director of PRTM, building it to one of the most successful consulting firms in the world. He is also an entrepreneur, founding several companies in addition to PRTM, and is currently in the process of expanding the *Decide Better!* line to include a new comprehensive Business Decisions Series.

Michael has extensive board experience, including public company boards. He is currently serving as executive chairman of Thomas Group (TGI) and recent chairman of Entrust (ENTU), and he has also served on the board of i2 Technologies (ITWO). He is former chairman of the board of trustees of York Hospital and is on the board of Aidmatrix Foundation and Saint Michael's College. In addition, he serves on the board of Sensable Technologies and has previously served on the board of several nonprofit organizations.

Michael has established a reputation as a strong, yet witty decision maker, and credits much of the success in his life to making better decisions. He has studied decision making for more than 25 years, building an extensive base of skills and techniques. He wrote *Business Decisions!,* the first book in his new Business Decisions Series, to share this experience to help businesses make better decisions and achieve greater success.

Michael founded *Decide Better!* in 2007 with the mission of helping people and businesses achieve greater success through better decisions. The first *Decide Better!* book, *Decide Better! For a Better Life,* was published in October 2008, and the second, *Decide Better! For College,* was published in March 2009. Since the launch of *Decide Better!* Michael has been in demand for national radio and television interviews as well as keynote speeches on how to make great decisions.

Michael has a B.S. in computer science from Boston College and an M.B.A. from Harvard Business School.